Business Thinking in Practice for In-house Counsel

Taking Your Seat at the Table

Catherine McGregor

Globe Law and Business

Author
Catherine McGregor

Managing director
Sian O'Neill

Business Thinking in Practice for In-House Counsel: Taking Your Seat at the Table
is published by

Globe Law and Business Ltd
3 Mylor Close
Horsell
Woking
Surrey GU21 4DD
United Kingdom
Tel: +44 20 3745 4770
www.globelawandbusiness.com

Printed and bound by CPI Group (UK) Ltd, Croydon CR0 4YY

Business Thinking in Practice for In-House Counsel: Taking Your Seat at the Table

ISBN 9781787423268
EPUB ISBN 9781787423275
Adobe PDF ISBN 9781787423282
Mobi ISBN 9781787423299

Table of contents

Acknowledgements

Numerous people have been instrumental in the different stages of this book – and also in my career, to ensure I had the ability to write it in the first place!

A big thank-you goes to Bjarne Tellmann, formerly general counsel and chief legal officer at Pearson and now senior vice president and general counsel at GlaxoSmithKline Consumer Healthcare, whose book *Building an Outstanding Legal Team* was an inspiration. Bjarne himself provided valuable conversations and advice on writing this book and a sense of direction when I had lots of competing ideas on what the book could be!

Kenny Robertson of Royal Bank of Scotland was a great sounding board for many of the ideas in this book. He also read many of the chapters in draft form and provided advice and thoughts on these at a critical stage. He and his team were also a great case study for the chapters on creativity.

Special thanks go to all of the general counsel and their teams who assisted me in the case studies for this book. I have already mentioned Kenny and Bjarne; big thanks also to Rob Booth at the Crown Estate; Alex Dimitrief, now at Zeughauser Group and formerly of GE; Maaike de Bie at EasyJet; Kevin van Tonder, now of Yewna Law and formerly at Schlumberger; and Bill Deckelman of DXC Technologies.

Many other general counsel, academics and experts provided content and ideas for this book, including Mo Zain Ajaz; Nilema Bhakta-Jones; Cornell Boggs; Nick Boymal; Jeff Carr; Luke Christoforidis; John Croft; Karen Dillon; Christopher Grant; Chris Fox; Howard Harris; Emma Jelley; Dan Kayne; Paul Lanzone; Alex Lazarus; Barry Matthews; Cat Moon; Richard Moorhead; Timothy Murphy; Annabelle Newman; Balder Onarheim; Rupa Patel; and Thomas Sager. The ideas and energy flowing from my Bionic Lawyer and O Shaped Lawyer tribes have also been an inspiration.

My career started out in a very different place and I wouldn't be writing about anything legal related at all if I hadn't been given the opportunity to take a job at *Chambers and Partners* many years ago. This was supposedly temporary, but led me into writing about law full time and becoming zealously interested in the role of the general counsel. Katrina Dewey and John Ryan at Lawdragon allowed me the scope to get comfortable with producing content on this and a magazine. My time at Legalease producing *GC Magazine* and a host of content and events for general counsel around the world solidified this interest and laid the groundwork for the ideas that have come to fruition in this book. Thank you to David Goulthorpe and John Pritchard for allowing me the space to explore these areas during my time with them.

Since I have been running my own company, many of my clients have provided opportunities to explore ideas via content which informed this book directly and indirectly. Content written for DLA Piper's *WIN* (What In-House Lawyers Need) and for *Global Leaders in Law* informed the sections on purpose and culture. Alex Dimitrief's case study on leadership originally appeared as part of my content strategy for DLA Piper's *WIN* and is reproduced here with kind permission. Thanks to

Zelinda Bennett and Karen Lees of DWF for continuing to support my work and vision in a number of different ways. Thanks also to Meg Sullivan and Karlie Ilaria of Paul Hastings for some great projects which have helped develop my thinking, especially around culture. And special thanks to Rhiannon Van Ross of *Global Leaders in Law* for giving me a number of different opportunities to produce content while supporting and being excited about this book. Thanks also to Christopher Hurst and the team at Carlyle Kingswood Global for introducing me to lots of great general counsel along the way and commissioning me to create content on them, much of which was very insightful for this book and fed into aspects of it.

My mentors Karen Dillon and Jason Glover have both been great listeners and have delivered sound practical advice when needed.

Pierre Gentin of McKinsey has always been a great friend and wonderful conversationalist about a wide range of topics associated with this book and more. Our discussions always inspire some creative thinking, for which I am always grateful.

My friend Lesley Wan of FBN Bank and founder of The Eagle Club, a great women's network, has always been a great professional and personal support and forever encourages me to see my own potential.

Gratitude to Sian O'Neill and Jim Smith at Globe Law and Business for seeing the potential in this book and providing advice and guidance where needed. The expert editing of Lauren Simpson and Carolyn Boyle helped to further refine my ideas.

Extra special thanks go to my long-time friend and an excellent writer and editor, Tracey Sinclair, whose expert eye helped me to shape many of the early drafts. Tracey also taught me to trust my own voice more.

Thanks also to Jodi Bartle for her help on publicising the book.

Last but not least, I would like to thank my family. My husband Andrew Eberhart patiently listened to my various ramblings on this topic.

Andrew also provided a wealth of insight and ideas for the leadership part of the book, based on his experience in the US Navy as a pilot and the commander of a squadron. Our son Matthew helps me to keep things in perspective by telling me that "All I do is write about lawyers and that's not really very hard!" My mother, Colette, has always inspired me to keep believing in myself. Peter the dog was also a constant presence – mostly just blending into the floor at the side of my desk, but valued nevertheless.

Introduction

··

If you don't like something, change it. If you can't change it, change your attitude.

Maya Angelou

Introduction: starting with *why*

I fell into legal research and journalism many years ago by accident. Something that was originally designed to be a stopgap between academic jobs teaching drama and performance ended up becoming a career. So while there was no compelling passion that initially drew me into the profession, what kept me there was understanding and writing about the world of in-house counsel. Even from my earliest days in the industry, working at a legal directory, it was clients' stories that fascinated me most. I was able to give this free rein when my roles in the industry allowed me to focus on telling these stories – in particular, as founding editor of *GC Magazine*. I developed this further in recent years as I started my own business focused on legal consultancy and thought leadership consultancy – a significant aspect of which involves examining the role of in-house lawyers and the future of the profession.

I was inspired to write this book by various conversations with in-house lawyers over the years, in both a professional and personal capacity. It has always surprised me somewhat that although its ostensible purpose is to advise businesses, business law is often so insular in terms of the frameworks of understanding that it uses. The law firms and lawyers I encountered were often focused purely on the law; although there were obviously some honourable exceptions. When I spoke to general counsel, however, they often said that they were much more interested in learning about business ideas, and in many cases were already doing this on their own.

Those lawyers who had moved in-house often felt a much more compelling need to understand the ideas driving businesses, and to fill the related gaps in their own education and experience. There are many key practical skills involved in running a business, which many lawyers feel it would be useful to grasp. The most obvious is an understanding of finance, such as the ability to read a balance sheet. This book does not aim to address these types of business skills. It is rather about the big ideas which drive the ethos of many businesses and are now becoming increasingly impactful in the legal profession.

Today, most legal departments and many law firms understand that they cannot remain cloistered in an ivory tower; instead, they need to operate in a way which is driven by the same factors that drive all businesses. And increasingly, for all businesses, this has become much broader than simply a conversation about profit.

In my career as a legal journalist and editor, I tested out some of these ideas over the years – most notably as the founding editor of *GC Magazine*. In launching that publication, I spoke to a number of general counsel about the type of content they wanted to read. There was a surprising confluence, in that most did not want to read about technical areas of law; they suggested that a plethora of information was already available in this regard, from legal briefings to more traditional legal publications. Instead, a significant number of the general counsel I spoke to stated that they wanted to learn about big business ideas and even the work of leading business thinkers. They were also hungry for practical insights into how other general counsel and their teams did things.

I have tried to combine both of these in this book. Each part takes a big idea in business and examines some of the key theories and ideas in influential or recent business books. Examples to illustrate these draw primarily on the experiences of in-house legal departments, but also reference other business examples where appropriate. Each part also features a case study, which examines in depth how an in-house team has taken one or more of these ideas and used them, in practice, to influence what they do.

I have focused on ideas in business that are broad, but that also seem to me to reflect the direction of travel in the legal profession. Innovation, for example, is now a significant theme in law; and legal departments and law firms are increasingly referencing purpose.

The seven themes I came up with are obviously not exhaustive. There is also overlap between them and each symbiotically affects the others. Other ideas and themes are also woven throughout all parts – the most notable being empathy, inclusion and diversity.

The first part of the book, to paraphrase Simon Sinek, starts with *why*. Thinking about your purpose and why you are doing something is generally a good starting point. It also underpins many of the endeavours described in the case studies: often, the stimulus for some of the big changes undertaken by these general counsel and their teams was a consideration of the reason for their continued existence and of what they do that, say, an outsourced solution could not.

There are a number of different ways of referring to purpose: 'vision', 'why', *'raison d'être'* ... I use some of them interchangeably throughout the book. In a way, it doesn't matter what term you use; but thinking about your fundamental reason for doing what you do – whether that's personal, team based or institutional – can throw a lot of issues into relief. It can reaffirm your joy and passion for what you are doing; or can help you to discover a connection to a new passion. It can also clearly show you what's not working.

The idea of purpose has had a longer tenure than some might think in business: a greater purpose than just profit was cited by early titans of industry, such as Henry Ford. The notion is gaining new currency with the 2019 declaration of the Business Roundtable group, signed by 181 CEOs, that business must have a higher purpose than just creating profit.

While this might seem like more of a focus for business leaders, it is interesting how much the concept resonated with the general counsel I spoke to. In any case, purpose or *why* is an incredibly useful starting point for a host of other developments. In our case study examining the work of the Crown Estate, for example, purpose was the starting point for its then-new general counsel, Rob Booth.

The behaviours that allow your *why* or purpose to play out are what create your culture. Lawyers have a special relationship with the idea of culture. It is one that's increasingly important, particularly for in-house lawyers: it's no longer enough to adjudicate on the legality of a certain course of action; you also have to consider whether it looks and feels right. Even if something is legal, will this attract censure from regulators, industry peers or the court of public opinion? This arbitration of broader risk factors is now a significant aspect of the general counsel role; and it is often where lawyers add most value to their C-suites and boards.

In the United Kingdom, the Financial Conduct Authority is now taking a special interest in the cultures of financial institutions and in behaviours which could be classified as 'non-financial misconduct'. The wider ramifications of movements such as #BlackLivesMatter, #MeToo and #TimesUp mean that boards and shareholders are also much more attuned to cultural factors than in the past. As general counsel and their teams increasingly have to act as arbiters of culture, it makes sense that the cultures of their own departments should also become a focal point.

In writing this book, I became increasingly aware of how interlinked many of the concepts I was considering are. Culture is inextricably linked to purpose. In our case study for this part of the book, focused on the legal team at educational publisher Pearson, we see how an exercise to consider team purpose evolved to become a broader focus on culture – essentially, how purpose can be reinforced by everyday behaviours. Culture is also a factor in ensuring that you attract and retain the right talent, and in stimulating, collaboration, creativity and innovation.

To coalesce teams around these ideas, leadership is fundamental. However, many lawyers have a challenging relationship with leadership; it's not something they traditionally think about until they are ready to assume the mantle of leader themselves. And generally, in doing so, they must deal with this shift in perspective while continuing to succeed in a challenging day job.

Leadership theory has shifted away from many of the stereotypes of a strong 'command and control' personality. It is also true that leadership has become an increasing focus of study over the last 30 years. The part of the book on leadership provides an overview of some theories and ideas that might be helpful for in-house legal leaders – particularly when trying to implement change relating to some of the other big-picture ideas we focus on. Our case studies look at two different general counsel with different experiences of finding their ways to leadership: Alex Dimitrief, former general counsel of GE; and Maaike de Bie, general counsel of EasyJet. Both case studies confirm that lawyers can no longer count themselves out of the leadership equation and that, for the modern general counsel, this is now a central part of the role.

What also becomes apparent from our case studies on leadership, as well as from recent research on the subject, is that leadership is not just about the individual. What is much more important is how, as an individual, you interact with others; how you get your team to work together; and how you develop the individuals within your team. The old truism about leadership holds that the best leaders hire people who are smarter than them. Talent is a continued area of focus for all organisations – research shows that this is a key area of concern for CEOs, and one on which many business leaders fear they are not focusing enough.

Given that how we work is changing, how we think about talent also needs to change. As increased use of technology becomes the norm, it is also noteworthy that many of the more 'human' qualities are what will define the search for talent in the future. Empathy and communication are skills which crop up again and again in this book, in relation to the influence of business ideas on the changing role of the general counsel. As more and more tasks are handed over to automation, qualities such as empathy and judgement become premium in the market for talent. There are particular challenges for in-house legal teams when it comes to talent management: opportunities for upward progression may be limited by historically flat structures. For many general counsel, nurturing talent also comes with the realisation that the logical outcome of success may be the loss of that talent.

Increased globalisation and digitisation are changing employees' relationships with their workplaces. Many general counsel now manage globally diverse teams; the logistics of doing this alone are challenging in themselves, let alone when you factor in ensuring that culturally diverse talent is nurtured in the right way. The increase in globalisation and digitisation is also affecting where and how talent works. This has both positive and negative ramifications. We can often choose where we work from and can be more in control of how we work; but is this also leading to a culture of being 'always on'? Lawyers may often need to be responsive to the needs of other stakeholders, and general counsel must strike a balance between adding value for their stakeholders and safeguarding the wellbeing of their teams. Generational shifts in the workplace demographic are also changing expectations around work – particularly for the younger generations, who expect more flexibility and greater use of digitisation.

How success is defined also has repercussions for the type of talent that organisations can attract. The historical billable-hour formula, whereby more hours worked equals more money for law firms, can lead to a culture of overwork – even in in-house legal departments. It can also disadvantage those who do not conform to the dominant template of success – often women and minorities.

The need for diverse talent is a compelling business imperative linked to the need for different perspectives to drive creativity and innovation in business and in law. In our case study looking at the talent strategy of Schlumberger's legal department, we see a number of narratives converging: the need to do more with less; legal teams being subject to the same business imperatives as other departments; the need to serve a global workforce; the need to increase digitisation and efficiency; and the need to attract more diverse talent. What is interesting about this way of approaching talent is how well it blends the human and the digital, as well as the need for greater diversity. Too often, the narrative of the future of talent in the legal profession can seem like a dichotomy between technology and human skills; whereas in reality, it involves both. We also need to be wary of conversations around the future of the profession being determined by certain groups; we don't want to replicate the same lack of inclusivity which is too prevalent.

We also need the ability to think differently. Creativity is needed to come up with new ideas; whereas innovation is the practical realisation of those ideas. What has often been missing from the legal profession is an understanding of the importance of a diverse range of perspectives, and of how to stimulate different ways of thinking and approaching problems – in other words, creativity.

But creativity is crucial if innovation is to be more than just a buzzword. In many in-house teams, creativity is being hampered by challenges such as budgetary and personnel constraints. However, it is important to remember that in its most traditional form, in the arts, creativity is often similarly bounded. Even with unlimited resources, trying to follow a stage direction such as that at the end of Euripides' *Medea*, where the titular heroine escapes by ascending into the sky in a chariot drawn by dragons sent by sun god Helios, would present some challenges; but in a student production, with a shoestring budget, there is definitely a need for some very creative thinking! In his book on animation studio Pixar, *Creativity Inc*, co-founder Ed Catmull likewise confirms that necessity can literally be the mother of invention; some of the studio's best work was produced under the most challenging conditions.

Many of the case studies in this book are characterised by the need to drive change, and by the realisation that how things have traditionally been done in the profession may no longer produce the optimum results. In a landscape where old certainties are being questioned, it is valuable to take a broader perspective, look outside the traditional context and make connections between different ideas. These are classic methods of creative thinking.

In my discussion of creativity in the in-house legal profession, I have focused on this notion of thinking differently. One method that is increasingly used to do this, both in business and now in the legal profession, is design thinking. Adopting the processes of designers allows us to understand the problems which we are trying to solve and apply creative ways of thinking to find potential solutions. The case study looks at an in-house department in the Royal Bank of Scotland, which regularly applies design thinking techniques and encourages the team to recognise the value of creative thinking and explore ideas from outside the legal profession.

This way of thinking forces us into a mode of continuous learning, which is a prerequisite for change and innovation in business. It also prompts us to access new ideas and work with others – often from outside our team or even our organisation. This leads us to another crucial building block in the process of reshaping our approach to legal services: recognition of the value of collaboration. Collaboration is acknowledged as a significant force in modern business; it is integral to many new business models and ways of working, such as cloud computing and blockchain.

However, as Heidi Gardner of Harvard Law School has shown, large law firms often struggle with internal collaboration – even though the evidence confirms that this leads to more favourable outcomes and greater profits. The compensation models and structures of law firms are not conducive to collaboration. And even when they move in house, lawyers tend to hang on to these mindsets, which position them as somehow separate, special and different, due to their focused training and specialised knowledge. Seeing oneself as different and special can result in a failure to recognise the value of ways of thinking and processes from other areas. But many innovations in the practice of law – both in-house and in law firms – draw on ideas that were initially made popular in other industries. The ability to work collaboratively with experts from outside our discipline is key to the successful adoption of these processes and methods, such as agile and Lean Six Sigma. Legal has also learned from other departments with regard to the use of shared service models and procurement expertise.

What is also integral to many of these models is that the people who work on them – whether members of the legal team, other internal stakeholders or external providers – must collaborate day by day to achieve the best results.

And sometimes these results are astounding. In the case study on DXC Technology, we see that collaboration was placed at the heart of an effort to drive reductions in workforce and budget, but ultimately yielded better results and better feedback from the business. Similarly, the purpose defined by the small legal team at the Crown Estate recognised the need for collaboration, both internal and external, as crucial to its success.

The final part of the book focuses on innovation, which in many ways has become the Holy Grail for both business and the legal profession: something both all-consuming and seemingly unattainable. This unattainability is partly driven perhaps by some misunderstanding of the innovation process – particularly as regards understanding the landscape and asking the right questions, rather than thinking of innovation as a race to the best, newest and shiniest technology. The legal sector must understand that innovation and technology are not the same thing. A piece of technology may be the answer to your question, but you need to know what the right question to ask is first.

You also need the ability to test and to fail. One underlying theme throughout this book is that lawyers find failure hard to deal with; but in an age when changes in business are occuring much more quickly, the ability to learn continually is crucial to success – as is the ability to fail and to learn from those failures. As one of Google's pillars of innovation states: "Never fail to fail."[1]

In the part on innovation, it became apparent that what is key to successful innovation is an understanding not of what the new idea is, but rather of the problem to which it may be the solution. So in many ways, our end is also our beginning: start with *why*.

Our final case study looks at a legal team which has taken many of the concepts in this book and applied them in perhaps the most extreme way to produce a new model of working. The case study reflects all the ideas that we consider in this book: purpose, culture, leadership, talent, creativity, collaboration and innovation.

While the parts of this book are arranged in what feels to me – admittedly, someone who may have been living with this for far too long – to be a logical order, the book could work equally well as a resource to dip in and out of; its shorter chapters within longer parts are designed for this. You can also focus on the case studies and use them as a way into other parts of the book.

Notes
1   www.thinkwithgoogle.com/marketing-resources/8-pillars-of-innovation/.

Part I: Purpose

∙∙

To know what a business is, we have to start with its purpose.

Peter Drucker

1. Why are we here? Why defining purpose matters

Does your legal department need a *why* – a purpose or a sense of inspiration? "We're lawyers – we don't do that sort of touchy-feely stuff!" you might exclaim. But purpose is now recognised as a significant factor in business success. It's also likely to become increasingly important, as millennials and Generation Z tend to focus more on the purpose and vision of organisations than prior generations – making this an important consideration in attracting talent. In the legal profession, given the increase in legal operations and a greater focus on how legal departments work, not just on what they do, doesn't a focus on why or purpose also make sense? Indeed, many who look at the *how* and the *what* of the legal team are now also finding that considering the *why* is a necessary first step to get a complete understanding of the current status before making changes.

Purpose; vision; mission statement; *why*: these have all become defining terms in business. What differentiates them from strategy is the sense of a unifying force which links with the ideas that are coalescing around culture at work. But what do we mean when we speak about purpose?

1. What is 'purpose'?

Purpose encompasses three different facets:
- It adds value to the lives of customers and society;
- It sets brands apart from competitors; and
- It provides clarification and a strong corporate culture.

To put it simply, purpose is more emotion driven, while strategy is more brain driven.

Therefore, the argument goes, just as 'culture eats strategy for breakfast', purpose will always trump strategy, as its appeal is more compelling and fundamental. Strategy can change and be subject to variables such as profit and loss and market conditions. Purpose is designed to be much more universal and long term, and based on fundamental human needs and desires – both those of end users or customers and those of employees.

The notion of the purpose-driven company, or even the purpose-driven team, is increasingly gaining currency. Some of this is due to the overwhelming influence of start-up culture in business thinking, and the desire to capitalise on the learnings and processes that have made many start-ups and disruptive businesses new market titans. It is also due to a realisation that inspiring employees to believe in a purpose produces better cultural alignment and greater productivity than monetary rewards or traditional methods of employee engagement. Finally, there is the influence of the more enlightened consumer – whether institutional or individual – for whom purpose and values are increasingly defining aspects and key differentiators of brands.

But what does this have to do with legal departments? Increasingly, as many organisations take the notion of purpose as a defining through-line, legal teams are finding that it is effective to align themselves with the organisation's wider purpose in order to be more fully integrated into its culture. This has been a significant factor for many general counsel in redefining their own roles and those of their legal teams. No longer wanting to be seen as the 'department of no', legal teams have found that by understanding the purpose and mission of the business, they can show how they can play a crucial part in achieving that mission – a key motivator for many modern general counsel.

Purpose allows you to align with business goals, inspire your people and achieve greater productivity. And you might even change the world while you're at it!

2. The history of purpose in business

In 1960, at an employee meeting, Hewlett Packard co-founder David Packard made a speech which set out his thinking about why Hewlett Packard existed. Despite its vintage, this speech resonates with the current thinking on purpose:

> *I want to discuss why a company exists in the first place. In other words, why are we here? I think many people assume, wrongly, that a company exists simply to make money. While this is an important result of a company's existence, we have to go deeper and find the real reasons for our being. Purpose (which should last at least 100 years) should not be confused with specific goals or business strategies (which should change many times in 100 years). Whereas you might achieve a goal or complete a strategy, you cannot fulfill a purpose; it's like a guiding star on the horizon – forever pursued but never reached. Yet although purpose itself does not change, it does inspire change. The very fact that purpose can never be fully realized means that an organization can never stop stimulating change and progress.[1]*

This reflects many themes in current business writing on purpose and how it aligns with leadership, culture, innovation and talent.

Packard distinguishes between purpose and strategy, suggesting that purpose is always just beyond reach; but even the very act of reaching for it can help to align the company.

His speech also illustrates that – contrary to what many may think – the defining usage of purpose in business is not a new phenomenon.

Admittedly, it has been stimulated by newer companies such as tech start-ups, which have similarly redefined the meaning of the workplace. But in many ways, it has been percolating throughout the history of the modern corporation – albeit to varying degrees.

The accepted wisdom is that businesses are there to generate money for their shareholders; but this wasn't always so. The defining 1919 case of *Dodge v Ford Motor Company* resulted in the Michigan Supreme Court declaring that "a business corporation is organized and carried on primarily for the profit of the stockholders"[2] – seemingly establishing that in corporate America, the interests of the shareholders are paramount. However, this is deceptively simple. If we look at what actually caused the case to come to court in the first place, it becomes clear that there has always been a strand of corporate life which recognises an overarching purpose as a means of inspiring growth – partly through energising and inspiring employees.

By 1916, thanks to the success of the Model T, Ford had accumulated profits of $60 million. Henry Ford wanted to put this money back into the business and maximise the dividends for shareholders. His vision for this was based on expansion, but also on the creation of new opportunities for the workforce, both present and future: "My ambition is to employ still more men, to spread the benefits of this industrial system to the greatest possible number, to help them build up their lives and their homes. To do this we are putting the greatest share of our profits back in the business."[3]

3. How purpose lost out to profit – and why it's coming back

Harwell Wells, writing in Temple University's business law magazine *The Temple 10-Q* in 2014,[4] stated that the social purpose driver for an organisation co-existed with the notion of driving profits for shareholders throughout the 1950s and 1960s, but subsequently began to disappear, to be replaced by the metric of shareholder profits. Wells quotes Theodore Levitt stating that: "It was typical for the corporation to show that it is a great innovator; more specifically, a great public benefactor; and, very particularly, that it exists 'to serve the public'."[5]

In general, however, this is no longer the case – aside from some businesses that make this integral to their vision by setting up as new types of legal entities, such as the low-profit limited liability company and the benefit corporation. But the quote from Levitt seems to have significant overlap with how many of the new industry giants that have disrupted their markets portray themselves.[6] It's about making a market more democratic and better for the end user; for some, it's also about literally doing good. But – as much writing in this area shows – purpose is a theory which unites a number of different key discourses in modern business. It is closely aligned with culture creation. It is also seen as a significant part of the leadership playbook. For many companies, it is closely aligned with innovation and disruption. And it is increasingly seen as a key differentiator in the war for talent – even as who, and indeed what, that talent is changes fundamentally.

Notes

1   David Packard (1960), cited in Bruce Jones, "The Difference Between Purpose and Mission", *Harvard Business Review*, 2 February 2016.
2   Harwell Wells, "The Purpose of a Corporation: A Brief History", *The Temple 10-Q*, 2014, www2.law.temple.edu/10q/purpose-corporation-brief-history/.
3   *Dodge v Ford Motor Co*, https://h2o.law.harvard.edu/cases/3965.
4   Wells (n 2).
5   Theodore Levitt, "The Dangers of Social Responsibility", *Harvard Business Review* 41 (1958).
6   Levitt actually views this in a negative light, and it is true that purpose and vision can have a negative aspect, particularly if governed by regulation.

"The increasing consideration of operational excellence in the legal department is more likely to succeed if it is framed within the wider question of 'Why are we here and why do we do this?'"

2. Bigger than you and me: purpose and values

What is clear from looking at the history of purpose in companies is that there is increasingly a significant overlap with values, as companies realise that these matter to customers. This also potentially means that the role of the in-house counsel becomes more significant where a more values-based or ethical purpose, rather than a purely financial purpose, is driving an organisation; which is why I believe that purpose is something in-house counsel can benefit from considering with regard to what they do.

Purpose is a clear differentiator in business success, and also aligns with the lawyer's key functions of concern for the greater good and ethical behaviour. Many legal departments that have defined a sense of purpose have approached this in relationship to the wider purpose of the company, considering how the legal team can contribute to this organisational purpose in the most meaningful way. Indeed, the increasing consideration of operational excellence in the legal department is more likely to succeed if it is framed within the wider question of "Why are we here and why do we do this?"

According to Peter Drucker's metrics, framing a legal department's *raison d'être* purely in profit terms via the 'adding value' equation will not be as successful as pointing to an overarching sense of purpose. To put it bluntly, 'value' is not the same as 'values'.

Purpose must likewise aim higher than strategy, which is linked to specific business goals. It is the somewhat intangible nature of purpose which makes it so compelling, forcing people to strive and to continually learn. Van Arsdale France – who created Disney's University of Disneyland, which trains many of its employees – stated: "My goal, as I saw it, was to get everyone we hired to share in an intangible dream, and not just working for a paycheck."[1]

1. Ethics and purpose

While purpose can be self-serving, it is increasingly linked to ethical values. Many companies are seeking to make this link more explicit, given today's more ethically conscious consumers. Significant examples include Patagonia: "Our Reason for Being. Build the best product, cause no unnecessary harm, use business to inspire and implement solutions to the environmental crisis"; and Google: "To organize the world's information and make it universally accessible and useful."

The link between why a company does something and how it ensures that it is doing the right thing cuts right to the heart of the modern legal department's *raison d'être*. Increasingly, the general counsel and his or her team cannot ask merely "Is it legal?", but rather "Is it right?" In a number of corporate failures in recent years, general counsel were seen as somewhat complicit, if not actively complicit, due to their failure to take action on corporate wrongdoing – even if that wrongdoing was not strictly against the law.

A sense of purpose running through the business is another tool in the general counsel's toolbox to help align function and behaviour with ethical best practices. For those who consider the relationship between business and ethics, the ability to align practices with purpose creates goodwill and is much more effective than profitability in shoring up corporate reputation in times of crisis. Julian Friedland, assistant professor of business ethics at Trinity College Dublin feels that capitalism is at a crossroads, where concepts such as purpose and ethics need to replace profit as the key motivator: "Businesses ultimately need to rethink their core functions so that they are not aiming solely at financial performance, but see this more as a byproduct of a fundamental commitment to providing social value through products and services that enhance human wellbeing. Once that identity is clearly articulated and sustained, it can be a formidable armour-plating against reputational threats."[2]

This thinking also aligns with some of the key business theories on the subject – notably Peter Drucker's maxim that unless a business has a purpose that is fulfilling a human need and has thought through that purpose, it can't succeed in the same way. Drucker is often credited as one of the first to start thinking about management as a specific area of study. His work is sometimes criticised for its lack of academic rigour and for being too journalistic; yet his pithy aphorisms have lodged themselves in the modern business psyche in a way that many more scholarly works have not. He is also seen as the forerunner of many of today's management thinkers, such as Clayton Christensen and Marshall Goldsmith.

While Drucker agreed that corporations should be profitable, he felt that seeing profit as a purpose gets the equation the wrong way around. Profit is rather a byproduct of success. And to succeed, you need to figure out your purpose – and that purpose must always lie in wider society.

Prefiguring theories on successful innovation, such as Christensen *et al*'s 'jobs to be done' theory, Drucker wrote in 1974 in *Management: Tasks, Responsibilities, Practices* that: "The want a business satisfies may have been felt by the customer before he or she was offered the means of satisfying it."[3]

To Drucker, the ultimate purpose of a business lies in creating a customer through marketing and innovation. Drucker saw 'sales' and 'marketing' as antithetical, not aligned or complementary. He believed that if an organisation puts in the requisite work to define its purpose and sets design and innovation objectives, along with effective marketing, then whatever it is offering should sell itself.

2. Purpose in a crisis – why purpose can help when your back is to the wall

While Drucker's view of purpose is more rooted in cold, hard business reality than Simon Sinek's, I would argue that both achieve the same aim. Drucker's writing on purpose is less focused on the brand associations of purposeful companies than Sinek's. Sinek discusses the iconoclasm that has made Apple such a success story; but whether the customer's need which dictates the purpose of Apple's business is obviously perceived or not, it is a need that the brand has often fulfilled through having a purpose aligned with its values.

This connection between customer need and desires and a sense of purpose which is conflated with the brand also reflects Drucker's maxim about the need for selling being null and void if all other factors are effectively configured. While Apple may market its products, it generally does so in a way that is very slick and that encourages consumers to buy into its purpose and the associations with this, rather than focusing on what specifically is being sold.

The pushbacks I often hear when proposing that legal teams think about these big ideas is time ("Who has time to consider purpose when up against the clock?") and whether this relates directly to their function ("Why do we need to consider purpose anyway?"). There is a constant need to be doing and reacting, which may well be engrained in lawyers' DNA from their private practice days. For many, carving out the time to think about these broader topics is crucial to the redefined role of general counsel, where there is a vital need to see the bigger picture beyond legal. But given these increased responsibilities, some might argue that thinking about seemingly abstract concepts such as purpose is a waste of time.

It may also be that a company's purpose is thrust to the fore in the darkest days of corporate crisis. Patrick Cook-Deegan and Kendall Cotton Bronk, writing in *Fast Company* in February 2018, cite the value of purpose during those challenging moments that increased risk in business brings:

> *We are often amazed at the level of pressure that leaders face on a daily basis – from bullish investors, disgruntled employees, or detractors on social media. It is so easy to always do, and never take time to connect with why you are doing. But it is during those deep, sometimes dark, reflective, and connected moments that purpose-driven leaders make their wisest and best long-term choices.*[4]

For general counsel, the ability not just to advise on legal and business risk, but to proactively scan for all possible risk, is now part of the job description. A more sophisticated corollary to this is the ability to situate those risks within wider societal debates on how their companies can be perceived positively. Some general counsel now count communications as part of their remit, showing how ethics and trust in business (and the perception thereof) are increasingly seen as a function for a company's lawyers to guard. Tim Murphy, general counsel at Mastercard, cautions that the general counsel of the future must make time for purpose to address the challenges of modern business and to better fulfil their role:

> *A common danger that many in-house law departments face is relying solely on management by lawyers who have spent their lives in private practice. That's where you fall into the trap of a client service, project-based mentality. Instead, every general counsel should be spending as much time thinking about the way they're working. Business leaders set strategy with a purpose. This is the core mindset that can truly engrain a law department into the business operations.*[5]

It is also interesting to consider the notion of defining purpose in the legal department within the wider debate on 'adding value'. In many ways, I wonder whether the notion of adding value is a facet of purpose, not an alternative. Considering the role of the modern legal department purely in value or cost-based metrics loses the nuances of the bigger debate within modern business aligned to purpose, values (not value) and ethics. If purpose is couched exclusively in those terms, this inevitably leaves general counsel on a road to nowhere, as the greatest value of the legal department is essentially a negative value: that of costs, monetary and reputational risk avoided through effective organisational risk management. Does the notion of 'value' trap the legal department too firmly within one vision of the corporate model – one based on the bottom line which is aligned purely to the model of profit for shareholders?

Notes

1   Bruce Jones, "Mission Versus Purpose: What's The Difference?" Disney Institute blog, 23 October 2018, www.disneyinstitute.com/blog/mission-versus-purpose-whats-the-difference/.
2   Interview with the author, September 2018.
3   Peter Drucker, "Management: Tasks, Responsibilities, Practices" in *The Essential Drucker* (Routledge 2007), p15.
4   Patrick Cook-Deegan and Kendall Cotton Bronk, "Want A Purpose-Driven Business? Know The Difference Between Mission And Purpose", *Fast Company*, 2 April 2018, www.fastcompany.com/40552232/want-a-purpose-driven-business-know-the-difference-between-mission-and-purpose.
5   Interview with the author, November 2018.

3. Simon Sinek: start with *why*

One of the most popular theories on coalescing a vision for an organisation around purpose is Simon Sinek's *Start With Why*. 'Start with *why*' as a business theory achieved cultural currency first as a TED talk, then as a book[1] and now as a consulting business developed by Sinek, a marketing executive. Sinek started out working for advertising agencies, but set up his own business in the early 2000s. His 2009 TED talk at a TEDX event in Puget Sound, outlining the key ideas of 'start with *why*', went viral.

Sinek's theory aims to determine why certain individuals or businesses are more successful than others. For Sinek, it's not just about market share, but also about influence. Sinek often returns to Apple as a key example. While Apple's overall market share is not as large as that of many of its competitors, its influence is much greater in shaping the use and cultural significance of electronic devices.

1. The golden circle of why

One of the most famous aspects of the notion of starting with *why* is the 'golden circle'. This was outlined in Sinek's original TED talk, which has now been watched more than 4 million times. The concept was inspired by the classic equation of the golden ratio in mathematics.

All companies know what they do. And most know how they do it – differentiated value propositions, USPs and so on. However, very few companies know *why* they do what they do – but inspired companies and inspired leaders do.

Sinek frequently uses Apple as an example because it is easily recognisable and a prime example of the benefits of starting with *why*. Apple is used to illustrate the golden circle proposition of how an idea can change if *why* is introduced at the start.

For example, if Apple approached its product marketing in the traditional way, it would go something like this:
- We make great computers.
- They're beautifully designed, simple to use and user friendly.
- Want to buy one?

There's nothing ground-breaking here that sets Apple apart from any other computer manufacturer. But how Apple actually approaches product market goes something like this:
- Whatever we do, we believe in challenging the status quo. We believe in thinking differently.
- The way we challenge the status quo is by making our products beautifully designed, simple to use and user friendly.
- And we happen to make great computers. Want to buy one?

The purpose, cause or belief has nothing to do with the products it makes. For Sinek, the example proves that people don't buy what you make, but why you make it. As an Apple devotee, I can freely confess that for many years I have bought into this aura of disruption. Another computer is probably just as technically good; but for me, something just feels a bit 'off' about using it.

What also sets Apple apart, Sinek argues, is its nimbleness – which he suggests is ultimately propelled by this notion of *why* driving everything it does. This leads to an overwhelming sense of brand differentiation and authenticity. In turn, this authenticity means that Apple can be trusted to deliver on a desktop computer, an MP3 player, a phone, a watch and so on.

2. No such thing as an i-lawyer?

But does this hold true for professional services – whether in an in-house team or in an external law firm? What if you're not selling an actual product? Arguably, this actually makes things even easier, as Sinek's argument on the pervasiveness of *why* is based on the idea that it is people with passion, purpose and credibility who succeed. It is also those people who think differently. This intersects with the focus in recent years on innovation in the legal profession.

But there's a key lesson here: does too much thinking around innovation in our industry currently focus on the *what* and not the *why*? Is this why, for many, change is increasingly difficult to embed? This would appear to be backed up by the ideas and learnings of many who have been driving change in this area – that often, what is missing is a crucial stage of reflection on why change is needed and what you are trying to achieve through that change. Too many operational change initiatives in law firms and legal departments can rush straight to a potential solution without doing enough groundwork to determine whether it is the right tool or solution.

Nilema Bhakta-Jones was a general counsel for many years, before moving to a CEO role at legal tech start-up Alacrity Law and then to a COO role at Farillio, which is a technology platform delivering legal and business solutions to small businesses and freelancers. Its mission is to ensure that no small business struggles or fails due to a lack of critical information or core materials that it needs to grow and thrive.

She has always been interested in broader business thinking and how to apply that practically in her roles. For Bhakta-Jones, Sinek's *Start With Why* has been fundamental. "I think you can apply his approach to pretty much anything," she says.

In her business roles in newer companies, having a blank slate and being able to set the vision have allowed for a very concentrated application of the theory of purpose: "We used this notion from the start and, interestingly, many of the start-ups who moved into our shared working space at the same time used it too. What problem are we trying to solve?" For Bhakta-Jones, this is a fundamental question that can be used for projects both big and small, to test validity and set the parameters: "This should be the question everyone asks themselves – whether it is to build a new brand, a new product or a new website; buy or invest in a new system or piece of tech; or revisit a process or devise a new one. Why are we doing it? How are we going to do it? For whom and for what benefit?"[2]

3. From *why* to *how* and *what*

One key issue that Sinek identifies is that, while the *why* sets everything else in motion, you cannot lose sight of the other constituent aspects. For the *how*, this involves articulating values and principles as verbs that are easier to follow. 'Innovation', for example, is an amorphous noun; but 'thinking differently' or 'looking at the problem from a different angle' sounds much more achievable. This way of thinking also reflects the fact that innovation is often incremental rather than earth-shattering.

When it comes to the *what*, the overarching value is consistency. For Sinek, the *what* defines the authenticity of the *why* and the *how*. For example, if you say, "We think differently," then everyone you hire must embody this in some shape or form. As Sinek states: "We live in a tangible world. The only way people will know what you believe is by the things you say and do, and if you're not consistent in the things you say and do, no one will know what you believe."[3]

Rob Booth, general counsel at the Crown Estate, has a core legal team of five – himself included – to manage an incredibly diverse set of assets, valued at £13.5 billion. Those assets range from deep sea rights to ancient castles and some of London's most valuable commercial property. When Booth entered the role, his *why* was "To create a sustainable competitive advantage for the Crown Estate"; and his mission was to do that by producing a world-class legal service for his CEO.

Booth is convinced that landing the purpose was the key to unlocking that mission: "I think the paramount thing is having a sense of purpose – that's definitely been a significant factor in getting this done and having the team completely behind it. It's a shared sense of purpose, and I hold myself and my team to the same value equation that we use for our external suppliers."[4]

For Booth, starting with purpose also made it much easier to undertake the task with limited internal resources, as the shared vision and passion counted for a lot: "You don't need that many people or that much time, if you have purpose – it's been proven time and again that purpose-led teams outperform those without purpose. And if you get your purpose right, it's amazing how quickly and elegantly you can build from there."

4. Lack of purpose = lack of success

Drucker suggested that the key responsibility of management is to determine what the purpose of the business is and what it should be. Otherwise, key decision makers in the business will lack direction, and competing theories and ideas from different decisions makers on the end goals of the business could derail any journey towards a shared purpose. Here, the notion of purpose overlaps with culture, leadership and innovation.

Drucker believed that the failure to give purpose and mission sufficient thought is the single biggest contributing factor to business failure. His theory of defining purpose is linked inextricably to fulfilling the customer's needs. However, a key question that must be asked in this regard is: who is the customer? How this is answered, according to Drucker, is a significant determining factor in how the business defines its purpose. The question also has much significance for legal departments, where there may be different layers of customers, such as different internal stakeholders, the CEO, the board and external consumers.

Drucker believed that all too often, leaders ask the question of what the company's purpose is at the wrong time, when it may be facing risks or under threat from market disruption. He felt it is preferable to ask this question at the inception of the business (though even asking it at a time of crisis is better than not asking it at all!). For Drucker, the purpose of a business should also be questioned when it is successful, as new realities and new problems will emerge. This aligns with more recent research (which I will refer to in more depth later) suggesting that purpose is an interactive process, not one set in stone.

5. Intersection of leadership, purpose and trust

"Reason not the need," declared King Lear before decamping to the heath – his point being that rationalisation can only take us so far and the heart wants what it wants. While Lear is not a role model I would advise anyone to follow (he would doubtless end up in front of a tribunal for his management style alone these days!), when thinking about purpose, it is this recognition of the importance of the heart which is at play in the impetus to start with *why*. Businesses that ignore this in favour of pure data and rational analytics do so at their peril.

Data can only tell us so much, according to Sinek. And more data doesn't always help – especially if a flawed assumption set the whole process in motion in the first place. Indeed, Sinek considers that the most effective business thinking and marketing have their effect not in our rational brain, but in our limbic brain. Without a *why*, which generally appeals to the emotions, a decision becomes harder to make. For Sinek, the significant point is to win hearts first, then minds. For him, "the art of leading is following your heart": "This is the genius of great leadership. Great leaders and great organizations are good at seeing what most of us can't see. They are good at giving us things we would never think of asking for."[5]

In *Creating a Purpose-Driven Organization*,[6] Robert Quinn and Anjan Thakor examine the notion of creating purpose from an organisational and leadership standpoint. They argue that many companies now find that "what got you here won't get you there" – the economic focus and incentives for how the company operates in terms of its mission and its treatment of employees will increasingly produce diminishing returns: "A higher purpose is not about economic exchanges. It reflects something more aspirational. It explains how the people involved with an organization are making a difference, gives them a sense of meaning, and draws their support."

The pair discuss the example of Gerry Anderson of DTE Engineering: "Like many of the leaders we've interviewed in our research, Anderson started his tenure as president skeptical about how much it mattered. The concept of higher purpose didn't fit into his mostly economic understanding of the firm." [7]

After the economic downturn of 2008, Anderson found that he needed employees to devote more of themselves to their work; the problem was that his employees were not very engaged. Anderson turned to Joe Robles, a board member of DTE and CEO of the United Services Automobile Association (USAA). USAA's focus on purpose and culture produced much higher engagement levels and success. Anderson's natural focus on economic success and incentives had hit a dead end; and Quinn and Thakor suggest that many modern industry leaders increasingly find themselves at this crossroads:

> *So you now face a choice: You can double down on that approach, on the assumption that you just need more or stricter controls to achieve the desired impact. Or you can align the organization with an authentic higher purpose that intersects with your business interests and helps guide your decisions. If you succeed in doing the latter, your people will try new things, move into deep learning, take risks, and make surprising contributions.* [8]

Notes

1   Simon Sinek, *Start With Why* (Portfolio Penguin 2011).
2   Interview with the author, January 2019.
3   Sinek (n 1), p87.
4   Interview with the author, September 2018.
5   Sinek, (n 1), p60.
6   Robert Quinn and Anjan Thakor, "Creating a Purpose-Driven Organization", *Harvard Business Review*, July–August 2018.
7   *Id.*
8   *Id.*

"While culture – like purpose –
may seem like an aspirational,
blue-sky concept, even very
operational tasks such as
creating process can benefit
from a purpose-driven approach."

4. Purpose in practice

Of course, it's easy enough to say all this – but how do you actually do it?

In *Creating a Purpose-Driven Organization*,[1] Robert Quinn and Anjan Thakor outline key points for leaders, but most of these focus on the fact that leaders should include their workforce and make purpose an iterative activity that infuses everything. To do that, the message must be authentic.

Authenticity often becomes most apparent during crisis or challenge. This is a theme that runs through Simon Sinek's *Start With Why*;[2] it is also echoed in Peter Drucker's message that when you achieve success, things will change, so this is also a great time to think about purpose.

But the message of authenticity must be consistent and ongoing. The authors share anecdotes that show many leaders think of purpose-driven work as another 'to-do' to be checked off a list, and argue that this approach is doomed to failure. Purpose must infuse everything and be consistently referenced.

Quinn and Thakor share the story of Tony Meola, former head of US consumer operations at Bank of America. Meola's purpose was operational excellence. To achieve this, he realised that a defining purpose was needed that infused everything:

> *When you hold it constant like that, when you never waver, an amazing thing happens. The purpose sinks into the collective conscience. The culture changes, and the organization begins to perform at a higher level. Processes become simpler and easier to execute and sustain. People start looking for permanent solutions rather than stop-gap measures that create more inefficiencies through process variations.*[3]

Quinn and Thakor's research makes clear that the successful development of a purpose-driven approach lies in the nexus of leadership and talent management. As Sinek's writing also highlights, the most successful leaders who utilise purpose use it to inspire.

Ultimately, for Quinn and Thakor, the benefits of a purpose-driven approach are multiple. Their research focuses a lot on engagement with individuals. Essentially, the message is to allow individuals to align their own sense of purpose with that of the wider organisation; this, rather than monetary incentives, seems to have the biggest impact on the bottom line. Research conducted across a number of different disciplines shows that those who find meaning in their work perform better than those for whom economic benefit is the sole motivating factor. So purpose may be priceless.

1. Using purpose to start your journey

Thinking about the order of chapters for this book was challenging, as many of the concepts bleed into each other; but it seemed to make most sense to take Sinek's advice to heart and literally start with *why*. And that can be true of many organisational changes – from the more ephemeral, such as culture, to operational thinking. For example, when discussing the case study on culture in Part 2 of this book with Bjarne Tellmann, former general counsel and chief legal officer at Pearson, I found that for Tellmann and his team, their culture change journey was dependent on earlier work they had done on purpose.

While culture – like purpose – may seem like an aspirational, blue-sky concept, even very operational tasks such as creating process can benefit from a purpose-driven approach. Currently, there is a lot of focus on operational thinking and its greater adoption in the legal profession; but would operational thinking benefit from a purpose and leadership around that in order to succeed?

Maria Passemard, former head of legal operations at the John Lewis Partnership, certainly thinks that having a purpose improves thinking about operations. In hindsight, she feels that when she initially took up her position at the partnership, she would have benefited from some thought about purpose: "When I first started this role, it was about doing whatever projects came up, so it was a little bit *ad hoc*. As I started working on those projects, I felt it needed a bit more top-down focus on strategy and purpose."[4]

The solution was to spend time as a leadership team off-site, discussing the partnership's purpose and what the legal team was aiming to achieve, rather than just dealing with whatever seemed most urgent on the fly: "Once we'd got that more strategic focus in place, it made my job easier because I could really see where we were going," Passemard explains. "So I agree that having a shared vision of where you are trying to get to is so important. If you don't have a clear direction, it can be a bit scattergun; and then you are probably not going to achieve a great deal and you are going to do lots of things not very well."

2. Tell me a story

In restructuring what legal departments can do to become more strategic, to ratify what is done and what is prioritised, decisions must be made. Drucker, Sinek and Quinn and Thakor's hypotheses of the importance of purpose are also studies in how we make decisions. In decision making, gut decisions have the edge over rational decisions.

Limbic brain decisions, which come from that part of our brain which is more emotional, tend to be faster, higher-quality decisions. Decisions made by the rational mind can often be overthought. This is what is meant by 'winning hearts and minds'. For all leaders, authentic communication and storytelling are increasingly key, and are crucial to bring about change successfully.

The ability to use stories to outline purpose and bring people on a journey is a significant tool in the leader's toolbox, and one that will feature in subsequent chapters. But as a function of defining and communicating purpose, it is crucial. Jack Ma, founder and CEO of Alibaba, suffered multiple failures before he founded the online marketplace. How did he manage to persuade so many people to come on board with his idea? It was how he communicated the story of its purpose. As Nathan Furr, author of *The Innovator's Method*, describes in a recent interview in the Harvard *Business Review* Ideacast podcast:

> *He was so able to pull people into Alibaba – not just investors but employees – because he was so good at telling the story of how they were going to transform China and he made the people who were around him part of that story... And he told this story and he drew even on this... historical text called Bandits of the Marsh and he drew on that story as well – like we're part of this group of bandits that are going to revolutionize the way commerce is done to help all the small vendors around us. And people just were drawn into that.*[5]

Ma's story framed the purpose of his company within a recognisable trope which is much more appealing than simply maximising profits: that is, the classic Robin Hood narrative of helping the little guy and smashing the system.

Bjarne Tellmann, former general counsel and chief legal officer at Pearson and now senior vice president and general counsel at GlaxoSmithKline Consumer Healthcare, has written extensively about the challenges facing the modern general counsel and how today's legal department should be run like a business, with the same focus on purpose and operations. For Tellmann, the keys to enabling general counsel, as leaders, to implement improvements and changes are having a defined sense of *why* and weaving in storytelling:

> *Where to begin? Start by discussing why. Make it dramatic and urgent. Use imagery... Start with a story, because stories appeal to the heart, not just the head. Whatever your story is, illustrate the consequences of not changing. There are many examples of firms or entire industries that did not adapt to change well: Wang word processing, Kodak film, Nikon cameras, manufacturers of typewriters, carbon paper and bottle openers.*[6]

For Tellmann, the implementation of new ideas can be fruitful only if this initial groundwork has been done: "The *why* can help you focus on the *how*. Only at that point can you begin openly discussing thought processes, trade-offs and alternatives considered. Always come back to the why until you are certain people have begun to accept it."

For Sinek, the definition of a great leader is not necessarily having great ideas, but being able to create the space for others to have great ideas. Establishing a culture where innovation can happen does not simply involve establishing a department that is responsible for innovation. Perhaps counterintuitively, it also involves establishing a culture where failure is allowed. When Edison was asked about how he made the lightbulb he said: "I didn't find a way to make a lightbulb; I found a thousand ways how not to make one."[7] This recognises the importance both of failure and of a culture in which failure is allowed as part of the process.

Much of the current debate around legal operations, data analytics and machine learning does not examine the failures which are often an integral part of the process. It is obvious why: many of those writing in this space have a solution to sell, so they focus on telling good news stories. What is interesting to me is those aspects of success and failure which are not purely technical glitches, but have a definitive human and emotional factor. In my original background in theatre and performance, the 'failures' in rehearsal and the process of working through them often produced great performances. Even after the first night of a production, the run is a continual work in progress, in which the performers learn from every performance. With regard to the theory of purpose, it is significant that the mantra of legal operations is 'People, process, technology'. The people must be won over first, and recognise the value of purpose to them as humans and how they can grow through working towards purpose. This where the emotional pull of purpose can help to drive success.

For Sinek and many other business thinkers, a significant factor of successful change is that employees buy into the sense of *why* change is necessary and have purpose, passion and trust. That is a function of leadership, but also of talent management.

3. Talent and purpose

There is an old fable of three bricklayers all working on the same wall. Someone asked the bricklayers, "What you are doing?" The first said, "I am laying bricks"; the second replied, "I am building a wall"; and the third answered, "I am building a great cathedral for God." The third bricklayer had a vision of how the daily task of laying bricks fitted within a broader, more meaningful purpose. Similarly, when John F Kennedy toured NASA in 1961 and asked a janitor mopping the floor what his job was, the reply came: "I'm putting a man on the moon."[8] Likewise, employees who envision the outcomes of their daily routines find more meaning from them (I am not just writing words on a page, but preparing the next generation of legal business leaders!).

Purpose has a strong overlap with leadership, but also with talent development and talent management. Talent management is a core skill that many general counsel cite as central to what they do – but also one they struggle with. They are not alone: CEO surveys frequently point to talent management as key strategic issue that all business leaders find a challenge. Purpose can be one of the most significant (and useful) aspects of talent management.

As Jeff Boss, a former US Navy SEAL and now leadership adviser, writes:

Purpose is a powerful force. Purpose was what pulled me through eight deployments as a Navy SEAL while getting shot on two of them, surviving four parachute malfunctions and losing more friends than some people can count. If employee performance isn't tied to purpose then they're operating on willpower and discipline – and each eventually run out. Don't get me wrong, willpower and discipline are important, but they're 'muscles' and like all other muscles in the body, they become tired. When willpower and discipline tire out, that's when you raise the white flag and say, 'Okay, I'm done here. Next!' If you want to attain, retain and sustain talent, you need to tie purpose into everything you and your company do.[9]

For purpose to be truly successful, it must resonate with the other individuals who make up an organisation. As Quinn and Thakor point out, purpose must bring the workforce along with it.

4. How do you manage talent to align with purpose?

It's got to be iterative. While a purpose such as the desire of Steve Jobs and Steve Wozniak to 'stick it to the man' – cultivated in the counterculture of San Francisco in the 1960s and 1970s – resonated with them, it also resonated with others. And it continues to do so today: so much so that Apple has managed to cling onto its aura of iconoclasm even after having transformed into a corporate giant – as much a part of the system as 'the man' Jobs and Wozniak rebelled against.

Quinn and Thakor suggest talking to others – your team, your colleagues, your leaders, your clients – to begin developing your *why*, and then come back to them to refine it. By doing this, although the leader may be driving the mission, purpose becomes everyone's co-creation.

Sinek echoes this, recognising that the *why* gains most power when it is shared. For Sinek, when *why* is clearly stated and thought through, it becomes a filter through which anyone in the organisation can make a decision – not just the founder or the CEO. It therefore becomes a clear tenet of good leadership and talent development, empowering others and giving them the tools to succeed.

For Quinn and Thakor, part of developing and integrating purpose is directly linked to stimulating individual learning. Giving individuals projects and stretch assignments that are connected to the purpose of the organisation helps them to grow, and they need less hands-on management.

This focus on purpose and developing autonomy has similarities with how the military operates, with learning, autonomy and purpose inextricably linked: "If soldiers know and internalize a commander's strategic purpose, they can carry out the mission even when the commander isn't there. This means, of course, that the leader must communicate the organization's higher purpose with utter clarity so that employees can make use of their local information and take initiative."[10]

This is important in talent management and leadership – both significant areas of focus for many general counsel. The military analogy is telling: we may erroneously think of military leadership as 'command and control', but it's really more purpose driven. Using purpose to develop autonomy in specific projects can also be incredibly helpful in talent initiatives for legal departments, which are often flat structures.

5. Managing from the middle

Quinn and Thakor make the point that in many organisations, the success or failure of a purpose-driven approach – perhaps surprisingly – lies with middle management. As an example, they cite KPMG, which began to explore the notion of purpose:

> Searching its history, its leaders were surprised to find that it had made many significant contributions to major world events. After conducting and analyzing hundreds of employee interviews, they concluded that KPMG's purpose was to help clients "inspire confidence and empower change." These five words evoked a sense of

awe in the firm, but KPMG's top executives avoided the temptation to turn them into a marketing slogan. Instead, they set out to connect every leader and manager to the purpose.

They achieved this by having leaders talk openly about their own sense of purpose and meaning. Their approach was then to cascade this down to all mid-level management – the partnership – to do the same with their teams: "When senior management shared these expectations, the partners were open to them but did not feel equipped to meet them. So the accounting firm invested in a new kind of training, in which the partners learned how to tell compelling stories that conveyed their sense of personal identity and professional purpose."

This links into the earlier points about inspiring the workforce and crafting a truly authentic message, and shows how leadership is fundamental in aligning the wider team to purpose. The most effective way to do this can be to tell a story which demonstrates your own connection to the purpose. A general counsel in a company where legal had merged with other related teams used the story of his father's love of hats to demonstrate a personal connection to the purpose statement he was using of 'one department, many hats'.

6. Time to face the change

For general counsel who lead a team, defining a sense of purpose for that team is about bringing people along on a journey of change.

If we think about what is currently happening in the legal profession, there is much talk about change and innovation, and much focus on introducing new processes and ways of doing things. In many cases, these changes strike at the heart of what a legal department or a law firm has traditionally been there for.

A significant factor in why many legal teams or law firms experience failure – or certainly, not outstanding success – in introducing change is the fact they don't manage the change particularly well, if at all. And they often don't try to win the hearts before the minds. That leaves their people to default to what they know and feel emotionally and psychologically comfortable with – for example, using a Word contract template rather than an online contract management system, or asking a lawyer rather than using the self-serve portal. According to the theories of purpose, what has gone wrong here is not starting with *why* and not appealing to the heart rather than the mind.

The challenge facing many lawyers – especially those working in legal departments – is to overcome the traditional service-oriented approach and adopt a more purpose-driven, operational mindset. For Tim Murphy at Mastercard, who spent 10 years in a leading business role at the company before returning as general counsel, this sense of purpose is fundamental to becoming a business-oriented legal department: "Every general counsel should be spending as much time as possible thinking about the way they're working, how they're using technology and, most importantly, why they are doing that. Business leaders set strategy with a purpose. This is the core mindset that can truly engrain a law department into the business operations."[11]

Notes

1   Robert Quinn and Anjan Thakor, "Creating a Purpose-Driven Organization", *Harvard Business Review*, July–August 2018.
2   Simon Sinek, *Start With Why* (Portfolio Penguin 2011).
3   Tony Meola, quoted in Quinn and Thakor (n 1).
4   Interview with the author, April 2019.
5   Nathan Furr, "Why You Need Innovation Capital and How to Get It", *Harvard Business Review* Ideacast 686, 11 June 2019, https://hbr.org/ideacast/2019/06/why-you-need-innovation-capital-and-how-to-get-it.
6   Bjarne P Tellmann, quoted in Catherine McGregor, "Start With Why", *DLA Piper WIN Insights*, March 2019, www.dlapiperwin.com/win-insights/articles/2019/start-with-why.html.
7   Quoted in Sinek (n 2), p101.
8   Tanya Jansen, "JFK and the Janitor: Understanding the Why Behind What We Do", beqom, 24 November 2014, www.beqom.com/blog/jfk-and-the-janitor.
9   Jeff Boss, "4 Talent Challenges That Every Leader Must Address", *Forbes*, 16 October 2016, www.forbes.com/sites/jeffboss/2016/10/18/4-talent-challenges-that-every-leader-must-address/.
10 Quinn and Thakor (n 1).
11 Interview with the author, November 2018.

5. Purpose versus… purpose? The challenge of wearing two hats

There is one caveat for lawyers who are trying to find their purpose: essentially, they are the servant of two masters. Lawyers working in-house are trying to balance being an effective business leader with fulfilling the professional obligations of a lawyer.

As Rob Booth at the Crown Estate summarises it:

> There is something special about the purpose of solicitors, barristers and other elements of the legal orthodoxy in the UK. That special element is a responsibility for the rule of law, drawn out in our regulatory framework and a fundamental part of why the profession can be trusted to advise in the way that it does. The rule of law feels often overlooked to me – but any report about the attractiveness of the UK as a place to do business, and certainly for FDI, will highlight the rule of law; our venerable unwritten constitution and all of its constituent parts, as a major global competitive advantage.[1]

The purpose of a lawyer is to uphold the law. Generally, it seems that this can run in tandem with a broader operational and business purpose linked to the wider organisation; but there can be challenges and tensions.

Sometimes these can come from the exciting and disruptive new ideas that are reshaping business. Many of these are ideas that lawyers are often told – even by books such as this – they should become more familiar with. However, the fact remains that in a number of jurisdictions, lawyers are bound by professional rules and standards which cut to the heart of what they do and are why they have been hired by their organisations.

Richard Moorhead, professor of law at Exeter University, has written and researched extensively on ethics and the role of the in-house lawyer. He feels that the drive to purpose, creativity and innovation can produce inherent conflicts:

> *This is partly because cultivation of the skills needed to excel in these areas – such as social decision making, creativity and innovation – can sometimes allow people to think themselves out of the obligation to adhere to rules and regulations. That conflict can often be found in newer industries, where companies are trying to challenge the status quo, as well as in elite firms that see themselves as pushing the boundaries of practice.*[2]

This is where having a purpose that includes a strong ethical component, rather than simply focusing on maximising profits, can assist. In determining the legal department's purpose, general counsel should align it with that of the company; but possibly also use the process as an opportunity to influence the wider organisation to ensure that its purpose includes an ethical component. Ethics are obviously sometimes different from the rule of law; but we increasingly see that organisations are often required to go beyond mere compliance with the law. And that is a further development in the role of general counsel and their teams.

1. Finding your *why*

Despite marketing which may suggest the contrary, purpose, vision or *why* is not handed down from a mountain writ large on tablets of stone. For leaders with a sense of purpose, it is often honed over many years to its final state of clarity.

> *Just as Apple's WHY developed during the rebellious 1960s and '70s, the WHY for every other individual and organization comes from the past. It is born out of the upbringing and life experiences of a small group. Every single person has a WHY and every single organization has one too. An organization, don't forget, is one of the WHATs, one of the tangible things a founder or group of founders have done in their lives to prove their WHY.*[3]

One crucial stumbling block often encountered in the endeavour to set a purpose is how to approach it – or rather, the myth that you cannot approach it: instead, it hits you like a divine revelation. If that doesn't happen, you might reason, perhaps purpose isn't for you and your team.

But this assumption masks the reality for most, if not all organisations that embrace purpose. A significant challenge here is that we frequently describe the process in terms of 'finding your purpose'. This does suggest some Damascene moment of revelation, when we chance upon the purpose, fully formed. One issue here is that in writing about purpose, we are often studying brands which have well-formed purpose statements that work; we're not embracing the reality that everyone struggles with this.

However, as John Coleman, writing in the *Harvard Business Review* argues, in practice this is rarely as easy as it may seem in retrospect: "In achieving professional purpose, most of us have to focus as much on making our work meaningful as in taking meaning from it. Put differently, purpose is a thing you build, not a thing you find."[4]

2. Does your purpose need to be permanent?

Although David Packard, in his speech about Hewlett Packard quoted in Chapter 1, stated that a purpose should last 100 years, in today's fast-moving business environment the failure to adapt your purpose, vision or *why* as needed could be as destructive as not having one at all.

Just as your purpose may not be singular, it may also not need to stay stable. Just as we all find meaning in multiple places, the sources of that meaning can and will need to change over time.

The conclusion of Coleman's article is helpful in approaching the notion of purpose at work. This is not a static goal, but rather an approach, which can then infuse lots of different things we do. This is particularly useful when considering the notion of purpose for a legal department. The legal department will always be in a service capacity to the business, so why and how that service is conceptualised will likely evolve in different directions as the company's operational or sales focus changes.

3. Taking it one step at a time

As with anything highly conceptual – be it purpose, innovation or creativity – breaking this down into steps as something that is built, rather than something that hits in a blinding flash of inspiration, can make it more achievable. And given the training and experience of many lawyers, this more logical, building block-focused approach will likely get more traction. For example, it may be that the legal department has an overarching purpose with regard to its key function as a service area to the business. If we look at our case study of the Crown Estate legal team, this was providing a sustainable competitive advantage to the business.

This overarching purpose can then inform sub-purposes, such as interaction with third-party providers. Crown Estate general counsel Rob Booth and his team, together with their external partners, came up with the idea of the 'bionic lawyer' to produce new approaches to how outside counsel could approach their work. Perhaps this purpose could be defined as 'collaborating to create new models for internal/external partnerships'. But that is inextricably linked to the team's overarching purpose statement for the wider business.

Yes, the initial catalyst for a purpose statement may come as a flash of inspiration; but the chances are that this becomes more of an iterative process, in which that initial inspiration is refined over time. Indeed, Quinn and Thakor's research suggests that this is fundamental to success.

As a former 'creative type', I am sceptical of the notion of the bolt of inspiration. In my experience of the creative industries, the odd flash of inspiration is always balanced by lots of practice and work in making it a reality. No matter how 'inspired' the final performance may look, a lot of time, hard work and practice go into delivering it. Revisiting an idea helps to refine it and helps to cascade the idea to the wider team and get them involved in the process, which often refines it further. Unless everyone in the team can own the purpose in their own way, it is doomed to failure.

4. Envision a purpose-driven workforce

The first step is to decide what you want to achieve, such as envisioning an inspired workforce. Experts such as Quinn and Thakor often advise clients that if you can find one example that embodies the inspiration you wish to engender more widely, it is possible to make the change: "If you can find one positive example – a person, a team, a unit that exceeds the norms – you can inspire others. Look for excellence, examine the purpose that drives the excellence, and then imagine it imbuing your entire workforce."[5] For any major change, having a specific internal example to point to will make that change more concrete to others.

It may be impossible to find all of your inspiration in one place; rather, different people or specific input on certain projects may embody different aspects of the inspiration. You may also want to look outside your own organisation at another team that has used purpose in defining what it does to embody this inspiration. However, when extrapolating from outside your organisation, you must take care to adapt ideas to your context, rather than simply importing them wholesale. This is why the iterative work in the next step is fundamental.

5. Explore your purpose

You then need to discover your purpose. It is worth emphasising that this is an interactive process, so iterative activities are key here. Engage with lots of different people. Listen to their stories about the organisation. Find common themes. Go back and explore these together. This has been a common theme in the legal teams I speak to which are exploring purpose and how to change or modify their strategies. Listening to the team and key stakeholders is a great way to start the journey; but it is also crucial to go back to them to refine the journey once it's underway.

6. Recognise the need for authenticity

As mentioned before, authenticity often becomes most apparent at times of crisis or challenge. This is a theme that also runs through Simon Sinek's *Start With Why*. In the iterative work you do with team members, don't just focus on your successes to identify themes that can help build your purpose; the failures are also key. Interestingly, some in-house lawyers report that sharing and speaking about the things that have not gone to plan is often much more valuable than sharing successes. You generally don't hear these stories in the legal press or at conferences, for obvious reasons; but often peers are more willing to share in smaller groups or closed networks. Learning from failures is another defining quality that start-up culture has brought to wider business.

7. A constant message

Turn the authentic message into a constant message. In many of the successful examples of purpose discussed here, what defines that success is the fact that purpose is seen as a journey, not a goal. Many leaders think of purpose-driven work as another 'to-do' to be checked off a list. It must also be balanced with a laser focus on ensuring that your purpose informs everything you do.

I recently interviewed a legal team which is doing a lot of work on culture change with regard to diversity and inclusion. The general counsel told me that the reason she felt it was working was because it was not a 'nice to have' extra; it was rather a component of every item discussed at the legal team's leadership meetings and had become a sense of purpose driving everything they did.

But you also need to balance that with an awareness that purpose will change and develop as your organisation and the world in which it operates change. In our case study on the Crown Estate legal team, a key issue flagged is that purpose needed to stay dynamic over time.

8. Connect the people to the purpose

Let people make the purpose their own. This may be via projects or stretch assignments that are connected to the purpose. Quinn and Thakor describe KPMG's journey to become a purpose-driven organisation and how it connected all of its people to the purpose. The company set its employees a challenge to design a poster that answered the question, "What do you do at KPMG?", capturing their passion and connecting it to the organisation's purpose.

Each participating employee created a purpose-driven headline, such as "I Combat Terrorism," and under it wrote a clarifying statement, such as "KPMG helps scores of financial institutions prevent money laundering, keeping financial resources out of the hands of terrorists and criminals". Beneath the statement, the employee inserted his or her picture. Each poster carried the tagline, "Inspire Confidence. Empower Change."

In this example, all employees were allowed to see how they contributed to the greater whole. Approaching this through an active, purpose-driven headline can be transformative to how employees see their day-to-day activities. A similar activity could be carried out in any organisation or team. Activities should be seen in terms of action statements that connect to a bigger purpose, rather than just going to work or making money.

Increasingly, the legal department's remit is much broader than simply advising on law. It encompasses risk management, crisis management, ethical values – many aspects which correspond heavily with a purpose-driven viewpoint. Thinking of such headlines for your legal team – which don't mention law, but are action oriented – could be a useful purpose-driven exercise. The really ambitious might want to create a video ad for the legal team! The possibilities are endless and this can also be a good way to use creativity to connect to purpose.

In the Crown Estate case study, general counsel Rob Booth used purpose to help define behaviours. With regard to buying legal services, this overarching purpose was used to create a smart buyer mentality. Empowering his team in this way "required us to build bridges between our business and external suppliers; creating clarity and transparency for our firms and other suppliers".[6]

In terms of day-to-day behaviour, this led to:

> a combination of clarity and transparency [that] generates confidence for our suppliers, which in turn benefits performance. Knowing what we want and what we expect from firms allows us to consistently manage our relationship lifecycles; bringing new firms onto our panel, managing those firms, rewarding those firms and ultimately giving them the chance to renew that lifecycle. We believe that we can now do that really well, supported by a good decision-making matrix, which we and our wider business are committed to.[7]

9. Spread the word

This taps into the power of influence and networking. Lots of studies on culture change confirm that it is crucial to have individuals who help to spread the word – or as Quinn and Thakor term them, 'positive influencers'.

Asking for ideas or assistance with the project can be a good way to tap into this pool of people. It is also a great way to empower and develop your team. Some lawyers have stepped into more of an operational role or helped to implement greater use of technology in their team by becoming the advocate who develops a passion, which brings others along on the journey.

Ultimately, the benefits are multiple. Both identifying the message and finding a connection to it helps individuals to align their own sense of purpose with that of the wider organisation or team. It is this, rather than monetary incentives, which seems to produce the biggest impact on the bottom line.

Notes

1   Interview with the author, September 2018.
2   Interview with the author, September 2019.
3   Simon Sinek, *Start With Why* (Portfolio Penguin, 2011), p215.
4   John Coleman, "You Don't Find Your Purpose, You Build It", *Harvard Business Review*, 20 October 2017, https://hbr.org/2017/10/you-dont-find-your-purpose-you-build-it.
5   Robert Quinn and Anjan Thakor, "Creating a Purpose-Driven Organization", *Harvard Business Review*, July–August 2018.
6   Interview with the author, September 2018.
7   Interview with the author, September 2018.

"Innovation can mean many different things to different companies. However, the quest for the new and the disruptive often fails due to a lack of understanding of what the real issues are before one starts to fix them."

6. Case study: setting a meaningful and sustainable purpose – The Crown Estate

Innovation can mean many different things to different companies. However, the quest for the new and the disruptive often fails due to a lack of understanding of what the real issues are before one starts to fix them. Innovation needs understanding and preparation. Too often, writings on new developments in law, such as legal technology, focus on a piece of software as if it were a magic bullet, designed to fix all legal department woes in one fell swoop. What often emerges in conversations with those who have undertaken the transformational journey in legal teams is that these journeys are much easier and more likely to succeed if they are backed up by a purpose, a vision or a *why*.

Too much focus on the new and disruption of the old can lead to a situation which is the professional equivalent of Christmas morning for a six-year-old, when the reality of the shiny new toy rarely lives up to the expectations.

There are notable exceptions to this, where legal departments have done the groundwork to consider where they are currently and where they need to get to. This work demands a holistic vision and a journey, which suppliers must be brought along on too.

An outstanding example of this is the work of the five-person team at the Crown Estate.

1. Defining the mission statement

The Crown Estate is the commercial property arm of the British monarchy's real estate portfolio. As a brand, it does not scream innovation; but appearances can be deceptive. Indeed, as we will explore more fully in the chapters on innovation, Clayton Christensen's recent work shows that successful innovation is primarily about the *why* of understanding your customers, not the *what* of what the new 'thing' is.

The purpose journey of the Crown Estate legal team had a pretty inauspicious start, as general counsel Rob Booth recalls:

> *A somewhat naïve and newly promoted general counsel (that's me…) confirmed to his new boss (Crown Estate Chief Executive Dame Alison Nimmo) that he would use the legal team to "create a sustainable competitive advantage for the Crown Estate". That wording was not crafted with the benefit of the tsunami of scholarly articles that try to eke out that Holy Grail of corporate resilience, but it felt about right. In post-rationalisation, it has survived our repeated examination and now has power in its longevity – we have found no reason to tweak it yet.*

As the team disaggregated this statement, it felt right because it could achieve the following:
- deliver ambition;
- be measured;
- be benchmarked;
- remain dynamic over time (ie, you can never truly know that it has been satisfied); and
- be understood and owned (it is pretty simple and contains no silly words or dizzying hyperbole).

There was one other aspect of the statement that Booth felt was really important – the 'sustainable' element. The statement had depth and could work as an ongoing mission. This depth meant it could also fulfil both the purpose of the organisation and the professional purpose of the legal team, as Booth explains: "While I am not a fan of lawyers who think that they are special, there is something special about the purpose of solicitors, barristers and other elements of the legal orthodoxy in the United Kingdom."

The purpose of the legal profession is an important part of that, suggests Booth, and the sustainable element of the purpose thus aimed to drive long-term resilience by respecting the rule of law and promoting its primacy:

> *From there, a series of behaviours and approaches cascade to ensure that our ethics, and the policies that embed those ethics, are also aligned to that rule of law element. This is a detail that needed to be explained; it is not called out in the purpose text, but for anybody who studies the "responsible business" agenda – embodied by the work of Colin Mayer – this should hopefully make sense. A legal team or firm that can't connect its purpose to protecting the rule of law has, in my humble view, missed something. Equally, for any team that is struggling with how to motivate millennials with a higher purpose, try hooking them with being a fundamental part of maintaining the country's constitution.*

Mayer's work is pertinent here, as he argues that the very structure of the corporation is fundamental to how it defines its purpose and the value it creates for wider society. Mayer is dismissive in his recent book *Prosperity* about the idea that 'purpose' can simply be slapped onto existing business models; it is the business model itself that must be modelled with purpose.[1] Otherwise, argues Mayer, 'purpose' merely becomes a meaningless slogan with no real value.

Some of these visions have been answered by the establishment of B corps in the United States in 2007. Corporations can apply for certified B corp status, which means that they meet the highest standards of verified social and environmental performance, public transparency and legal accountability to balance profit and purpose.[2] Mayer's solution to the demise of trust in corporations is similar to the notion of the B corp: that mission statements should be enshrined in articles of association. Corporate law would then be "a commitment device" rather than a set of rules. It is this marriage of vision, depth and sustainability that the Crown Estate legal team was aiming for.

Back to the practical task of defining purpose for the legal team, as Booth describes it: "Having almost blurted out the purpose in a fit of enthusiasm, evolution had now inexorably begun. This was definitely a change; and whether you are a fan of John Kotter or not, that change needed adoption and embedding if it was going to work. It being right in my head did not mean it would be successful." Two immediate steps followed, both centred on securing collaboration and buy-in from others to the purpose statement.

2. Collaboration

The first step was to take the proposed purpose back to the team and give them a chance (in a psychologically safe space) to take it apart. This aspect draws on some of the other ideas we will encounter in this book – notably in the part on culture, which is inextricably linked to purpose. Successful culture change requires both psychological safety and the ability to fail, and the change journey must be both iterative and inclusive.

The same held true for the Crown Estate legal team in starting to develop a workable purpose statement. As Booth recalls:

> *In openly and honestly sharing our thoughts on the proposed purpose, we forged something that was manifestly more valuable than my simply dictating it and relying upon my legitimacy and power to entrench it. Perhaps born of a team that was already pretty well aligned and in the exciting pioneer stage of a new way of working, the purpose did not change at the point. I guess if you are setting a purposed that draws on the values of an organisation (the Crown*

Estate's are commercialism, integrity and stewardship), you would hope that you could get quite close to a good answer first individually and then collectively.

The next step was more difficult and involved taking the purpose through the Connected Leaders layer – the Crown Estate's collective executive programme, facilitated by Dr Simon Hayward of business management consultancy Cirrus. This presented the perfect opportunity to see whether the team purpose was something that the wider organisation could get behind. It also happened to coincide with the Connected Leaders deciding to re-enunciate the corporate purpose, so as Booth humorously recalls: "The group was all purposed up and ready to go!" A bigger, more diverse group was always going to be a more challenging play for the legal team's nascent purpose; but it was released into that group and survived. Booth explains: "It was clear from their reaction that some of my senior colleagues were surprised that we thought we could do this; and there may have been a hint of it suggesting some self-importance on our part – but in discussion, it became clear that it was something that they would support. Result."

Booth feels that his collaborative approach in taking the purpose mission to other leaders was key in getting traction for what the team wanted to do. Lateral support from other colleagues and leaders in the organisation was fundamental both in taking it to the next stage and in confirming that it had the necessary rigour to resonate throughout the wider business and was not solipsistic. As Booth explains:

While I am loath to generalise about an industry which has a lot of volatility around its averages, lawyers do perhaps tend to create clever answers in isolation and purpose doesn't really benefit from that. If you are going to go far with it, you really do need as many people as possible to be going with you. A good opportunity to share, taken with some thought, was a massive boost to taking our purpose forward.

3. Making it happen

For the legal team, there were several key stages in the journey to make their new purpose a reality.

The first was to share it. Booth points out that the collaborative aspect of this was a crucial part of the process – but also practical, given that his legal team is so small:

> *We took a conscious decision that our team purpose would also act as a purpose wrapper around all of our external relationships. We have a very neat panel system which is part of delivering our purpose, and our panel firms are very clear that their role is to be entwined with that purpose and to act in partnership with us to deliver it. That sharing has also acted as an effective platform to enable collaboration. By that I mean genuine collaboration – not the cooperation peddled as collaboration that the industry seems rather transfixed by at the moment.*

A significant part of the collaboration piece, both internally and when taken to external relationships, was the ability to explain it meaningfully and succinctly. Booth continues:

> *We put together a short explanation of the purpose that we could roll out to partners and use for internal purposes too. An elevator pitch was important – partly for utility and partly to show we understood it. If you can't explain it quickly and insightfully, you probably don't understand it yourself... With that done, we could embed the purpose and the explanation in all of our conversations and missives, helping adoption with its ubiquity.*

4. Theory into practice

However, the next steps would be the most challenging: turning the more academic vision statement of their purpose into tangible ways of working, which could be repeated and refined day by day.

Booth was well aware of the dangers of becoming too preoccupied with the purpose itself, without giving enough attention, thought and praxis to the living of that purpose: "In a world which is fixated with purpose and its ability to drive outperformance, a neat fit and a few nodding heads are not of themselves enough. Inspiration from a statement exists in a moment or series of moments; and self-evidently, this purpose needed to have impact and to do that in a meaningful and long-term way."

It helped that the new purpose statement had fully resonated with the legal team and had survived being shared across the broader organisation. Booth and the team next needed to break down the purpose into levers which could then be operationalised:

Turning purpose into a way of working that delivers that purpose is difficult and requires a very focused, yet very broad view of all the levers that can and should be pulled in order to create impact. The advantage of having a resonant purpose is that it acts as the guiding principle (we describe it as a laser guidance system), to ensure that each of those levers is indeed pulled in a consistent and coordinated way, giving the best chance of achieving the purpose itself.

Having both a resonant purpose and an understanding of which levers to pull to action it allowed the team to switch between a big-picture view of what they were doing and smaller workable applications of this holistic view. Or as Henry Ford once stated: "Nothing is particularly hard if you divide it into small jobs."[3]

The team therefore focused on building an architecture around the purpose, wholly driven by the goal of achieving it. This was a herculean effort that required real focus and determination, as Booth explains: "The process to operationalise our purpose was definitely a 'go hard or go home' moment and involved a concerted effort over a period of about two years. Anybody who tells you this is easy is probably trying to sell you their services or a book – it is not easy, and it requires a lot of discipline and alignment to achieve."

In approaching the value equation and operational process of their purpose, the team collaborated with the wider business to get a top-level sense of the purpose before getting into the detailed transformation. The challenge with many of the concepts discussed in this book is that they are quite amorphous. What makes the difference between success and failure in using these concepts is the introduction of ways to measure them. As Peter Drucker apocryphally declared, "If you can't measure it you can't manage it."

This was equally true of the Crown Estate's purpose journey – they had to be able to measure it, as Booth explains:

> *Shortly after landing the purpose, we went to work on creating a measurement framework that could be used to work out whether we were delivering it. Our 'value equation' is an eight-factor model, seeking to deliver a science-based validation of competitive advantage. We talk about it being a 'knowledge butterfly' – it learns as more and more information is pushed through it, and as we learn more about our environment. That model and the way we collect information around it have changed quite a bit over the last three years; the model gets more and more reliable as we use it and learn what it is capable of.*

5. Breaking it down

The team based this value equation on what resonated both with themselves and with the wider business. They then broke this down into eight different levers which could have specific actions and outcomes associated with them:

- Delivering legal excellence;
- Maintaining business alignment;
- Anticipating and preparing for change;
- Increasing administrative efficiency;
- Optimising knowledge transfer;
- Leveraging market knowledge;
- Managing cost; and
- Delivering service excellence.

The key to making this work, Booth believes, was creating a smart buyer mentality as well as a heightened awareness of the need for collaboration and partnership outside of such a small team. As mentioned earlier, Booth is scathing about some of the iterations of collaboration which have been lionised by the legal industry. But he is equally scathing of the propensity of some clients to constantly complain about the paucity of solutions given by legal suppliers without ever considering whether they are part of the problem by not asking the right questions. To ask the right questions, of course, requires a very clear sense of your own needs. Here collaboration comes to the fore, says Booth:

One of our significant findings is that for value-based partnerships like this, what you both get out is directly related to what you both put in. Structured and strategic communication is so important in that context. It astounds me how many other GCs, with significant external spend, I see moaning about how their firms don't really understand them; but when you probe a bit, you find they're not proactively bridging the knowledge gap. This won't be a popular comment, but the lazy GC thing doesn't work; we need to give firms inroads into our businesses and guide them to what is important.

Thinking about purpose helped to instil what Booth terms 'a smart buyer mentality' in the legal team. On a daily basis, the team is required to build bridges between the business and external suppliers, creating clarity and transparency for their law firms and law companies. The change has been transformative for these suppliers too, as Booth outlines:

That combination of clarity and transparency generates confidence for our suppliers and in turn benefits performance. Knowing what we want and what we expect from firms allows us to consistently manage our relationship lifecycles; bringing new firms onto our panel, managing those firms, rewarding those firms and ultimately giving them the chance to renew that lifecycle. We believe that we can now do that really well, supported by a good decision-making matrix, which we and our wider business are committed to.

6. Shaking up the traditional buying model

So how did these changes look in practice? Booth explains:

> We are five lawyers looking after £13.5 billion of assets, so we knew that our approach had to focus on the performance of our external ecosystem if we were to genuinely create a sustainable competitive advantage. Our value proposition reflects that, seeking to get the best from a model which relies heavily upon outsourcing. We believe that the best way to do that is to create genuine and invested partnerships, with firms and organisations that we believe will respond to that partnership model.

The team achieved this by looking for the synergies and value arbitrages that sit between their own value equation and the value models of the various organisations they work with. As Booth elaborates: "It's not just about an old-fashioned buying model based on a transfer of money in exchange for fluid capacity and legal knowledge. There is a much wider potential to partner and to make meaningful transfers in that wider relationship."

Crucial to this was thinking not just about what the legal team wanted from these external partners, but also about what they could provide to those partners, beyond cash. What did they have that other firms would value?

Says Booth:

> Our brand is a start; but the unique work we offer, our power to convene, our partnering approach on diversity and inclusion, and even our inspirational CEO are all there for the firms that work with us. If you want a client voice for a junior cohort or somebody who will find the time to provide credentials for an award nomination – that's all there too. While some of that may sound quite granular, it's packaged up as a complete buying model, not just, "I have money – please provide advice."

Prioritising partnerships with external suppliers as an approach to tendering now centres on identifying those firms with which there is the greatest potential to maximise delivery through the legal team's value equation and in turn those that we feel will respond best to what we have to offer to them.

That might sound high minded, but it can be practical too, as Booth outlines:

We typically work with firms not on a matter-by-matter basis or via annual or two-yearly panel reviews, but by offering longer-term exclusivity on meaningful individual mandates. Within a mandate, we can deliver relative certainty on fees – let's say £1 million per year in work; and we will commit to partner on that for five years. The icing on the cake is that if a firm hits a hurdle in its three-year rolling average scores within the value equation, it can 'win' an extra two years without having to retender.

The difference in the offers that the team receives splits broadly into three levels of service focus, as then does the extent of the partnerships. Short-term outlook firms will pitch based on a series of one-year fee positions. Medium-term outlook firms pitch their investment based on £5 million. Those taking a longer-term view pitch based on £7 million and will therefore tailor their performance throughout the period to achieve that. "The offer therefore quite dramatically highlights an immediate value transfer for the longevity arbitrage that we create," Booth explains. "It still takes a lot of work, but the difference is massive if you get it right. Imagine what you would invest for £1 million against what you would invest for £7 million! It's fair to say that we still get pitches in all three camps."

Building a series of arbitrages in buying models allows the team and its suppliers to work on a basis of certainty and generates a very clear picture of who the team really wants to work with.

7. What's in the box?

The team also approaches the purchase of legal services according to a 'gold and silver box' model, which was developed to ensure that buying behaviour is aligned to its purpose. Suppliers are divided broadly into silver or gold boxes, depending on the types of problems they will be solving. This categorisation – which is broader than just deciding whether something is high volume and low risk – allows for more multifaceted decision making by the internal lawyers and a much more collaborative approach between them as buyers and sellers. Different types of work can be categorised according to whether they fit into the gold or the silver box, and both sides are aware of the process through which this designation is determined.

7.1 The silver box
Silver box problems are characterised by being (relatively):
- rules based;
- stable and predictable;
- repeatable; and
- scalable.

Silver box problems are therefore amenable to:
- the application of collaborative problem solving to create a model;
- the application of a process and lean thinking;
- the application of data-driven knowledge and insights;
- the application of technology; and
- a 'train, maintain, sustain' approach.

Silver box problem solving is therefore delivered and priced specifically to the underlying requirements of the silver box itself, creating the model and using/maintaining it.

Silver box problem solving is a 'no lose' play if you get it right.

7.2 The gold box
Gold box problems are characterised by being:

- complex, multifaceted and ambiguous;
- unpredictable and uncertain;
- rapidly changing or chaotically decaying; and
- affected by irrationality, emotion, dishonesty and bias.

Gold box problems are therefore amenable to:
- the application of collaborative problem solving;
- the harnessing of diverse thinking and sources of insight; and
- agility and responsiveness.

Gold box problem solving is therefore delivered and priced specifically to the underlying requirements of the gold box itself and the value that the problem solving creates.

Gold box problem solving is a 'win' play if you get it right.

8. Managing purpose

The eight-lever value equation by which the team defined the constituent parts of its purpose statement now functions as a lifecycle management tool.

The legal team uses this to manage its own workflow and pick partners, manage partners and reward partners externally. It is used both specifically for individual partners and at a holistic level to validate the entire panel system. The legal team uses these eight levers to refine its approach, learn from others, cross-fertilise ideas and approaches, and give feedback for improved future performance. "Stepping back, we can make most decisions that we need to as a team (and there are thousands of them) by pointing the value equation at the purpose," says Booth. Translating the theory of the purpose into manageable levers has helped to refine decision making and has also empowered team members.

9. Live the purpose

This is the point at which purpose intersects with culture: when it infuses all behaviours and thinking. As Simon Sinek has written, it involves making sure that the *why*, the *how* and the *what* are all aligned. For the Crown Estate legal team, extrapolating this series of levers from the purpose statement in turn allowed the team to extrapolate viewpoints and behaviours from those levers which could then drive performance both for themselves and for external partners. This isn't primarily about metrics, but rather behaviour and ethics. As Booth clarifies:

Our purpose is not just about measuring hard metrics and setting scientific KPIs. In fact, we still don't have that many purely data-driven elements within the value equation that translates the purpose. The purpose requires a series of behaviours and a commitment to an underlying ethical stance. These chime with the values of the Crown Estate, and we look for those behaviours and ethics across our partners and within our team. The result is far from perfect; but what it has done is allow us to identify the good and link that good to reward – all driven by an overarching purpose that is now three years old and really getting into its stride.

There are a whole series of further models that we have implemented in order to complete the architecture. We have a model for legal service definition (relying upon gold and silver boxes); we have a model for structuring our buying (based on 'capitalising' our buying model to maximise longer-term performance) and we have a model for collaboration (utilising set pieces to foster background collaboration). It might sound a little overcomplicated, but actually it makes our lives much simpler. It is very, very difficult to generalise how to approach situations, unless you have a model or series of models that allow you to connect the situation back to your purpose. Given I was a scientist before I was a lawyer, I also have a pathological need to understand what is going on behind the activity.

Purpose is, of course, aligned to strategy – although, as the quote from David Packard at the beginning of this chapter pointed out, purpose must be something with more longevity and something that is sustainable. When setting strategy and goals for the legal team, the notion of gathering diversity of thought and collaboration informs this and makes the legal team's partnerships with external counsel a central pillar of how this is approached. This is done via a series of quarterly meetings with individual panel firms – each of which lasts about 90 minutes and, crucially, has its own specific purpose:

- Q1 – performance: The legal team and panel firms discuss what drove performance at the Crown Estate over the last 12 months and what is anticipated will drive performance over the next 12 months. Or as Booth puts it, "It seeks to lift the lid on our annual report to provide context for our firms."
- Q2 – strategic risk: This is not about granular risk management, but rather involves an analysis from the macro environment all the way down to how risks manifest and affect the delivery of the legal team's strategy. This is used to push for a deeper understanding of the issues the Crown Estate faces as a business, and how the internal legal team and their outside counsel must work together to tackle the risks and seize the opportunities that arise.
- Q3 – strategy: This is a run-through of the detailed strategic planning that comes out of the Crown Estate board strategy session. Having this executive perspective is really helpful, suggests Booth: "We do this because I am convinced that it helps to explain the decisions that we are making and gives our firms insight into likely activity levels. It also enables them to draw out what is really important within the more tactical transactional delivery."
- Q4 – the value equation: This is a deep dive on each firm's performance during the year. That is carefully calibrated and firms are benchmarked (on an anonymised basis) both against their peers and against the team's view of the legal market. The internal lawyers try to draw broad input on firm performance at a qualitative level, including taking feedback from non-legal members of the business, other firms and the Crown Estate's wider supplier base. They also draw on a small number of important quantitative metrics and frame all of the feedback around the value equation derived from the purpose statement. "It's very much a forward-looking exercise," says Booth. "But it does also cover the delta between performance and expectation.

I'm not a fan of being a slave to metrics, but we do look at cost volatility, litigation volatility, service level trend and panel performance volatility to help us with validating our feedback. Beyond that, we try to score as scientifically as we can on our qualitative metrics, hanging those qualitative metrics off the value equation." But this is not just a one-way street: the legal team uses the session to gather panel-wide feedback on its own performance, so that insight can be used to refine and develop the value equation. "After some initial nervousness, our firms are now open and transparent with their reflections on our approach," says Booth. "The upshot is that we believe we are getting better performance from our firms than we have ever had before and we have the science to prove it to our business."

But it goes a deeper than that. Having embedded these sessions, the legal team can now draw on each firm to provide input to the team's own strategic planning, both at an individual level and in collaboration with other firms. This coalescing around the purpose has been significant, feels Booth:

I'm very proud of how our firms have responded to that, including their participation in a 'material issues' panel session that I co-led with my CEO and CFO. That session generated content on macro-issues that went to our board and was ultimately recognised in our annual report. It was a great example of the power of holistic thinking and purposeful collaboration, which produced a think piece with real teeth.

Booth firmly believes that having a shared sense of purpose has been transformative, allowing the team to do more and collaborate more effectively with external partners: "You don't need that many people or that much time if you have purpose – it's been proven time and again that purpose-led teams outperform those without purpose; and if you get your purpose right, it's amazing how quickly and elegantly you can build from there."

But, cautions Booth, purpose should be set with empathy to its environment. Purpose can drive outperformance, but only if it is connected to your activities. That is where a lot of the work lies, but also where the true value will come. As Booth concludes: "Inspiration alone is not enough. But do I think starting with *why* is worth the effort – yes."

Notes
1   Colin Mayer, *Prosperity* (Oxford University Press 2018).
2   Certified B Corporation, "About B Corps", https://bcorporation.net/about-b-corps.
3   Flavio Medrut, "25 Henry Ford Quotes to Make You Feel Like You Can Achieve Anything", Goalcast, 24 December 2017, www.goalcast.com/2017/12/24/henry-ford-quotes/.

Part II: Culture

....

Culture eats strategy for breakfast.

Peter Drucker

7. Why culture?

'Culture' is defined as the ideas, customs and social behaviours of a particular people or society. When we consider this in organisations, it encompasses the ideas, customs and beliefs that shape how people work together. This seemingly intangible phenomenon has dominated a lot of business thinking in recent years: how to create a good organisational culture; how to re-engineer a culture which isn't so great; day-to-day hacks to maintain or shift a culture; and so on.

Culture is now seen as fundamental to business success, but also incredibly difficult to quantify. As an idea, it intersects with many other qualities that are significant for modern business success, including purpose-driven leadership, talent management and strategy, to name a few.

As Peter Drucker is apocryphally supposed to have declared, "Culture eats strategy for breakfast."

But the elusiveness of culture as a concept can deter rationally minded lawyers from engaging fully with it. "Isn't it all a bit too touchy-feely?"

they might ask. However, culture definitely does matter: a Harvard Business School report by John Kotter and James Heskett showed that in a 10-year study of 200 companies, those with strong corporate cultures increased their net profit by a staggering 765%.[1] Kotter and Heskett attempted to quantify organisational culture and how this can affect profits in their book *Corporate Culture and Performance*.[2]

As legal teams – like their colleagues elsewhere – must increasingly look to the bottom line, being more mindful about culture seems to be a must-have: not merely a 'nice to have', but something that can create both profitability and efficiency. When we talk about culture with regard to the legal department, this can variously refer to the department's own culture; the wider culture of the organisation of which it is part; and indeed the cultures of other departments. As Kotter and Heskett show, while these constituent parts may contribute to the holistic culture, they can also diverge significantly: "Although we usually talk about organizational culture in the singular, all firms have multiple cultures – usually associated with different functional groupings or geographic locations."[3]

But to what extent is culture an imperative for general counsel and their teams? In a presentation for Pearson's legal department, Bob Mignanelli, COO for the legal department and executive sponsor of the team's culture change initiative, laid out the reasons why today more than ever, legal departments need to think about culture:

- *A legal department's culture is a critical factor in determining its success as a business partner to the broader organisation.*
- *A strong, positive culture will attract top talent and create an environment of elevated performance across the organisation.*
- *A weak, negative culture will drive away top talent and create an environment of mediocrity.*[4]

Sean Roberts, former general counsel of GlaxoSmithKline's consumer healthcare business, agrees that culture should be a central focus of the modern legal department and its general counsel: "For me, thinking about culture is incredibly important. As a threshold matter, I would not want to work in an organisation that didn't have a clear articulation of its purpose and vision that you can help shape. That is fundamental – and how you enact that vision, that's your culture."[5]

Kenny Robertson, head of outsourcing, technology and IP legal team at Royal Bank of Scotland (RBS), feels that a focus on culture is fundamental not only for organisations, but also for those who run teams within those organisations, such as general counsel: "The fabric of the team and the culture is a big piece for us, in terms of who we are and building engagement both within the team and more broadly."[6]

Kenny's team has created a document outlining its culture, the genesis of which was collective:

We ran a session last year on culture: what we think our culture is and where it should be; where the gaps are. The reason I wanted to have something like that was that, while it's not always plain sailing, I did want us to appreciate how good we have it. It was also an exercise to codify where we think we are already, as well as to deliver objectives for where we want to be.

This cultural engineering is key. In the chapters on culture, I will consider first, the ways in which leaders can shape cultures; and second, what I believe are unique changes to the role of the general counsel in shaping organisational culture specifically. I will then look at the building blocks of great organisational culture – specifically, safety, shared vulnerability and shared purpose – and how these align with the changing role of the general counsel and his or her team. Finally, we will consider a case study showing how a legal department is using these ideas both within its own team and within the wider organisation.

1. Leading culture

Leading culture is a fundamental aspect of effective leadership. James Heskett, professor emeritus at Harvard Business School, advises leaders that working on culture is a game-changing part of their role: "The task of nurturing and changing culture is an important responsibility of the CEO; it has to be led from the top."[7]

This is not something that is confined to the biggest organisations or legal teams; in his first day as part of a two-person team of co-founders at Intuit, Scott Cook started by writing a handbook about the company's culture! There is an important lesson here for sole or small team general counsel who might think that culture is a luxury reserved for larger legal departments. That can be a huge mistake, as Bjarne Tellmann, former general counsel and chief legal officer at Pearson and now senior vice president and general counsel at GlaxoSmithKline Consumer Healthcare, warns: "Many people in this position consider themselves to be too busy building the business or department to be conscious about how they are building their cultures. That is a big mistake. Poor culture will kill your organisation as quickly and efficiently as poor products, lousy service or a maladaptive strategy."[8]

The importance of culture is aligned to a range of other key drivers in organisations and teams. And it has fundamental importance for the leader of a team, as Booz & Company's Jon Katzenbach and DeAnne Aguirre outline in an article published in *Strategy + Business*: "Your role as cultural leader is, more likely than not, the single thing you will be most remembered for. That's why so many CEOs refer to culture as their highest priority; it is the primary vehicle for establishing their legacy."[9] This legacy is essentially the effect that you as a leader have had on people, and is also why culture is so significant in both talent and collaboration strategies.

Culture change is an interesting phenomenon to study: when it works, it is a unique dance between the needs of the individual and those of the organisation. Leadership is pivotal in aligning these two drivers and ensuring that there is organic interaction between both. Research into successful culture change suggests that the best leaders are fully aware of their influence on culture and how they help to set the balance between the needs of individuals and the organisation.

Boris Groysberg of Harvard Business School, along with Jeremiah Lee and Jesse Price of executive recruiter Spencer Stuart, conducted extensive research into how organisational cultures can change, which revealed that leadership is a significant factor:

> *For better and worse, culture and leadership are inextricably linked. Founders and influential leaders often set new cultures in motion and imprint values and assumptions that persist for decades. Over time an organization's leaders can also shape culture, through both conscious and unconscious actions (sometimes with unintended consequences). The best leaders we have observed are fully aware of the multiple cultures within which they are embedded, can sense when change is required, and can deftly influence the process.*[10]

In creating and changing culture, leaders are crucial. They set the scene and show that a sense of belonging, a shared purpose and shared risk taking and vulnerability are priorities. They function as role models – whether that is a conscious choice on their part or not. Leaders can also demonstrate the professional importance of key cultural markers and belonging by changing the conversation around what success at work looks like, both internally and externally, and by driving difficult conversations where that's not happening. This is where the general counsel and his or her team can come to the fore: helping to define the culture of an organisation in a way that says certain behaviours are unacceptable and that return for shareholders cannot be achieved at all costs while ignoring ethical behaviour.

While leadership is fundamental to culture, culture cannot be dictated from the top down. But neither can it be purely a grassroots phenomenon – if there is no leadership buy-in, change is much harder to effect. What is crucial for leaders in creating a culture is establishing an environment in which it is okay to try things and fail, or simply in which all voices can be heard. Google is often cited as a great example of culture, and the focus here is often on the tangible markers of a work culture that differs from many others in blending aspects of work and non-work life. This has certainly influenced many people's ideas of what a culture-driven workplace looks like.

Much of this focuses on freebies or paid-for services provided on Google campuses around the world, including shuttle rides to work and free food and drink. However, as Laszlo Bock points out in his book *Work Rules!*,[11] these freebies were based on suggestions from Google employees. What is actually much more significant, for Bock, is the cultural aspect: the fact that Googlers know they can suggest such programmes and therefore shape their own workplaces.

What comes across forcibly in the discussions on leaders in texts that look at unique organisational cultures – such as Coyle's *The Culture Code*,[12] Catmull's *Creativity Inc*[13] and Bock's *Work Rules!* – is that many of them are not leaders in the traditional sense of the word; and indeed, that many of them display contradictory attributes even among each other. We discuss this in more detail in the chapters on leadership.

But what is significant about them all is that they can create situations or cultures where teams can work most effectively together. As former Navy SEAL Dave Cooper states in *The Culture Code*:

> *Having one person tell other people what to do is not a reliable way to make good decisions. So how do you create conditions where that doesn't happen, where you develop a hive mind? How do you develop ways to challenge each other, ask the right questions, and never defer to authority? We're trying to create leaders among leaders. And you can't just tell people to do that. You have to create the conditions where they start to do it.*[14]

In many of the legal teams I focus on in this part of the book, the leader or the general counsel plays a pivotal role in driving the creation of culture and often the initial understanding that this is something that needs to be focused on. In the outsourcing, technology and IP legal team at RBS, the impetus for much of this work sits with general counsel Kenny Robertson. He feels that, to paraphrase Marshall Goldsmith: "What got you here won't get you there." For the majority of legal teams to be truly fit for purpose for the future, much of what they must focus on is not legal *per se*, but rather the business of law. And building and maintaining a top-notch legal team comes down to the culture you create with that legal team, as Tellmann explains: "Your legal department's culture is the essential medium in which your team works. If the culture is polluted or suboptimal, your team will be unable to perform at their best."[15]

2. General counsel as cultural engineers

Is good leadership really just about creating the conditions for people to flourish?

And is good legal leadership about not just managing the legal department *per se*, but also finding ways to empower a corporate culture that becomes compliant naturally? Increasingly, general counsel see their role as creating a culture which is ethical and compliant beyond the traditional sense of promoting and maintaining adherence to a set of rules and regulations. That is obviously still a key part of it; but there is also increasingly a need to adopt proactive strategies to create corporate cultures in which laws and regulations will not be contravened. And that involves empowering everyone in the organisation, rather than the general counsel and his or her team simply policing them. This is partly a result of the fast pace of business and the fact that in many newer industries, characterised by start-ups, high-growth companies and cutting-edge innovation, the law is sometimes not able to keep up. Therefore, proactive risk management, rather than mere adherence to the letter of the law, is what sets apart the modern general counsel from the traditional concept of the role.

But is this achievable? Writing in her book *Powerful*,[16] Patty McCord – former chief talent officer at Netflix – agrees that the move from aspiration to reality can definitely be challenging. The inspiration for her book – and for much popular debate and writing about the culture at the company – was Netflix's 'culture deck': an unadorned PowerPoint which quickly achieved mythic status on the Internet. This is not something McCord ever expected, as she admitted in an article in the *Harvard Business Review* in 2014:

Sheryl Sandberg has called it one of the most important documents ever to come out of Silicon Valley. It's been viewed more than 5 million times on the web. But when Reed Hastings and I (along with some colleagues) wrote a PowerPoint deck explaining how we shaped the culture and motivated performance at Netflix, where Hastings is CEO and I was chief talent officer from 1998 to 2012, we had no idea it would go viral.[17]

Outlined in the deck were the key principles of Netflix's culture and talent management approach, which could perhaps be summarised as: "Don't add, but subtract." Much of this resulted from the decision not to privilege a style of leadership that has arguably lost its way, particularly regarding transparency and communication: an attitude of top-down command and control, where the assumption is that everything leaders do is right, but this is shrouded in secrecy. McCord argues that this lack of transparency and communication is often masked by rules and schemes that purport to foster employee engagement, but can end up doing the opposite.

A key aspect of the Netflix culture deck was its recognition of the inherent tension in navigating aspiration and reality. This tension informs much of the creativity, but also much of the challenge, of the role of the general counsel and the legal department in engineering culture: "It's easy to write admirable values; it's harder to live them. In describing courage, we say, 'You question actions inconsistent with our values.' We want everyone to help each other live the values and hold each other responsible for being role models. It is a continuous aspirational stretch."[18]

This is perhaps a perfect description of the evolving role of the general counsel and the legal department: having the ethical courage to question actions that are inconsistent with both the company's values and the wider ethical mores of society. Increasingly, these are coalescing as companies appreciate the economic consequences of being held accountable for their actions.

Rachel Walker – general counsel at Gazeley, a leading developer, investor, owner and manager of logistics facilities and technology-led solutions – would agree: "This 100% resonates with me. As general counsel, I am often asked to talk about Gazeley's corporate culture and I absolutely see it as one of my responsibilities to lead with integrity and to set the tone for the rest of the business."[19]

For Rachel, the leadership attitude to compliance is defining for all leaders – not just legal leaders – in helping to create a corporate culture that promotes alignment and collaboration:

> *In some other organisations, the perceived tension between legal and the rest of the C-suite can be focused around approach to compliance. We're different – commitment to compliance is something that is upheld in all areas of the senior leadership team, although it's my job to ensure that we have a robust programme in place and that our colleagues are trained properly.*

> *In today's social media-driven world, reputation can be shattered in an instant… So I really don't see us a being a company where on the one hand the deal teams want to take certain risks and legal says "No!" – we are so much more aligned than that.*

For Rachel, creating this shared accountability means that leaders are co-creating a culture in which the right discussions are taking place. Tensions can arise; but the alignment at Gazeley, Rachel feels, produces healthy tensions: "To the extent there is any tension, I welcome it. Tension leads to decisions where you have considered every angle – therefore, good decisions."

As the role of the general counsel and his or her team has shifted from being mere lawyers to business leaders who happen to have a legal background, the delineation of what this role entails is likewise shifting. It is no longer just legal work they undertake; this has now merged into ethics and compliance, social responsibility, crisis management and risk management.

Increasingly, where the general counsel and his or her team add real value is on proactive work rather than reactive work. To a great extent, this has always been where the true remit of the legal team lies and has been a contributory factor as to why 'value' is so hard to prove. In legal departments, value must often be measured by what does not happen or is avoided, rather than what actually occurs.

I would argue that the shift to a more proactive stance is accelerating as the notion of the general counsel as risk and cultural arbiter gains prominence. This is also how the culture creation aspects of the general counsel role are coming to the fore. The remit is not limited to dealing with the ramifications of a toxic culture, but also includes collaborating with other key executive officers to ensure that the culture of the organisation works and blends together as effectively as possible. And as the modern consumer is increasingly driven by ethical choices, this focus also adds value to the bottom line, as Kotter and Heskett demonstrate in their study.

But what does 'good' look like when it comes to culture and how do you get there? Every culture, like every innovation, is unique to the organisation's starting point, the make-up of its teams and its purpose.

General counsel are now considering both how to create cultures within their own teams and how their goals as a legal department impact on the broader culture within their organisations. We can clearly see this in the example of the Crown Estate in Chapter 6. For the modern general counsel, the cultures of their own teams and those of their wider organisations are based on an agile, forward-thinking, horizon-seeking perspective that is reflected in the departments they are creating or want to create. This could be relative to process or to risk taking and general counsel modelling good corporate behaviour.

Notes

1　John Kotter, "Does Corporate Culture Drive Financial Performance?" *Forbes*, 10 February 2011, www.forbes.com/sites/johnkotter/2011/02/10/does-corporate-culture-drive-financial-performance/.
2　John P Kotter and James L Heskett, *Corporate Culture and Performance* (e-book, Free Press 2008).
3　*Ibid*, location 83.
4　Interview with the author, August 2019.
5　Catherine McGregor, "Is the Key to Business Success Cracking the Culture Code?", *Global Leaders in Law Current Awareness*, February 2019.
6　*Ibid*.
7　Sean Silverthorne, "The Profit Power of Corporate Culture", *Harvard Business School Working Knowledge*, 28 September 2011, https://hbswk.hbs.edu/item/the-profit-power-of-corporate-culture.

8   Bjarne P Tellmann, *Building an Outstanding Legal Team* (Globe Law & Business 2016), p216.
9   Jon Katzenbach and DeAnne Aguirre, "Culture and the Chief Executive", *Strategy + Business*, 28 May 2013, www.strategy-business.com/article/00179?gko=0fb40.
10   Groysberg, Lee, Price and Cheng, "The Leader's Guide to Corporate Culture", *Harvard Business Review*, January–February 2018.
11   Laszlo Bock, *Work Rules!* (John Murray 2016).
12   Daniel Coyle, *The Culture Code* (Cornerstone Digital 2018).
13   Ed Catmull, *Creativity Inc* (Transworld Digital 2014).
14   Coyle (n 8), p138.
15   Tellmann (n 5), p212.
16   Patty McCord, *Powerful* (Silicon Guild 2018).
17   Patty McCord, "How Netflix Reinvented HR", *Harvard Business Review*, January–February 2014, https://hbr.org/2014/01/how-netflix-reinvented-hr.
18   Netflix Jobs, "Netflix Culture", www. Jobs.netflix.com https://jobs.netflix.com/culture.
19   Catherine McGregor, "A Place For Radical Honesty in leadership", *DLA WIN Insights* 2019, www.dlapiperwin.com/win-insights/articles/2019/a-place-for-radical-honesty-in-leadership.html

"For the modern general counsel, the cultures of their own teams and those of their wider organisations are based on an agile, forward-thinking, horizon-seeking perspective that is reflected in the departments they are creating or want to create."

8. What creates a good corporate culture?

A variety of research suggests that there are some universal factors which help to build effective cultures. These are fundamentally rooted in the ways that teams work together. So there is obviously significant input with regard to providing leadership and promoting collaboration, as well as coalescing around a shared purpose or vision.

Daniel Coyle – author of *The Culture Code*,[1] which analyses the building blocks of successful organisational cultures – became fascinated by culture when writing his earlier bestselling book *The Talent Code*,[2] in which he analysed what talent was and debunked the myth that talent is innate, positing instead that it can be created and nurtured. As part of his research, Coyle investigated what aligns highly performing teams and organisations. Sports teams, tech businesses, Navy SEAL teams, high-achieving schools – all have a unique cohesiveness and speak of themselves as though they are family. What inspires this cohesiveness and how it is described are often similarly unquantifiable: "It's just the way things are"; "It's the secret sauce" and so on. In this sense, culture is a bit like a pair of shoes: when they fit, you don't notice them; but when they don't fit, you can't think about anything else!

In *The Culture Code,* Coyle studies a range of organisations to identify the factors that cause cultures to work and what happens when they are missing. Coyle identifies three core skills which contribute towards building a cohesive culture:

- Build safety: This explores how signals of connection generate bonds of belonging and identity.
- Share vulnerability: This explains how habits of mutual risk inform trusting cooperation.
- Establish purpose: This explains how narratives create shared goals and values.

The three skills work together from the bottom up, first building group connection and then channelling it into action.

These three focus points clearly align with the ideas outlined by Patty McCord and Ed Catmull when describing the unique cultures at Netflix and Pixar respectively. In the case of Netflix, its success was down to a nimble, high-performance culture; in the case of Pixar, a sense of collaboration, creativity and possibility. What is interesting in both cases is that the authors point to a sense of togetherness, safety, the ability to fail and shared purpose. Also underpinning both cultures is a sense of honesty and a willingness to face up to problems. And it is here that general counsel can be a fundamental catalyst to creating culture not only in their own teams, but also in their wider organisations.

1. Building safety

A feeling of safety is not a byproduct of a strong culture, but rather the foundation on which it rests. This is something that all my general counsel interviewees on this topic feel is fundamental to a cohesive culture.

Coyle recalls that all in of the groups he visited when researching *The Culture Code* which exemplified strong organisational cultures, members used the term 'family' to describe their relationships with each other. This was also reflected in certain external factors exhibited by these groups, including physical proximity; active listening; short, energetic exchanges; lots of questions; and few interruptions.

These behavioural codes speak to our primal sense of safety by signalling belonging and answering the questions, "Are we safe here? Is there danger? Is there a future with this group of people?"

Safety is one of our primal needs, as reflected in Maslow's hierarchy of needs,[3] represented as a pyramid with the most basic needs at the bottom – of which safety is the second. When it comes to safety in an organisation, Coyle suggests that this is secured through a feeling of belonging. According to Coyle's analysis, belonging is coded through investing energy in:

- interactions – showing that they matter;
- individualisation – showing each person that he or she is unique and important; and
- future orientation – signalling that the relationship will continue.

Leigh Kirkpatrick, who works for Kenny Robertson at Royal Bank of Scotland (RBS) and leads a unit within his broader team, feels that this sense of safety is a prerequisite for cohesive cultures and must be tangibly demonstrated:

A key way that safety is demonstrated, and that I have been really aware of in the wider team, is that people have the ability to come to you and share issues, problems or talk through ideas. I would contrast that with the experience, which to me is typical in private practice, where partners may often say they have an open door policy but the conversation is handled in such a way as to not make you want to go back! Whenever someone asks to run something by me, I always prioritise that, as I feel that's how we demonstrate safety and caring for each other.[4]

In the law firm example, the 'belonging' is merely window dressing; and importantly, there is a lack of individuation and feeling that there is any real investment in the relationship or its continuation.

As a team which has a significant focus on culture, the outsourcing, technology and IP legal team at RBS also endeavours to build safety through a blended focus on both the greater group and the individual.

Central to this is coaching. Kirkpatrick explains: "In the coaching framework that is in place with my sub-team, there is the expectation that we will have two coaching sessions a week. That might involve having a call with a business stakeholder and getting feedback at end. There's also a lot of peer-to-peer coaching. One of the team has just been coaching Kenny this morning."

For Robertson, being coached by someone junior is a significant piece of role modelling in building the culture: "One of the key aspects is that you need to be able to be coached, especially as a leader, and to demonstrate that you don't have an ego. Different perspectives are key."

In Robertson's team, there is a strong sense of group belonging, but also of individuation. In his analysis of an Indian-based call centre business, Wipro, in *The Culture Code*, Coyle shows that this balance is fundamental to building culture. When Wipro decided to try to fix its atrocious employee retention rate, the most effective method was not to build a sense of the advantages of the organisation, but rather to build a strong sense of the individual as situated within that organisation and what each individual brought to it.

Sean Roberts, former general counsel of the consumer healthcare business at GlaxoSmithKline (GSK) concurs with this notion that the whole is more than the sum of its parts, and suggests that a sense of safety – far from breeding complacency – plays a vital role in this equation: "A safe environment doesn't mean that you don't face challenges or you can't challenge yourself. But if you are bringing your true self, that allows for real growth potential for yourself and the team." As an example, Roberts points to the lesbian, gay, bisexual and trans (LGBT) experience at GSK:

> *I have for many years been a straight ally to our LGBT group and have seen them grow from early beginnings to a point where my LGBT colleagues have flourished through an organisational culture that quite rightly sees them as valuable colleagues, along with all others. It makes us all feel very proud to be working in a place where we can be who we are and contribute our best without fear or inhibition. We are safe.*[5]

Roberts also points to the fact that such safety allows individuals to reflect on the bigger picture: "These cultural foundations generate some fantastic conversations about how we as a team, and how we as an organisation, operate. That is particularly important in an industry like ours, where ethics and values are such a central component."

That notion is echoed by Damien Atkins, general counsel of global confectionery company Hershey, who suggests that there are definite commonalities within legal departments and companies regarding psychological safety: "When people say, 'We are family,' they are really expressing that psychological safety and ability to be who they are and live their own values." A defining aspect of this for Atkins – and something which can be really significant for the legal department – is the ability to disagree: "It's key that I can express differences and, if I disagree with leaders, that I can do so without being punished. That to me is the strongest indicator of a cohesive culture."[6]

This reflects what Coyle points to in high-performing cultures: a sense of belonging seems to work best when it involves a dance between the needs of the individual and those of the group, rather than a binary either/or. One tactic that Coyle hones in on is how leaders situate the individual and the group both in relation to each other and in the wider world context – both of which are further cemented by the next two building blocks in the culture code.

2. Share vulnerability

If creating a sense of safety is the foundation of a great culture, the next building block – which is equally important – is shared vulnerability. This might seem counterintuitive, particularly for those who assume that professional situations require a display of infallible competence. However, this is countered by evidence which shows that revealing vulnerabilities and receiving a reciprocal show of vulnerability in return enhances the ability to work together. Coyle quotes the work of Harvard professor of organisational behaviour Jeffrey Polzer, who has shown that a 'vulnerability loop', as he terms it, is the best mechanism for building cooperation and teamwork: "Vulnerability loops seem swift and spontaneous from a distance, but when you look closely, they all follow the same discrete steps: Person A sends a signal of vulnerability. Person B detects this signal. Person B responds by signalling their own vulnerability. Person A detects this signal. A norm is established; closeness and trust increase."[7]

Coyle's thesis is that organisations that do not allow people to fail, be vulnerable or get things wrong don't have great cultures. One common characteristic of those that do have great cultures, however, is greater cooperation and teamwork, stimulated by safety and thus the freedom to display vulnerability. A key example of this is the coaching system at RBS, where Robertson – the general counsel and team leader – is also being coached by team members and thus displaying vulnerability. This sends out an unequivocal message that vulnerability is okay. I will discuss this in more detail later in this chapter in relation to the 'Failure Camp' established by Cat Moon, who runs the Programme on Law and Innovation at Vanderbilt Law School in Nashville.

Coyle frequently points to Google as an organisation that has institutionalised vulnerability into its culture. The uniqueness of Google's culture and its focus on cultural fit has been the subject of many books – most notably *Work Rules!* by former chief people officer Laszlo Bock, which is referred to throughout this part of the book.[8]

Google's overwhelming ethos was designed as anti-bureaucratic. As Coyle details, its seminal breakthrough with AdWords came not from a strategy meeting or a project taskforce, but rather from an employee randomly responding to Larry Page's Post-it Note left on the kitchen fridge.

The cornerstone of creating a safe context in which vulnerability can be shared has persisted within the company as it has grown and as it has expanded to include different departments such as legal. I spoke to Emma Jelley, Google's former head of legal for the United Kingdom and Ireland, about the importance of safety, shared vulnerability and purpose in creating the culture that has become so famous.

"All of those things are true for Google – the sense of safety, shared vulnerability and a common purpose – and also within the legal team," says Jelley. "It wasn't written down; it was more little rules of thumb that built up to this sense of the culture."[9] Common company aphorisms included "Launch and iterate" and "Fail fast and learn". There is an interesting creative balance between freedom to fail and the knowledge that incompetence would never be tolerated: how this translates into the legal department is not set in stone. Nonetheless, these aphorisms increased the psychological safety of everyone, including the legal team.

As the company exponentially grew and consultative decision making in legal became difficult to manage, it was this safety to fail, she feels, that kept the team from grinding to a halt. There was a general sense of: "An appetite for now. Get on and do it – acknowledge you might put a colleague's nose out of joint, but in many circumstances it is better to act first and ask for forgiveness later." If actions turned out to be less successful, culture kicked in again: "We would always assess and try to understand things that didn't go so well: if you had bad press or an unsuccessful product launch, the team would have a constructive post-mortem to extract learning. It was just in the culture."

Even in legal, there was a sense that action and moving forward were better than inactivity, and that striving for perfection could actually hamper action: "In legal, we had an 80/20 rule, meaning that after 80% of effort, another 20% was likely to bring diminishing returns. So 80% and meeting a tight deadline would likely be more commercially valuable than indulging in a 100% Rolls Royce job."

Emma agrees that this was reinforced by a strong sense of shared vulnerability, including from the most senior leadership: "One executive sent a big *mea culpa* around the company after his review with Larry Page, in which he talked through the fact he could be quite acerbic and harsh, and was going to do X, Y and Z about it. Having that public an admission of vulnerability from someone at the top of the tree sends very strong cultural signals to everyone."

Jelley believes that examples such as this show that Google got the culture of shared vulnerability just right.

The interplay between safety and vulnerability is something that Sean Roberts also believes is fundamental to understanding risk and developing a culture of smart risk taking as both lawyers and business partners:

> *As a legal team, if you feel something is crossing the line into breaking the law, you have no choice in closing that down. That, by contrast, is different from legal risk, such as the risk of being sued, which might not be certain. That's where we – as with our all business colleagues – want something punchier. What we are trying to do, through examples, is to emphasise as a legal team that we support creative risk taking. We reinforce our support of this in our culture through examples shared at monthly team downloads, where we have Eastern Hemisphere lawyers on in the UK morning and Western Hemisphere lawyers on in the afternoon. These examples are intended to demonstrate not only where smart risk taking has succeeded, but also where it has failed. Taking a smart risk where it was sensible and well thought out is something to recognise and celebrate as an advancement of a culture, regardless of whether it succeeds or fails. Doing something that is not sensible or well thought out – well, we all know that in any setting, that is not a good thing.*[10]

This ability to foster a culture where failure is seen as part of the process can also make colleagues more comfortable about sharing personal vulnerabilities, suggests Roberts. And leaders have a key role to play here: "We foster a culture where people love coming into work; they feel they are supported and that leadership won't tolerate unreasonable behaviour. If it happens, I will genuinely go to bat for my team if business colleagues are unreasonable."

At RBS, "playing into the vulnerability piece", as Robertson terms it, is significant in getting new people to buy into the idea of culture that the team is building: "We're trying to get across the sense that fallibility is okay. We convey that through coaching and team meetings. Leaders give examples of when we screw things up."

Robertson believes that this sort of mindset should be central to legal teams, but often isn't: "From an operational risk perspective, it's very good to share near misses and see there isn't perfection and where we need to work on things. Generally, in the law game, it can be hard because lawyers are inherently competitive."

Although RBS is a more traditional company, just as at Google, Robertson and his team at RBS are trying to instil a notion of iterating quickly, failing quickly, learning and moving on. "We are doing quite a lot on design thinking and agile and scrum methodology, and a lot of that is around failing fast," he says. "That is very challenging for lawyers – the idea of iterating something that is very much the first cut of a document and showing the work in progress; but I think increasingly, this way of working will become more and more relevant." It is also very significant in the next building block of the culture code – creating a sense of purpose – and in the notion of Failure Camp.

Failure Camp

Caitlin (Cat) Moon, director of innovation design for the Programme on Law and Innovation at Vanderbilt Law School in Nashville, is a passionate advocate for the need for greater innovation in the legal profession. But to achieve this, she feels that what is needed is a change in culture in the profession and in how we think of the role of the lawyer. A key issue in redefining lawyers and how they work, suggests Moon, is confronting lawyers' fear of failure.

Moon discussed this with colleagues and collaborators and decided to design an event based on bringing a diverse group of legal professionals together to safely explore their own failures and then link that into a different conceptualisation of the role of the lawyer: "It was designed to explore our human relationship with the fear of failure, the power of intelligent failure, its necessary role in driving innovation across the legal industry, and more."[11]

One of the driving forces for Moon was what she has described as her "unrelenting focus on asking why as we are trying to move forward in the profession". Moon believes that there are systemic factors which mean that innovative change is not really taking hold; and that most of these are rooted in the human elements of the profession – namely the lawyer personality and the work structures that this personality creates. This has a number of ramifications, explains Moon:

Lawyers struggle with innovation and the reasons for this are part of why we also struggle to maintain our mental wellbeing. It's largely our struggle with perfectionism. Much of that comes from the way we train lawyers and what I see manifest in students at such an early point: namely, the strive towards perfection. These characteristics are constraining us. What leaders in innovation exhibit – and most lawyers don't – is the ability to experiment and learn from what doesn't work.

And at the core of this need for perfectionism is a fear of failure. For Moon, the starting point in changing the culture of lawyers was to explore and reframe this fear of failure: "People deal with fear of failure on a personal human level and unless you deal with it on that level, you can't reframe it."

However, given the legal industry's growing realisation that innovation is a must, Moon also makes explicit in Failure Camp the link between confronting failure and innovating: "Innovation requires us to experiment when we won't know what will happen. We tied the exploration of failure to efforts to be intentionally creative and smart." Moon wanted to realise this exploration through an event that brought diverse perspectives together to engage on these issues:

The idea of camp (like the summer camps that kids in the United States go to) came to me as a way of bringing lightheartedness and fun, and giving people a way to tap into their creativity. If it were a lighthearted event, people wouldn't take it too seriously; but the flipside was that I designed it to create as quickly as possible a safe space for people to be vulnerable.

The day started with people telling a personal story of real-world failure in groups of 10 to 12. Just a person on stage with a mic, no slides – more storytelling than TED talk. "I just sent out a call to share stories," says Moon. "This created an opportunity for vulnerability and set a tone of safe culture, because everyone was being authentic and transparent."

Moon had seeded this beforehand by creating a Slack group for attendees: "This gave them opportunity to think in advance of things they were interested in addressing with smaller groups of about 10 to 12".

The event was loosely designed like a conference, but with more fluidity, as Moon explains: "There were about 50 people in total, and folks were free to move in and out of sessions as they chose, or simply to have conversations with people they had just met."

What was key for Moon was how she messaged the event: "I did not involve people who were less interested in this kind or work or try to engage with sceptics to 'convince' them to participate."

As a result, a group emerged from all over the United States who came from diverse perspectives, but who really wanted to grapple with this topic. The day also featured a scavenger hunt and an art project, to give people a fun way to connect creatively into the event and help prepare them for sharing stories. The session ended with the participants developing challenges for themselves as how to move forward, either personally or in their institution; and the original Slack group is still active around this.

The concept of Failure Camp is resonating more broadly across the profession, as Moon has been contacted by a number of groups of people who are interested in hosting similar events. "What does it look like if you take Failure Camp into a law firm or a legal department? Kenny (Robertson at RBS) has run a mini Failure Camp for his team."

Moon sees this interest as evidence of just how much the cultures created by lawyers need to be redefined to allow for safe spaces to explore failure and therefore to challenge lots of preconceived expectations around what being a lawyer means.

Notes

1   Daniel Coyle, *The Culture Code* (Cornerstone Digital 2018).
2   Daniel Coyle, *The Talent Code* (Cornerstone Digital 2010).
3   Abraham H Maslow, "A Theory of Human Motivation", *Psychological Review*, 50, 370–396 1943, reproduced in Classics in the History of Psychology, http://psychclassics.yorku.ca/Maslow/motivation.htm.
4   Catherine McGregor, "Is the Key to Business Success Cracking the Culture Code?", *Global Leaders in Law Current Awareness*, February 2019, www.law.com/global-leaders-in-law/2019/02/11/is-the-key-to-business-success-cracking-the-culture-code/.
5   *Ibid.*
6   *Ibid.*
7   Daniel Coyle, *The Culture Code* (Cornerstone Digital 2018) p104.
8   Laszlo Bock, *Work Rules!* (John Murray 2016).
9   Interview with the author, January 2019.
10 McGregor (n 4).
11 Interview with the author, November 2019.

9. A sense of purpose and culture creation

Ordering the chapters for this book proved a challenge, as many, if not all of the overarching business and organisational concepts discussed are symbiotically linked in a 'chicken and egg' relationship. Which comes first? And does it even matter – maybe they all organically work together? This is very much the case with purpose and culture: each intrinsically informs the other. Purpose definitely helps to set culture; but can you even set a purpose without a culture that is amenable to both your purpose and indeed the notion of having a purpose in the first place?

Emma Jelley, former UK and Ireland legal director for Google, told me that at Google, culture was defined via a series of rules of thumb, mostly expressed through various aphorisms. This mirrors the characteristics of many successful cultures, where certain markers can help to drive a creative movement for an organisation from where it is to where it wants to be.

From the earliest days of culture, storytelling has continually reinforced shared cultural values. Markers such as the aphorisms at

Google can consciously and unconsciously move an organisation towards the same goal. For Jelley, Google's statement of purpose was all-pervasive and was something she never lost sight of during her time in the legal department: "It's very clear – Google's mission is 'to organise the world's information and make it universally accessible and useful'. After a while, you get cynical at points; but nothing ever really knocked my belief in the fact that this sense of purpose did really infuse everything."

Many of the cultures discussed in Daniel Coyle's book *The Culture Code*[1] have not been consistently successful and some have experienced significant failures. The difference with successful cultures seems to be that they use the crisis to crystallise their purpose and often use that purpose statement or story to guide them through both good times and bad. This gives us insight into building purpose and building culture. It's not as simple as carving a mission statement in granite or encouraging everyone to recite from a hymnal of catchphrases: "It's a never-ending process of trying, failing, reflecting, and above all, learning. High-purpose environments don't descend on groups from on high; they are dug out of the ground, over and over, as a group navigates its problems together and evolves to meet the challenges of a fast-changing world."[2]

That's something that Sean Roberts, former general counsel of the consumer healthcare business at GlaxoSmithKline (GSK) has seen in his years at the company – particularly in how the culture has evolved: "It feels like it moved from being much more of a rules-based organisation in the mid-2000s to become a more values-based organisation. This does force you to follow your gut a bit more."[3]

Roberts suggests that in companies that focus on culture, there has to be a healthy balance between purpose and performance: "The downside with a value-based culture is that you don't want people using values as an excuse for failure in performance." As former general counsel for GSK's consumer healthcare business, Roberts tried to balance the overriding company culture and purpose with that within his own legal team, which is co-created by those who live it: "As GC, I try to make cultural adjustments from the bottom up, from the grassroots. We pay a lot of attention to our survey scores; there's a lot of listening to our teams. When we have ideas put to us, we will act on them if we can and let the team know, and give feedback on those we can't act on."[4]

It is in this symbiosis between leadership and teamwork that Roberts sees the building blocks of culture – a safe space, shared vulnerability and common purpose – come together: "It's being heard and being part of it – that is why the team are prepared to participate and be vulnerable, not just having their ideas flushed away. In crowdsourcing ideas, we are all shaping ourselves as lawyers for the future."[5]

Similarly, at Royal Bank of Scotland (RBS), the theme of being future-ready informs the need for cultural cohesion, with everyone working together to create a team that is more than just a group of lawyers. "Our purpose and our *why* go hand in hand, if you are trying to think of something you can do more easily with purpose; but equally, if there are cultural deficiencies, we won't be a market-leading in-house legal team," states Robertson.

Robertson feels that a purpose-driven mindset is increasingly something that all in-house teams need – and part of this means being progressive and competitive:

> While currently every piece of work we do internally is still cheaper than externally, changing market forces could mean that is not always the case. Our value to the organisation has to be more than just monetary. We have to be more ambitious than just sitting on our backsides and being technicians. Our why is being a market-leading, progressive in-house legal team. Looking at a lot of market-leading companies such as those described in Simon Sinek's Start With Why – such as Apple and Southwest Airlines – it's that sense of purpose which defines their success. We, as a team, need to understand who we are to drive the team forward.

Leigh Kirkpatrick, who works with Kenny Robertson at RBS, suggests that it's hard to delineate the different aspects of the culture code –

they all work together to create a culture. "It's helpful to establish your purpose first and the other aspects can then fall into place," she says. "Because knowing what you want the team to be about and the organisation to be about is important before you start thinking about how the culture behaviourally plays out."[6]

1. How do you do it?

As Bjarne Tellmann points out in his book *Building an Outstanding Legal Team*[7] – which provides a framework for developing a legal department, including a roadmap for the general counsel's first 100 days – culture is fundamental for a legal team; but it is also subservient to the wider culture of the organisation. There is also a significant difference between creating a culture from scratch and changing an existing culture. In many ways, changing a legacy culture – which is likely to be where most general counsel find themselves – is more difficult. But whether changing a legacy culture or defining and building a new culture, a shared vision is key.

2. Culture change ideas

2.1 Find an opening
Tellmann advises legal leaders who wish to change a legacy culture to ensure they do this at the right time and find an opening to do so – essentially, creating the *why* for the culture change.

This could be a positive event, such as entering a new market or industry; or a negative event, such as a crisis or setback. Tellmann advises against new general counsel trying to implement full-scale culture change in the first 100 days of a job; although the exception may be if your hire coincides with or was prompted by an event that might make the organisation ripe for change. But generally, to approach culture change, you first need to establish credibility within the organisation.

2.2 Take stock
Tony Hsieh is CEO of Zappos, whose unique culture has become a

defining part of its brand and success. In his book *Delivering Happiness*,[8] Hsieh shares an anecdote about a time when a group of employees who were hanging out with a new hire in a local bar each gave his or her definition of the company's culture; afterwards, Hsieh regretted that he hadn't recorded the discussion. From this, the idea of the *Zappos Culture Book* was born, which lists employees' definitions of the company culture and is handed out to new recruits, vendors and even customers. What can be eye opening about defining your culture as a group is that it allows you to try to identify the different building blocks and therefore what is working and what isn't.

Research on culture change conducted by Boris Groysberg of Harvard Business School and Jeremiah Lee and Jesse Price of executive recruiter Spencer Stuart reveals that while culture change can be challenging, you must begin by mapping the existing culture.[9] This can be done through surveys and interviews. If you feel that cultural constraints may not be conducive to individuals being truthful, mechanisms such as anonymised surveys and interviews undertaken by third parties can help. Here, the leaders being seen to speak up openly and honestly can be a significant catalyst.

Groysberg *et al* advise using an analysis of the current culture that can be spoken about openly throughout the organisation. The analysis should also look beyond the organisation to consider the broader market conditions within your industry. For general counsel, this may require a dual focus on what is happening both in the organisation's industry and in the legal industry – for example, process efficiency, alternative staffing, flexible working and so on.

Groysberg *et al* also advocate the use of a culture change map, to show where your culture currently is and where it needs to get to. For example, it is hard to instil a culture of learning alongside authority, as this does not allow for the requisite flexibility and independence to make this work.

2.3 Articulate an aspiration
Your analysis of where the current culture is should also give you

tangible ideas of what needs to change. You will probably enter into the process with some sense of these, but going through the analysis process will make you certain of them and begin to draw others into the process.

As Groysberg *et al* point out in their analysis on levers for culture change, this stage allows you to point to tangible problems versus ambiguities.

2.4 Choose leaders who align with the target culture

At both RBS and Pearson, having members of the team who were part of the change was crucial for success. Training can be helpful here. Going through the first two steps listed above will make this an iterative change and give other leaders the opportunity to get on board with it. However, be aware that culture change can inevitably lead to turnover.

2.5 Use organisational conversations about culture change to underline the importance of change

Using a framework such as that proposed by Groysberg *et al* situates culture change within the bigger picture beyond just the team or the organisation. It also allows for the articulation of what the change is – not just that it needs to happen. For example, if you work in an industry which is innovative and facing disruption, this could be a learning culture to promote innovation. What this model proposes is the same as that advocated by Tellmann at Pearson: iterative changes that give everyone a chance to be part of the change. This could happen through roadshows, likening sessions, structured group discussions workshops or similar initiatives. Social media could also be used. Culture change champions could be identified in a group and become peer advocates for change.

3. Structures need to support change

Linked to the above points about understanding your culture type, it is worth looking at the work of Henry Mintzberg, which shows how organisational structures can fundamentally shift how people think about their cultures and how they behave. It also shows that how people behave can become formalised into new organisational structures.[10]

If your structure is actively mitigating against change, this needs to be addressed. For example, to achieve greater unity, collaboration and efficiency, a legal department needs central reporting lines to the general counsel, rather than one where the lawyers are embedded in business units.

4. Conclusion: does culture ultimately eat strategy for breakfast?

It would seem so – both in legal teams themselves and within the wider organisation. It makes sense that if in-house legal teams are increasingly being judged on metrics common to the wider business – such as profit and loss, efficiency and use of talent – then the same factors for success in the wider organisation will need to be a focus. For many successful businesses, the intangible building blocks of culture can make or break the bottom line.

As automation increases, the human factor will increasingly differentiate the professions. How we perform and interact as humans at our fullest potential, in cultures that work well for us but that also allow us to be creative, should be front of mind for all business leaders, legal and otherwise.

Notes
1   Daniel Coyle, *The Culture Code* (Cornerstone Digital 2018).
2   *Ibid*, p229.
3   Catherine McGregor, "Is the Key to Business Success Cracking the Culture Code?", *Global Leaders in Law Current Awareness*, February 2019.
4   *Ibid*.
5   *Ibid*.
6   Interview with the author, January 2019.
7   Bjarne P Tellmann, *Building an Outstanding Legal Team* (Globe Law & Business 2016).
8   Tony Hsieh, *Delivering Happiness* (Grand Central Publishing 2011), p155.
9   Boris Groysberg, Jeremiah Lee, Jesse Price and J Yo-Jud Cheng, "What's Your Organization's Cultural Profile?", *Harvard Business Review*, January-February 2018.
10   Henry Mintzberg, *The Structure of Organizations* (Pearson 1979).

"If in-house legal teams are increasingly being judged on metrics common to the wider business – such as profit and loss, efficiency and use of talent – then the same factors for success in the wider organisation will need to be a focus."

10. Case study: the Pearson legal department – from Project Roadmap to Ethos

Over the last 12 to 18 months, Pearson's legal team has been rolling out a blueprint for a process to rework its culture and ensure that considering culture becomes part of its DNA.

The exercise was kickstarted when the team began considering the purpose of the legal department. "We had just gone through this whole exercise of identifying our purpose and our mission," recalls Bjarne Tellmann, Pearson's former general counsel and chief legal officer. "I asked my leadership team: 'If McKinsey came and told our CEO that they could come up with a plan that would replace 100% of the legal department and save them 50% of costs, why should he say no?' A provocative question – but one definitely designed to get us thinking about what we were there for!"[1]

And it definitely focused the team, recalls Tellmann:

> *They came back and said, "There are two things we do that no external legal hire can do. First, we can be preventative – we can stop*

things from becoming problems in the first place, rather than just react once they exist. And second, we can be pragmatic in terms of taking legal advice that final mile and blending it with the risk appetite, culture, values and aims of the company." So we developed this purpose that rested on being preventative and pragmatic, as well as enabling and protecting the company; these became the four corners of our mission.

1. Assessing the culture

'Project Roadmap', which developed into 'Ethos', began as a process to align the department's culture with that mission.

Practically, this meant that Project Roadmap was rolled out in two waves. The first wave involved the assembly of a group of people from all across the function, who were asked to help define the department's culture more generally. Tellmann defines 'culture' as "the values and beliefs that drive behaviour": "We've got these values and beliefs that underpin everything. Both drive behaviour and they can be toxic or inspirational, depending on what they are."

The success of the project depended on drawing people together, explains Tellmann:

Wave 1 had to be about figuring out what our culture was. I told the team, "I want you to go away and come back and tell me what values and beliefs actually do drive our behaviour." So they went away and surveyed the rest of the function, and they came back and had a whole list of things they identified as the values and beliefs that drove behaviour. When you join Pearson's legal team and somebody takes you to lunch on day one and they tell you how it really works around here – these are the things that drive our behaviour.

The second wave involved identifying which of the listed values and beliefs would help the team to achieve the department's identified mission of enabling and protecting by being preventative and pragmatic, and which were hindering it from doing so.

Bob Mignanelli, Pearson's legal department COO, led the first phase of Project Roadmap and is the executive sponsor of Ethos. He agrees that the starting point had to be an examination of the state of play – what worked and what didn't: "The underlying tenet of both Roadmap and Ethos didn't change – it was always to examine our culture. The aim was to build a better culture and build our culture through the input of our folks in the department; they were never designed to be top-down."[2]

A team of 10 was pulled together from around the department. Its first task was to identify and then assess all of the unwritten assumptions that underpinned the current culture. As Mignanelli explains: "The key focus had to be looking at what was working but also identifying issues that were preventing us from getting to where we wanted to be."

On the positive side, the group identified a lot of collegiality and found that people wanted to do the right thing for the business. "However, on the negative side there were unwritten assumptions that everything had to be perfect; also that the lawyers had to stay in their lanes or not express opinions outside of the legal remit," continues Mignanelli. "The key issues that came out of that assessment included how to break down historical silos and how to get people to be more willing to take risks. Tactically, the team also wanted tools to enable them to do their jobs better, and to have greater transparency and communication from leadership to the rest of the department."

What followed was a process to come up with concrete steps and projects, budgets and timelines that would help drive the culture forward and stop people doing those things that were mitigating against the team's purpose. In Tellmann's view, what was most significant about this process, as the starting point for a culture change project, was that it was iterative and driven by the team from the bottom up, not just by the leadership:

That effort was successful in the sense that it flushed out what we're all about; it flushed out what we were doing well and what we were not doing so well. It engaged people and it energised the team. Ultimately, at a time of great transition, it enabled me to go back to people and say, "It's not me telling you that we need to do these things – you're telling me. You're telling me what the culture is, what the values and beliefs are; you're telling me what needs to change to get them aligned with our mission."

The net outcome of the first and second waves was a desire to focus on the team's culture in a more lasting fashion. As Tellmann explains: "That ultimately resulted in the team coming back and saying, 'We really want this to be a permanent standing feature of what we do.' And we said, 'Great, let's do it' – and then they rebranded themselves 'Ethos'."

The desire to focus on culture change as an ongoing project reflects both the reality that change is a continuous process and the fact that organisational culture itself is not static. In a 2015 article in the *Harvard Business Review*, Raghu Krishnamoorthy – GE's then vice president of executive development and chief learning officer – attributes the company's longevity to its ability to adapt its culture to the appropriate external and internal contexts:

At GE, we have stayed competitive for more than 130 years because of our relentless quest for progress on all fronts, including culture. We believe that there is no such thing as a 130-year culture. In our opinion, culture is contextual, and what would have been appropriate in the 19th century, when the company was a one-product, one-country organization, is very inappropriate in today's far more globalized environment. (GE now operates in 175 countries across the globe.) So, a constant reengineering of our business portfolio, operating model, and culture has been a key to our evolution.[3]

The rebrand of Pearson's culture effort as 'Ethos' also reflects this need to identify culture change as a continuous process – something that is bigger than the team and even the organisation; something that relies on and must adapt to the spirit of the age. '*Ethos*' is the Greek word for 'spirit'; and the use of this term speaks to a form of culture change that has particular resonance for lawyers, in the sense of doing the right thing.

2. The culture code

A key feature of the Ethos project is its iterative, collaborative nature. The lawyers who are part of the project are involved in key strategic decisions, such as working on the Pearson legal team's Culture Code. The inspiration for this came from a conversation that Mignanelli had with the head of technology and strategy at Hershey. Mignanelli recalls:

> *He had a credit card-sized card with the five points of his department's culture on it. He explained that everyone in his department had agreed to live by those five points and be held accountable to them. I thought that was fabulous – it was a bit of an epiphany for me. What I was so struck by was that they were written down in a concise and simple way which was easy to understand and remember; they were obviously not written by lawyers!*

One of those tenets was respect for time, continues Mignanelli: "The gentleman I was speaking to had a habit of meetings running over. As one of the tenets of their culture code is respect for people's time, he will have people standing outside his glass office wall looking at their watches if his meetings are running over. What's great as well is that the most junior person can hold him accountable; there's no fear of reprisal."

This notion of a code which could permeate everything and become so entrenched that employees at all levels would feel empowered to enforce it was inspiring to Mignanelli: "I had this idea that if we could come up with something like that and socialise it broadly, how powerful would that be?"

Tellmann continues:

> *We have designated Ethos representatives from different parts of the legal function and they collaborate on proposals and initiatives. We had them work on our Culture Code – that was the first project that they did. We said, "We want you to boil down those values and beliefs – the ones that we want to keep." So they boiled these down to about 10*

to 15 things, and then I said, "We need to refine that and refine it and refine it." So, wave after wave, from 15 to 10; from 10 to seven; from seven to four. And then I said, "Three is a good number" – so they came back with the final product of three, which we're rolling out now.

This refining of the Culture Code was the initial step in clarifying a whole range of proposals and initiatives for the legal team. Tellmann believes that, like a purpose statement or a *why*, a culture statement should be simple and to the point, so that people can keep it front of mind and not have to refer to a primer or list – hence the continued refinement down to just three values and beliefs:

- *We do the right thing.*
- *We have each other's backs.*
- *We are innovative.*

As discussed earlier in this part of the book, the final aspect of Pearson's Culture Code is very much dependent on the first two. Creating an environment of support and shared safety is a fundamental aspect of a great organisational culture. It's pretty much impossible to have true innovation or creativity without a feeling of safety and that you are allowed to fail: failure and innovation are inextricably linked. The first building block of the Culture Code is also intrinsically linked to the purpose of the legal team and their function as lawyers; but it is also a universal aim that isn't just about their professional function. In a way, like purpose, culture must speak initially to the heart and the emotions, not the intellect; it's got to be fundamental.

As Tellmann clarifies: "These were the three things that they felt were critical to who we are – our DNA, what we're all about. There are subsets under each of those headings; but we've decided that these are the three things we're going to hire against, to fire against and to promote against."

Mignanelli agrees: "I think its simplicity is great, because it provides an anchor: what are the three things which are fundamental to us and what behaviours follow from those?"

The creation of the Culture Code also galvanised the whole legal department. Mignanelli convened Culture Code focus groups, to which all members of the department were invited: "People got so passionate in the focus groups that it stimulated some of them to join the committee and work on this in a more concerted way."

Increasingly in business, the notion of cultural tenets and the closely linked aspect of purpose provide a link for employees between the significance of their function and the wider business. They also help to empower people to make decisions – particularly when those decisions need to be made quickly and possibly with imperfect knowledge – by ensuring that they know what is central to the team and the organisation, and can assess whether something feels right. As Tellmann explains: "It's easier to have a shorter list, as everyone can keep it in mind. The 10 to 15 things that they had initially listed were great, but nobody will remember that many things. That is a significant part of working on your culture. Your culture has to be so simple that anyone can tell anyone in 10 seconds what it's all about."

The simplicity of the Culture Code is definitely a two-way street – it is also about keeping management focused, as Tellmann is well aware: "It keeps us honest as management, too. People will ask: 'Is this the right thing? Do you have my back? Is this truly innovative?' So, it keeps our feet to the fire as well."

Creating a sense that management has the team's back is central to the concept of psychological and emotional safety; but as interviewees such as Alex Dimitrief – the former general counsel of GE – point out in the chapters on leadership, it is also a central characteristic of a good leader who can inspire people.

In his book *The Culture Code*,[4] Daniel Coyle points out that reminders of what makes a culture different are generally found scattered around organisations. For Coyle, this demonstrates that continual reinforcement and calibration of culture are essential to who we are. In the same way, the legal team at Pearson is focused on reinforcing the Culture Code.

"We're now thinking of ways not just to launch the Culture Code," explains Tellmann. "We're asking the marketing team to find a way to really brand it. I want it to be everywhere – screensavers etc. We now have awards based on living our values, but I also want to find formal ways to make sure we're hiring against them. If we're thinking of hiring or firing someone, we can ask whether they are living our values – is this compatible with the culture?"

3. Hacking culture

One concept that Tellmann has spoken and written about, and that is used as a way to produce culture change – whether overtly or covertly – is culture hacking. I was first introduced to this concept in Jessica Bennett's book *Feminist Fight Club*,[5] which explains how women can make their workplaces more female friendly through day-to-day actions and nudges that produce change in perceptions and behaviours. Similarly, Tellmann feels that day-to-day culture hacks are crucial to engender behavioural and therefore culture change. Key to reinforcing this at Pearson is the notion of rewarding actions that conform to the Culture Code. At the request of the legal team, this scheme has evolved to incorporate more *ad hoc* awards for different types of behaviours that exemplify living the team's values. As part of this project, the team also tells the stories of those behaviours on the intranet and in the team newsletter. Tellmann feels that this focus on day-to-day behaviours is fundamental to the success of the project: "I think over time, based on creating those awards and telling stories about how people live our values, we begin to hack the culture and we can move it in the direction we want to get it. Then it's not just words on a piece of paper – we have champions; we have stories; we have lived examples. So that's a big part of it."

This gets to the heart of culture change, countering what management psychologist John Amaechi has called 'cultural littering', where a lack of proactive intervention in the event of bad behaviour means that this can become normalised as part of the culture. One of Ameachi's favourite sayings is "People make choices, choices make culture."[6] As discussed above, the Ethos project focuses in particular on small, day-to-day hacks that tackle behaviours that are not conducive to the aspirational culture; but it also rewards good behaviours that might not be earth shattering, but still make a difference. Promoting recognition of this has been a key aspect of the initiative.

As Tellmann explains:

> We had an awards system in place already, but it was a very high-level award that the leadership team vetted formally. We still have that in place, but the team said, "We would like to have small, spot awards that we can give, in our discretion, without necessarily the leadership's involvement." So we've started doing that for people who live our goals and culture in small ways. This is not recognition for above-and-beyond, medal-of-honour type stuff – this is the day-to-day living our values; somebody who did some small thing that was reflective of what we're trying to do. And we called these awards Bravos. A colleague sitting beside that person says, "I want to call her out, because she did a great job." They're spot awards – £50, £100, a free dinner, that sort of thing. Take your spouse out to dinner on us. But it's more about that recognition, saying, "You did a great job and you're living our values"; it then reinforces those behaviours.

The next stage, suggests Tellmann, is to develop the culture project to a place where people can feel comfortable calling out "the little things that are not compatible with the culture. We haven't gotten there yet, but I think we will as the effort matures".

4. Continuous culture

One significant aspect that has been built into the Pearson legal department's culture is the fact that culture is organic and is constantly changing; therefore, the work and focus on culture must evolve as well. A key learning from both Project Roadmap and Ethos is that culture initiatives cannot be discrete, one-time projects – they must be ongoing and become part of the organisation's DNA.

One way in which the department has made the initiative organic and continuous is by rotating personnel on the Ethos Committee. Leadership rotates each year and at the point when leadership changes, other members are given the option to rotate off the committee and open up slots for new people and, crucially, new ideas.

The Ethos committee also always has an open call for membership. As Mignanelli explains: "We want to refresh leadership and give opportunities to new people, and allow others who may want to exit to roll off so they can do other things."

A key aim for Mignanelli is to make Ethos more representative of the Pearson legal team's international demographic and ensure that the culture is not exclusively US-centric, but reflects perspectives from Europe, Asia, Latin America, the Middle East and Africa.

"If your culture does not have that diversity of thought," Mignanelli clarifies, "it is being driven by a sub-culture of people."

Rotating who works on the committee keeps it fresh and emphasises that culture is continually changing rather than something that is set in stone. Mignanelli cautions: "I have seen this in other committees – if the leadership and membership never change or get refreshed on a regular basis, they have a tendency to stagnate and become myopic."

Rotating leadership also gives more members of the team the opportunity to stretch themselves and step into a leadership role or gain valuable extra experience. Mignanelli himself is a walking example of this: "Bjarne asked me to lead Project Roadmap in 2016; the success of the project led to me taking on more operational leadership responsibilities, which ultimately led to him appointing me as COO. So culture change has also provided talent strategies."

5. Imagined communities become real connections

Meanwhile, the Bravo awards tap into the need to reinforce behaviour or behavioural change through stories. Since the earliest days of civilisation, stories have been used to build and shape cultures by changing some behaviours and reinforcing others. In folk and fairy tales, there is often a subtle (or not so subtle) didactic function or moral. As Marina Warner writes in *From The Beast To The Blonde* – her extensive analysis of fairy tales, why they were told, how they changed and who told them – "fairy tales are often told in the optative tense: announcing what might be".[7]

In the same way, the stories rewarded at Pearson are shared internally via the team newsletter. This newsletter has been a significant factor in the development of the Ethos project across the team, which is spread out around the globe, as it allows people to tell their own stories. For Tellmann, this is a key way to bring people together and a crucial aspect of cultural change:

> *There was a book I read during studies for my master's degree that stayed with me. It's called* Imagined Communities, *by Benedict Anderson.[8] It considered the rise of nationalism and the surge of national romantic movements in the late 1800s. What happened in the late 1800s that caused nationalism to surge all at once? Many of these countries that had never been nation states, like the Philippines and Norway, suddenly had this moment of, "Oh my gosh, we're a nation." Anderson's answer was that the media and the telegraph began to rapidly disseminate news across geographies, so that you suddenly had this moment in time when everybody was reading the same things together on the same day. That resulted in these shared national narratives and people began to imagine themselves as one community, because of the stories they were telling each other.*

Connecting team members across the world by sharing stories through the newsletter and scheduling regular monthly calls has been a fundamental part of the culture shift in the team, both for Tellmann as the leader and for members of the team. As Tellmann puts it:

> *We all have this imagined world. In this imagined community in the late 19th century, peoples' imagined spaces went from their farms to this massive geography where they realised suddenly that they all shared the same language, history, traditions; that they all saw*

things in the same way, which was different from how the overlords who ruled them saw things. That notion, I think, can also be used in the legal profession – even for people who will never meet each other. If we're putting a conversation online once a month and telling each other stories, and we have a newsletter that's beautiful – that's actually not only about work, but also about who they are as people, or what they think is important about Pearson Legal – something amorphous suddenly becomes an imagined community.

This sense of sharing, being in something together and – most importantly – co-creating is how a culture is reinforced: it gives a group a commonality that they own together.

To reciprocate this sense of connection, the team has been pioneering micro-assignments. In a global organisation such as Pearson, to move an employee from one location to another – even temporarily – can be expensive and potentially cost prohibitive. So the legal team has introduced micro-assignments, which are short and almost like an extended business trip. As such, they do not involve the logistics and expense of a permanent move. Tellmann cites the example of a maternity cover, where an employee from Minneapolis went to Cape Town for six weeks. The experience was transformative: "She was completely changed when she came back. She said, 'Wow, I'm learning so much from working alongside this new team' – and the Cape Town team felt the same. They both gained new ways of looking at things."

In another example that Tellmann recounts, another employee from Minneapolis came to cover a sabbatical in London:

He was there for 30 days, maybe a little more – it was over the summer, so he was able to bring his family. We didn't give him any extra pay; we gave him a small subsidy for housing. He was so profoundly changed by it that about a year and a half later, when we had a vacancy in Manchester, he raised his hand and said, 'Based on my London experience, I'm prepared to move and localise to Manchester.' He is still there and operating very successfully.

These flexible ways of moving people have been fundamental, Tellmann believes, in reinforcing this sense of an imagined community, which then becomes a real community. It's an area where Tellmann feels that most general counsel are missing an opportunity:

They look at the cost of sending someone on a business trip to Jordan, wherever; they're like, "My budget's tight; I can't afford it; what's the real return on the investment here?" My advice is: just do it. Because the value of those few days in terms of them coming back and having made a connection, and building that community, and saying, "Well, I know so and so now; he sits in Dubai and I sit here and we worked on this thing together in Jordan" – that's so powerful for your culture.

This is a fabulous point, because it illustrates the breaking down of silos and the creation of community in a global organisation, which can be very difficult for geographically diverse teams whose work doesn't normally cross over.

6. Taking it to the top and back

A significant aspect of the feedback from the first wave of the Ethos project was a desire for greater transparency between the leadership of the company, the leadership of the legal team and the rest of the team.

The legal team's initial work on this in fact pre-dated a cultural initiative in the wider business, which reached the same conclusion. As Tellmann explains:

The funny thing was, we did this before the business did. The business had a large-scale organisational health initiative and greater transparency was one of the key things that came back. We had already known this for quite a while, because Ethos had told us that we needed to be less siloed; we needed to be more transparent. Part of the reason for that was that historically, Pearson was somewhat siloed because it was a holding company with a portfolio of different businesses. We had these legal teams sitting in historic businesses. That feeling of siloisation meant that – especially at a time of great change – employees felt that leadership was off somewhere coming up with things and didn't really understand the whole picture.

This resulted in a series of proposals to tackle the sense of separation between leadership and the rest of the organisation. One was to have global conversations every month and to change the format that the legal department had historically used, which Tellmann describes as a "Eurovision Grand Prix broadcast format, which was very scripted, with the corporate affairs people kind of just parsing through everything I would say."

That has now been completely revised; the format is now a true conversation, with very little input from Tellmann. Each conversation focuses on one theme – the Culture Code was one recent theme and diversity will soon feature as another. The calls are run by the team members and can number up to 130 participants; but the format and the way they are run mean that many participants weigh in and feel empowered to do so.

The other move towards greater transparency was to have an Ethos representative present at the department's weekly legal leadership team meetings. Leadership pushed back a little on that, feeling that in practice, they needed some time ring-fenced off for them to come together as a team. But a compromise was reached whereby two Ethos representatives now sit in on the leadership meetings once a month. Again, this is rotated, with different Ethos members joining each time. They introduce themselves, listen in, add input and then report back to the whole legal department in a blog post, explaining what the leadership team spoke about and providing the minutes from the meeting.

7. Culture to create the future

Culture is central to innovation and it has been a big part of the Ethos project too, with the legal team and its leadership asking, "How can we be innovative? How is this innovation being defined?" Tellmann explains that they are using a fairly broad and user-friendly definition of 'innovation': "We think of innovation as basically new and better ways of doing things. It doesn't have to be technology. 'How can we make this better?' And we've now got a team that's looking at how we do things and how we can be more innovative. They've really been thinking about playing that role: being drivers of new thinking, changing how we do things."

One innovation that the Ethos team suggested was to break the silo effect by creating a special ops team which could work in an agile way on projects around the legal team and save duplication of effort. The team asked for volunteers, who then created talent cards for everyone, setting out their skills and capabilities together with their picture. When the legal team has a project that requires more people and resources, instead of hiring an external consultant, the first port of call is to see whether it can use its own people. These opportunities empower the entire team, as Tellmann explains:

The original proposal was to create a defined team of special ops people, but we thought that might create an A team and a B team. So instead, we just let people volunteer for special ops projects. We had a compliance project recently where we had a £500,000 budget to hire consultants to do this deep-dive risk analysis, but we decided to save the money and see if people would volunteer. They were not getting paid anything more; they just raised their hand for the opportunity to be part of something different and learn something new. And we had way more people raise their hands than we could take! We had to filter them out and identify those who were best suited for that particular job. So far, it's working out quite well: we're saving money and people get to learn something about a different part of the business.

In the longer term, Tellmann is keen to introduce additional rewards for the special ops teams, such as certifications of their skill sets, so they can badge themselves as having expertise in a particular area or project. But this is certainly a creative way of managing talent, working on culture and providing 'value' to the department and the wider organisation.

8. Being courageous

The Ethos culture project is still in development. But according to Tellmann, the key to the entire initiative is ownership. His top tip for other legal leaders – indeed, for any leaders – is to ensure that "if you are doing something like this, it's not owned by the leader: it has to be owned by the team". This requires a lot of risk taking – particularly for a leader, as the team's perceptions of what your culture currently is and/or where it should be might be at odds with those of management.

This means that leaders must have the courage to engage in dialogue with those whom they manage about these gaps in perception – and must then be prepared to set what might be audacious goals or engage in herculean tasks to ensure that change actually happens.

This echoes other reflections on successful leadership. Writing on the website of Harvard Business School, Bill George, former chair and CEO of Medtronic, declares: "Courage is the quality that distinguishes great leaders from excellent managers." He goes on to elaborate: "Courageous leaders take risks that go against the grain of their organizations. They make decisions with the potential for revolutionary change in their markets. Their boldness inspires their teams, energizes customers, and positions their companies as leaders in societal change."[9]

Changing culture and changing behaviour in an organisation can produce even more wide-ranging change; but it is clear that our other areas of focus – leadership, purpose collaboration, innovation, creativity and talent – all play a part. Certainly, having leaders with the courage to address change is a catalyst. In the next part of the book, we will deconstruct leadership, examine what this means for general counsel and delve into some different examples of leadership to demonstrate that leaders are not all created from the same template.

Notes

1   Interview with the author, August 2019.
2   Interview with the author, August 2019.
3   Raghu Krishnamoorthy, "GE's Culture Challenge After Welch and Immelt", *Harvard Business Review*, 26 January 2015, https://hbr.org/2015/01/ges-culture-challenge-after-welch-and-immelt.
4   Daniel Coyle, *The Culture Code* (Cornerstone Digital 2018).

5   Jessica Bennett, *Feminist Fight Club* (Portfolio Penguin 2016).
6   Noah Frank, "John Amaechi still has plenty to teach the sports world", wtop News, 6 July 2018, https://wtop.com/nba/2018/07/john-amaechi-still-has-plenty-to-teach-the-sports-world/.
7   Marina Warner, *From The Beast to the Blonde: On Fairy Stories and Their Tellers* (Vintage 1995) pXVI.
8   Benedict Anderson, *Imagined Communities* (Verso 2016).
9   Bill George, "Courage: The Defining Characteristic of Great Leaders", *Harvard Business School Working Knowledge*, 24 April 2017, https://hbswk.hbs.edu/item/courage-the-defining-characteristic-of-great-leaders.

Part III: Leadership

· ·

Let us all be the leaders we wish we had.

Simon Sinek

11. Leading versus managing

What is the difference between a leader and a manager? Is it just a matter of semantics or is it fundamental? In the military, the word 'manager' is never uttered; it's all about leadership. Leadership is aspirational and is essentially bigger than a role held by one person; it is also collaborative and is as much about other people as it is about the one individual who happens to be in charge.

As Maaike de Bie, general counsel of EasyJet, defines it:

> *A manager is more task oriented. When you are a leader, it feels more important because it's about others. You look at the work and figure out who is best placed to do that. You are a coach, a mentor and a facilitator: the person who will go out there first and take the difficult step. You are a role model to a lot of people: everything you do and say is so important. It's about being humble about that and understanding that it is not you, it's that position.*[1]

1. "What got you here won't get you there" – the need for new skills

The essential wisdom of this quote by Marshall Goldsmith[2] defines in six words the fraught relationship that many general counsel have with leadership. Leadership is something that many general counsel – and indeed, lawyers in general – struggle with and feel unprepared for. Many do not feel they have the adequate tools to become leaders. Others feel unsure and uncomfortable about leaving the role of lawyer behind and moving into a role that predominantly involves leadership and depends more on emotional intelligence than technical knowledge. They are aware that others in the C-suite may be MBA graduates and therefore have studied leadership in some form; whereas their own training will generally have focused purely on legal skills and will likely have continued to a narrower sphere of specialisation before they moved in-house.

There is a wealth of material out there on leadership – books, coaching and courses – but these goalposts are not stable, as the business world is constantly changing. Neither is there a 'one size fits all' template of a 'good leader.' What works in one organisation may not work in another and culture plays an incredibly important part here. Moving into leadership cannot be done in a way which is at odds with the essential culture of your organisation, unless you are planning to undertake a culture change programme. (In that case, a new style of leadership may be a defining factor.)

But establishing and developing your sense of self at work is a significant factor in developing yourself as a leader. Marshall Goldsmith's seminal work on leadership, *What Got You Here Won't Get You There*, essentially explores how to relocate this sense of self at work. This can undergo seismic shifts as your career evolves – even if those changes are positive, such as promotions. Goldsmith's work, based on his extensive experience in coaching, considers how to hone your interpersonal skills to become the best leader you can be and explains how an authentic sense of self is a crucial part of that. This definition of 'leadership' is therefore very personal and defined by how relationships at work are handled, rather than some immutable conception of what a leader looks like.

But is concentrating on your authentic sense of self always helpful? What if, essentially, you feel that you cannot be an adequate leader? Herminia Ibarra of London Business School argues that rather than looking to personal insight, you need to develop 'outsight' – to some extent, fake it until you make it. Others such as Simon Sinek maintain that what leadership requires most is a focus on developing others and putting the experience and development of the team above all else – an idea based on the 'servant leadership' concept that is used in the military.

So how to know which of these theories will work best for you, in your environment? In this part of the book, I will discuss some of these theories with regard to the experiences and common problems faced by lawyers moving into leadership and look at how they can be practically applied for leadership success – however that is defined in your life and business.

2. The changing environment

The changing environment for leadership can refer to two different aspects. The first is that the business environment in which leadership now takes place is much more complex and changeable. The second is that theories of leadership are now much more cognisant of the complexity of factors that create leaders and the importance of relationships. Most contemporary leadership theory doesn't focus on the idea that there are specific attributes or behaviours that will make a good leader no matter what. But this is a relatively novel approach – and the hangover from earlier ways of thinking can produce roadblocks for individuals as they move into leadership roles.

3. Moving on from old ideas – a timeline of leadership theories

The earliest theories of leadership, which were popularised during the 19th century, centred on Thomas Carlyle's theory of the 'great man' (and, yes, they were usually men). In this theory, leadership is seen as something innate, giving rise to the idea of 'natural' leaders that persists today. Essentially, the theory goes that, irrespective of the situation or context, these individuals are so heroic and inspiring that they will naturally rise to the top of a group.

During the 1930s and 1940s – partly due to the rise of psychology as a discipline – the theory of traits-based leadership emerged. This highlighted a number of personality traits which, in certain combinations, would make for great leaders. Over many years, various studies have attempted to analyse whether there are certain qualities and characteristics that all great leaders share. However, the traits-based theories were based on sample sizes that were quite small and did not take into account cultural and contextual differences.

Although experts now consider these theories as unsophisticated and outmoded, the precepts can still affect how we view the idea of leadership – both within ourselves and in others. The notion of not being a natural leader or not having the right traits can be pervasive in women, for example (and is often an argument used against them). And indeed, I often hear lawyers who are moving into leadership question their innate suitability for the role. It would seem that the judgement of effective leadership and leadership potential is often still based on rather superficial elements. In a widely shared *Harvard Business Review* article of 2013 and subsequent book, Tomas Chamorro-Premuzic posed the question: "Why Do So Many Incompetent Men Become Leaders?"[3] The answer, he suggests, is that leadership is too often conflated with superficial traits such as confidence, rather than the skills that actually make great leaders in terms of measurable outcomes. Instead, successful 'leaders' project a myth of leadership confidence – one which they themselves may believe. This echoes many of the ideas in Goldsmith's work. Goldsmith analyses a number of case studies which show that many leaders become over-enamoured with their own mythology and perceived success, and lose the all-important relationships and communication with their colleagues and teams.

The behavioural theories of the 1950s started to look more at what leaders *did* rather than who they were or what innate qualities they had. These theories also started to consider the relationship between the leader and others. In the 1960s, this led to more contingency-based theories that suggested that there is no 'one size fits all' theory of leadership success; rather, success is contingent on a number of factors, including the context of the organisation and the relationships in teams.

What both of these theories introduced to the equation is the notion that anyone can become a leader with the right training and development.

The 1970s saw the introduction of even more relationship-focused leadership theories. The transactional theory posited that leadership success is based on a mutually beneficial exchange between a leader and his or her team. In transactional theories, to be effective – and as a result, have motivational value – a leader must find a means to adequately reward (or punish) his or her followers for performing (or not) leader-assigned tasks. In other words, transactional leaders are most efficient when they develop a mutually reinforcing environment where the individual and the organisational goals are in sync.

Around this time, the notion of the transformational leader also came into vogue. The essence of transformational leadership is that a leader is charismatic and inspires a solid relationship with his or her followers, based on trust.

In recent years, leadership thinking has evolved to posit that the role of the follower is key to the role of the successful leader. This has also placed a greater focus on consensus-driven decision making and empowerment of teams. Also layered into the mix is a recognition that continuous learning is needed throughout one's professional life, and that the leader is not the one with all the answers.

Leadership coach Alex Lazarus suggests that when you layer in the increased complexity of the modern business environment, self-leadership is key.[4] For leaders, the message is: know thyself before you can be fit to lead. For Lazarus, this involves creating a culture at work that enables other people to think creatively, beyond the existing expert knowledge:

This is especially pertinent in today's dynamic marketplace, which shortens the lifespan of what we define as 'expertise', when new business models and technological developments are popping up in all sectors. We are also tapping much more these days into the worldview and the wisdom of young people: with knowledge being increasingly democratised and access to education made easier in the history of humankind, we are seeing that young people have raised the bar on an innovative and agile mindset. This calls upon senior leaders to adopt and inspire in others what I call the 'inner game of entrepreneurs', whose raison d'être *is to challenge the norm. What we can learn from them is to embrace the paradigm shift from highly esteemed 20th century 'know-how', with all its status and hierarchical rituals, to today's 'learn-how' and being an EFTO (expert on finding things out).*

Our leadership style is a significant determinant as to whether we foster that curiosity in others, explains Lazarus: "If we do, it turns into a business advantage, as people will be empowered to make leaps in their thinking, make incremental improvements with continual innovation and place creative problem-solving at the heart of their organisation. Is it easy? Not always. Leaders who have a good grasp of human psychology and make everyone feel that they are their thinking partners lead the way."

Meanwhile, the maxim "Leader, know thyself" links to research that proves that self-awareness and emotional intelligence are hallmarks of successful leaders. According to Lazarus:

Leaders should demonstrate the ability to evolve and share with their team examples of how their own moments of growth led them to make better decisions. Essentially, it's about inviting others into your thinking space – people are inspired, and some feel even honoured and valued, by leaders who openly reflect stories of their mistakes and share practical examples of what they will do differently next time as a result.

But do lawyers face particular challenges in getting to grips with leadership, whether of themselves or others?

Notes

1   Interview with the author, December 2019.
2   Marshall Goldsmith, *What Got You Here Won't Get You There: How Successful People Become Even More Successful* (Profile Books 2010).
3   Tomas Chamorro-Premuzic, "Why Do So Many Incompetent Men Become Leaders?" *Harvard Business Review*, 22 August 2013, https://hbr.org/2013/08/why-do-so-many-incompetent-men; and Tomas Chamorro-Premuzic, *Why Do So Many Incompetent Men Become Leaders?* (Harvard Business Review Press 2019).
4   Interview with the author, October 2019.

12. The need for self-leadership

Experts such as Marshall Goldsmith believe there is a need to develop self-leadership before one can successfully lead others. However, in today's fast-paced corporate environment, there is little time available to develop this. Therefore, business thinkers such as Herminia Ibarra suggest that those moving into leadership roles need to find ways to work on building these skills in the job.[1]

But the job of general counsel doesn't allow for a lot of spare time. So how do you find ways to cement your leadership skills while undertaking such a demanding role? And how do you start to practise self-leadership?

Goldsmith suggests that you should try to get a truly rounded 360-degree view of yourself at work:

If you want to know how your behaviour comes across to your colleagues and clients, stop looking in the mirror to admire yourself. Let your colleagues hold the mirror and tell you what they see. If you don't believe them, do the same with your loved ones and friends – the people in your life who are most likely to be agenda-free and who truly want you to succeed. We all claim to want the truth. This is a guaranteed delivery system.[2]

Allon Stabinsky, chief deputy general counsel at Intel, recalls undergoing a 360-degree view of his leadership style as part of a coaching exercise:

My style of leadership is being wired to take charge. I did one of these leadership value assessments with my coach where you look at 360-degree input. This was incredibly helpful. Some of my values were broadcasting too loudly and drowning out others' views: this taught me I need to change the way I behave in meetings and the way I work in personal interactions. The key learning was: I need to listen more. My natural inclination is to get the problems out there and vigorously attack them, but not everyone is comfortable with that.[3]

Stabinsky's comments reveal something which, for Goldsmith, is at the crux of the matter: most leadership skills are about behaviours and relationships. Indeed, as Goldsmith asserts, the higher you move up an organisation, the more the problems that you deal with become behavioural. Everyone who ascends to the executive ranks will be a technical expert on something, but the ballgame then changes completely: it is now your people skills that will make the difference between success and failure. To paraphrase one of Goldsmith's questions: who would you rather have as your general counsel – a moderately good lawyer who is great with people outside the firm and skilled at managing smart talent; or a brilliant, technically adept lawyer who is inept with outsiders and alienates colleagues and direct reports?

1. Empathy and leadership

The importance of relationships and communication in leadership again brings up the importance of empathy. In his book on leadership, *Leaders Eat Last*,[4] Simon Sinek posits that empathy is at the heart of great leadership. Here, Sinek is heavily influenced by leadership ideas practised in the US military. He begins his book by telling the story of Captain Mike Drowley's flight over Afghanistan to monitor the progress of a special forces mission in 2002. Drowley went with his gut and performed actions which might have seemed risky, but which were inspired by his ability to empathise and intuit what might be going on with the special forces operatives below. His actions ultimately went on to save the lives of the 22 special forces operatives on the ground. For many who have been through officer training in any military group, it is the leadership aspect of this that stands out, rather than the particular technical expertise of a specific military unit. The style of leadership practised by most military units is so-called 'servant leadership', where the leader focuses on the needs and psychological (and physical) safety of his or her reports.

I will discuss this in more detail later; but at its heart, servant leadership is based on empathy. And this is increasingly seen as a defining factor for successful leadership in the modern world.

2. The need for empathy in a changing world

Why is empathy so important? As discussed by leadership coach Alex Lazarus,[5] the increased pace of change and the uncertainties as old realities crumble make the work environment more fraught than ever before. The increased use of technology means that 'work' is also harder to define and switch off from; therefore, leaders who can empathise with the toll these demands are taking will be more likely to inspire better performance. This fact is not lost on general counsel.

Maaike de Bie, general counsel at EasyJet, places significant importance on bringing a human aspect to her leadership. To assist with this, she has also undertaken training as a coach. Empathy, she feels, is at the heart of successful leadership:

> As a leader, I think it is really important to bring empathy to the business culture of your organisation. We need to not forget that when we go to work, we are surrounded by a group of people; we are all human, and we all have a brain and a heart, and we need to engage

with the whole person. I am interested in all of my individual team members. I do not treat them as a unit; everyone is different and will have different motivations and interests.[6]

Logical as this viewpoint may seem, it is still not how many organisations are run. In *Leaders Eat Last*, Sinek cites the lack of empathy and humanity in much of business today. He contrasts the excess of smart executives with the dearth of strong leaders. There is too much focus, he feels, on being the leader, rather than on the task of leading.

If we look at the etymology of the word 'leader', it comes – unusually – not from a Latin or Greek root, but from the Old English '*lædere*', "one who leads". But the root for '*lædere*' is the verb '*lædan*': "to guide, bring forth." This places the emphasis much more on the *act* of leading and the leader's relationship with others, rather than on the leader himself or herself. But given that the training and early experience of many lawyers foreground technical excellence, and that the professional law firm environment often prioritises the ability of individual partners to 'eat what they kill' and build a book of business, will leadership always be a challenge for most lawyers?

3. Leadership and emotional intelligence

In his provocatively titled book, *Why Do So Many Incompetent Men Become Leaders?*,[7] Tomas Chamorro-Premuzic considers the gender bias affecting many leadership appointments. Men, he argues, are more likely to be overconfident, narcissistic and psychopathic than women; and while these traits might help them to secure a leadership position, they are detrimental once actually in the role.[8] You can get pretty far in many corporate settings through being vocal and appearing confident, even if such behaviour is masking insecurity and a lack of ability.

Chamorro-Premuzic cautions that while there are generally more similarities than differences between men and women, one substantial difference concerns emotional intelligence (EQ). EQ is definitely the flavour of the moment. As Chamorro-Premuzic notes, in the last 20 years more than 43,000 research studies on EQ have been published, versus just 90 in the 1990s.

EQ produces calmer, more resilient workers. It is also needed for roles that involve a high level of interpersonal interactions, such as sales, public relations, customer services and, of course, leadership. In producing a more balanced, less overconfident and less over-excitable personality, EQ counterbalances the negative traits that Chamorro-Premuzic has identified as correlating to some types of leadership: narcissism and psychopathy. EQ also helps you to manage yourself and access the right mindset to be a leader – skills that leadership consultants such as Goldsmith and Lazarus have identified as key to successful leadership.

Notes
1   Herminia Ibarra, *Act Like A Leader, Think Like A Leader* (Harvard Business Review Press 2015).
2   Marshall Goldsmith, "Self-assessment: Leadership Excellence",
    www.marshallgoldsmith.com/articles/self-assessment/.
3   Interview with the author, September 2019.
4   Simon Sinek, *Leaders Eat Last* (Penguin Random House 2014).
5   Interview with the author, September 2019.
6   Abigail Harris and Maaike de Bie, "Q&A", *Global Leaders in Law Current Awareness*, 5 November 2019, www.law.com/global-leaders-in-law/2019/11/05/maaike-de-bie-group-gc-of-easyjet-on-the-importance-of-human-leadership-for-business/.
7   Tomas Chamorro-Premuzic, *Why Do So Many Incompetent Men Become Leaders?* (Harvard Business Review Press 2019).
8   In Chapter 3 of *Why Do So Many Incompetent Men Become Business Leaders?*, Chamorro-Premuzic cites a meta-analysis of 355 studies covering 500,000 individuals, which finds that narcissism is the psychological trait for which the highest gender differentiation is found. The meta-analysis is Emily Grijalva *et al*, "*Gender Differences in Narcissism: A Meta-Analytic Review*", *Psychological Bulletin* 141:2 (March 2015), pp261–310.

"[Given] that the professional law firm environment often prioritises the ability of individual partners to 'eat what they kill' and build a book of business, will leadership always be a challenge for most lawyers?"

13. Lawyers and leadership

The outdated notion that there is a perfect template for leaders, and that some people are simply not properly equipped for leadership, arguably underpins lawyers' struggle with the concept of leadership. For lawyers in in-house teams, this is also linked inextricably to the struggle over how what they do is perceived among the wider business.

This tension often stems from a sense that lawyers' value comes only from their legal advice. It also stems from traditional conceptions of the legal department as a team that is divorced from the workings of the wider business, and that exists only to rubberstamp deals or say no to opportunities – the classic designation of 'the department of no'. This can make lots of lawyers feel that they "have to stay in their swim lane", as one general counsel put it, and focus on issues pertaining to legal advice in executive meetings. But is this a result of how lawyers are perceived or how they perceive themselves – or a complex mix of the two? The answer will depend on a range of factors, including the organisation they work in; the historical role of lawyers there; the attitude of the CEO; and the individual lawyer's own mindset.

Another factor which sometimes makes lawyers apprehensive about leading is the sheer amount of time and effort required to fulfil the role of a lawyer. Many can struggle with the push and pull between technical specialism and broader business skills such as leadership: management consultants and coaches who work in other industries with a similarly high bar for technical training (eg, medicine and technology) report a similar phenomenon in those fields.

Management consultant Alex Lazarus runs her own company, Lazarus & Maverick, which helps a range of professionals – including lawyers – to become leaders. She is one of the coaches involved in Marshall Goldsmith's 100 Coaches initiative. This is Goldsmith's 'pay it forward' project, where he teaches 15 people for free who then agree to pass their learning on to 15 others and so on. The initiative includes people such as Alan Mulally (former CEO of Ford) and Jim Yong Kim (former president of the World Bank Group). Collectively, they are working to advance the leadership practice around the world.

Discussing leadership and lawyers, Lazarus suggests that professionals such as lawyers with high levels of expertise can experience the greatest struggle in the current business environment: "People who were in the past tasked with expertise and know-how no longer have the ability to be so sure."[1]

This is also due to the fast pace of change in the world of work. In many businesses, change and innovation are at a premium; globalisation has produced new ways of working and selling. Organisational structures are also much flatter – a fact that is certainly true of many legal teams. This does not just mean a lack of promotion prospects or a limited number of vice president titles: the very architecture within which people work has changed. Remote working is much more likely to be either the norm or a proportion of professional workers' daily experience. There is also increased travel at all levels in organisations – not just at the top. These changes may not seem immediately relevant to the idea of leadership; but – as we will discuss in the talent chapters – globalisation and different ways of working are changing people's relationships with their workplaces. This can lead to a disconnect between their sense of self, their sense of self at work and their relationships with colleagues and team members – all of which can make leadership a challenge.

But being a leader is no longer optional. The demands and requirements of the general counsel role are changing, and the idea of the general counsel acting as a leader is no longer 'nice to have'. Tom Sager – who, as general counsel at DuPont, paved the way for more operational thinking and inclusive leadership – feels that leadership is now an essential quality in the role of general counsel or chief legal officer: "Historically, there was very little emphasis on leadership; but now the role of the chief legal officer is much more leadership-driven. Not to diminish the importance of legal acumen, but in order for the CLO to succeed now, he or she has to build a team that has a global footprint. He or she has to be cognisant of risk management in anticipating risk and developing strategies to eliminate these risks."[2]

Given that there is a difference between management and leadership, it might be that lawyers are generally more comfortable with management than leadership – partly perhaps because management can be more technical and detail orientated, and less big-picture and emotional, than leadership. But the need for leadership skills also cuts to the very core of the lawyer's professional obligations in the modern corporation, says Sager: "Governance is also of increasing importance. We still see so many instances where corporations put themselves at risk because they do not have a grounding in the importance of governance. Or the CLO or general counsel doesn't have the leadership strength to tell the board or CEO that they have these obligations."

1. IQ versus EQ – a lawyerly dilemma

As discussed previously, emotional intelligence (EQ) is now seen as a fundamental skill for leadership. But lawyers often have a problematic relationship with EQ because of their high IQs. While many lawyers do naturally have EQ and can use their emotions in the right way at work, there can still be an – often unspoken – perception that these 'soft skills' aren't 'real skills' in the way that hard, technical legal knowledge is.

The terminology often used – 'soft skills' – certainly does not help with this. Many also feel that this is an either/or equation: you are good at one or the other. But there is very little real scientific evidence to support this. However, there is a significant correlation between effective leadership and EQ. This is due not only to the interpersonal skills associated with EQ, but also – as Chamorro-Premuzic points out – because there is a positive association between EQ and organisational citizenship behaviours. While Chamorro-Premuzic cautions that EQ is not a failsafe against bad behaviours, if organisations focused more on EQ when hiring for leadership positions, they would end up with leaders who were more honest and ethical.

Chamorro-Premuzic states that leaders with more developed EQ have stronger abilities in three key areas: transformational leadership, personal effectiveness and self-awareness. As discussed earlier, Goldsmith cites self-awareness as a crucial skill for leadership. Both Goldsmith and Chamorro-Premuzic suggest that this is not introspection, but rather a sense of how you affect others and how that influences what others think of you.

Transformational leadership involves taking a vision and turning it into an actionable plan for change, and functioning as a strong role model for reports. EQ is fundamental here, as the ability to transform vision into action depends on active management in the form of assigning tasks, managing performance and setting rewards and incentives. This style of leadership is more commonly found in women, according to Chamorro-Premuzic's research – even if it is more popularly associated with men through entrepreneurial or disruptive approaches.

Personal effectiveness is linked to the ability to navigate interpersonal challenges, again correlated with a more developed EQ. In professional life, this tracks into the ability to see problems from others' perspectives and a flexible approach to problem solving. Again, Chamorro-Premuzic's research indicates that these are more commonly found in female leaders – although, as he admits, the fact that female leaders generally face much tougher selection processes than many male leaders may mean that they are actually better-skilled candidates. He goes on to suggest that we should apply similar rigour in the selection to all leaders.

While there are some aspects of the law which are all about technical aptitude, there are significant aspects of the practice of being a lawyer – or perhaps, being an effective lawyer – that track the skills associated with EQ. Alex Dimitrief, former general counsel at GE and CEO of its global growth business, maintains that the EQ-focused aspects of lawyering – particularly in a trial scenario, where you need to understand and anticipate the other side – can be very valuable in a leadership role:

> There's a huge benefit to thinking like a lawyer. We're taught in law school to evaluate the strengths and weaknesses of a particular position, but also to respect and hear out the other side. I've encountered a lot of leaders who don't want to hear bad news and/or who don't want to hear contrary opinions. Therefore, I think your training as a lawyer to solicit advice and hear out the other side, to make sure that you aren't missing some weaknesses in your own position, really helps.[3]

Increasingly, newer generations of general counsel are approaching how they interact with their teams in different ways – partly by tapping into behaviours which feel more authentic and are based less on what they think they are supposed to do. This is particularly evident in high-growth companies, where traditional hierarchies are challenged as part of everyday working practices. Says Chris Fox of online gaming technology company Kambi:

> From a management perspective, I tried to build a high-rapport, high-growth credibility relationship with my team. My current role has a casual dress policy, so I'm sitting here in a hoodie, T-shirt and jeans; I cycle into work; I don't look 'smart' in the traditional sense. Hopefully, my team feel like I'm credible because of my input on the issues they face; the way I help them deal with things; the way I assist them on personal and professional matters. I have a very collegiate

approach to decision making, where I can; but where I need to say what I think is best, I will assert myself as well.[4]

2. Winning too much?

One challenge for many legal leaders in trying to develop the sort of collaborative and empathetic mindset that Chris Fox at Kambi discusses above is deprioritising the sense of yourself as 'A Leader' and instead focusing on the importance of others or the cohesion of the team. Assuming the mantle of leadership can certainly feel like a big deal: who could be blamed for feeling somewhat self-satisfied; that they are – or ought to be – the most important person in the room?

For lawyers, this sense may well be enhanced by the rigours of their education, which prioritises academic excellence. Given that most in-house lawyers start out in private practice, the earliest markers of professional success to which they are typically exposed are based on winning and individual success: profit per equity partner. The 'eat what you kill' mentality – increasingly the mantra for many large law firms and replacing the more collegiate lockstep model – prioritises the success of the individual lawyer over the needs of the many (the firm). Directories that rank and rate lawyers in certain practice areas also seem uniquely prominent in law, compared to other industries – and also in contrast to their actual utility as a business development tool, the purpose for which they are supposedly designed.

Even in-house, where the structure is radically different, the mindset engineered both at law school and in private practice can cause some general counsel to focus on their individual importance, title and compensation at the expense of more collaborative leadership. This is not confined to lawyers, of course; but the notion of winning, being the best and achieving perfection seems particularly hardwired into the legal mindset. This may have detrimental effects when trying to find the best way to move into leadership.

The very basis of much of the entire practice of law is adversarial. Even negotiation – which experts such as Natalie Reynolds show works best when undertaken collaboratively – is still too often seen as a battle. Reynolds argues that the number one mistake in negotiation is making it about winning. Of course, it is always possible that one party may come out with an advantage over the other; but being obvious about winning is detrimental to the relationship with the other side, which may cause issues – if not immediately, then perhaps in the future.[5]

Legal education and legal practice condition lawyers to strive to be the best. However, this focus on perfection can be detrimental to creativity and innovation, where iterative thinking is needed; and can inhibit the development of a culture which promotes psychological safety. As Kenny Robertson at Royal Bank of Scotland (RBS) explains: "A lot of lawyers come from a background where they are used to being praised for perfection. That's their currency. They are used to being academically strong; to being praised for being academically strong. You're delivering pristine essays, theses, doctorates – whatever. And that is the tailwind that has guided you to a certain point in your career."[6]

This need for perfection can potentially undermine trust and the ability to give others the space they need to develop their own skills, and thus hamper lawyers' development as leaders.

While this can be a challenge at any level as an in-house lawyer, the trajectories of those in the key leadership roles of general counsel and chief legal officer very much involve moving away from the use of their legal skills. Given the highly focused and specialised nature of their previous experiences, this can create a crisis of confidence as to where their expertise and value actually reside.

Dimitrief enjoyed a long and successful career at GE and was both general counsel and ultimately CEO of GE Global Growth. Reflecting on his role as a lawyer and a leader, Dimitrief suggests that too many lawyers become their own worst enemies, clinging to their legal expertise:

It's all about how you communicate. If you're always talking about the legal issues and the legal risks, people are going to view you as always being 'just the lawyer'. But there are a couple of ways to break out of this mould. First, really dive into the business. Understand your customers; the business model; what's important for commercial success. Don't think of yourself as 'the lawyer'; think of yourself as a member of the senior leadership team. Don't hesitate to express well-informed opinions on personnel, commercial, strategic and reputational matters. Don't limit yourself to the types of issues on which lawyers are asked to weigh in. I got some great advice from Jeff Immelt [CEO of GE from 2000–2017] when I was general counsel. He was frustrated with how I was limiting my comments at a particular series of reviews to legal issues. He said: "I really want to hear your opinion on some of these business issues that come up. I have you around the senior leadership table because I like your judgement and I want to hear your views. I don't want you to always be the lawyer."[7]

The problem is that once you move out of your primary area of expertise, you are asked to create strategy. Once again, due to the training and prior career experience of many in-house lawyers, this may be the first time they have ever had to think about strategy. "It's about learning how together," suggests Lazarus. "Yes, you were an expert on something; but your expertise gets diluted very quickly as you progress upwards in your organisation." And the more you defined yourself by that expertise, potentially, the harder you may find having to leave it behind and move into an area where you do not feel you are automatically winning all the time. Lazarus says that the ability to ask questions is key here: "How I will be an expert on asking questions? Together we will be comfortable and have a culture of being able to ask questions together."

Here we see the importance of culture: you have to feel safe with people to be able to ask questions. This relationship aspect of culture – driven by empathy and communication – is now a key component of successful leadership, especially in a world which is in much greater and faster transition than it has ever been before. Lazarus works across a range of industries and has seen evidence of this trend across them all:

Clients often bring to coaching a sense of being lost in a changing world. We almost never talk about the fact that people come into work and it does not always let them be their best. Leaders who understand that work is just one of life's activities are more inclined to care about the wellbeing of their employees and not assume that people leave their private selves as they step into the work mode, or that their private lives are nothing but a blissful perfect picture. These leaders don't take for granted their employees' contribution or the stress that the job comes with.

How do I recognise these leaders? They typically know most of their employees' names, something about their private lives learned through casual comfortable conversations; they first connect with someone's potential, not the current job title; they communicate in a manner that says "I'm ok/You're ok" (the Eric Berne model); they champion humanistic policies – training that strengthens people's psychological growth, not just technical skills; they demonstrate values in action and keep others accountable to do the same. Ultimately, they understand that adult development continues past our 21st birthday. Since people spend most of their free time at work, they understand their organisation's opportunity to foster a culture of meaningful human connection and growth mindset. It's a win-win for all.

3. The CEO effect

The relationship between the general counsel and other colleagues in the C-suite – specifically, the CEO – can be fundamental to how the general counsel approaches leadership. For example, Dimitrief's CEO, Jeff Immelt, sensed why he was holding himself back and gave him the encouragement needed to change his narrative and become more than 'just the lawyer'.

For Rupa Patel, now general counsel at Awaze and formerly general counsel at both BPP and Exterion Media, the influence of the CEOs she has worked with has broadened her viewpoint from beyond being 'just a lawyer' to being a business leader. Like Dimitrief, Patel was exhorted to trust her ability to make decisions and contribute on matters beyond the purely legal:

My CEO at Exterion Media, Leon Taviansky, was very much of the mindset that my opinion on wider issues counted as much as anyone else's. After my first board meeting, he said, "If you attend another board meeting and you don't speak, you won't attend again." He believed that if I was attending the board meeting, then I participated fully. That's been a key learning for me: participate fully, not just as a lawyer. That means understanding and getting to know the business, which is as much your responsibility as the CEO's, to make sure that you are heading in the right direction and to add value beyond your immediate remit. That is what makes a general counsel; it's understanding the big picture for the business. You can make better decisions because you know the strategic sectoral impact, the financial impact and so on.[8]

This experience was part of a journey which Patel began in her first in-house legal role at BPP, a private university which provides business-focused training, including for lawyers (via its Graduate Diploma in Law and Legal Practice Course). As the first general counsel for the institution, Patel had a steep learning curve – both in the transition from private practice and in creating the legal function. However, her CEO was also influential, not least because he himself had also made the transition from lawyer to CEO:

I was thrown into the deep end when I took my first in-house legal role at BPP. This role was to create the in-house legal function at BPP. My CEO at the time, Carl Lygo, made a habit of pushing me out of my comfort zone, because he wanted to develop me and recognised my potential. There was a tricky immigration issue that I felt needed outside counsel support on, but he questioned why and convinced me to take the challenge on. Carl instilled a lot of confidence in me and gave me faith in my own abilities. He was a barrister who had made the transition from lawyer to CEO. I think his advice resonated with me more because of what he had achieved.

It was clear to me from the way he operated that a legal career path could be broader than being 'just the lawyer' and I found this inspirational.[9]

Patel's experience confirms that the relationship between general counsel and CEO can be transformative as to how you develop as a leader. But as General David Petraeus has discussed in relation to strategic leadership, you can only have one person in an organisation (or a military operation) in the supreme strategic decision-making role.[10] While a general counsel may increasingly have to function as a leader in relation to his or her own legal team, in the wider organisation he or she will always be subordinate to the CEO and the board. However, it also behoves the CEO and the board not to waste a valuable resource by not allowing the general counsel to act more broadly. As a former general counsel and now adviser to boards, Cornell Boggs sees this as key: "The leadership journey for general counsel often begins with insight and leadership from the board and CEO. Very wise CEOs have given their lawyers a sense that they are a broader member of the business team and not just there solely to address or respond to legal matters, but are a contributing member of the leadership team."[11]

In one regard, however, the general counsel is different: as an officer of the court, he or she is also committed to maintaining the rule of law. Navigating the synergies and potential conflicts of these different allegiances has made the general counsel role increasingly complex. A stereotype for in-house lawyers is being seen as the 'department of no'; but as Sager's quote above shows, there is also a fundamental need as leaders for general counsel to be able to say no when they need to.

4. The department of no

The 'department of no' stereotype of in-house lawyers essentially comes from a lack of communication and understanding. Lawyers can't demonstrate strategic thinking and be given a seat at the decision-making table if they can't step out from behind their shield of legalese. Currently, lawyers are not being empowered enough in their training to explore further possibilities beyond law, as Lazarus explains: "The narrative around what lawyers are and how they are trained traditionally is too focused on legal expertise; we need to change that narrative now."

But as Lazarus acknowledges, changing the narrative can be uncomfortable: "What's really needed in leadership is a core ability to look at yourself from the foundation of being a human being and how that translates into being the leader in an organisation. This can produce uncomfortable feelings, as we feel we have certain capacities in which we work and if the system is now asking us to do something else or consider ourselves in a different way, we feel uncomfortable."

One initiative that Lazarus has been working on with a general counsel and his team involves introducing a framework for 'conversational intelligence' – bringing emotional intelligence (EQ) into difficult communications to help those who need to act as leaders (and therefore sometimes to move out of their comfort zone) find frameworks from which to have interactions that may not come naturally.

Lazarus notes that while lawyers may be aware of the need for EQ, having the tools to make EQ apparent in social situations is sometimes quite a leap. Lazarus notes that teaching conversational intelligence – this application of EQ in difficult interactions – is a big component of her work, especially in industries where professional standing is based on expert knowledge, such as medicine, insurance, technology and law.

Lazarus adds that conversational intelligence is not a natural human ability and is also harder to practise when under pressure:

If we agree that innovation, creativity and collaboration are imperative for the future of the legal profession, we have to ask ourselves, "What kind of conversational skills do lawyers have?" Lawyers are known for their ability to dissect a problem with great logical assessment; but do they have the kind of oracy skills that get the best out of all stakeholders? Traditional school curriculums in the United Kingdom did not include oracy skills; hence, they don't come naturally to many of us adults. Innovation, however, requires completely different speaking skills to what we've become accustomed to and which – even if unintentionally – feed a fixed mindset and labelling: "Who's right?" "Who's wrong?" "Who's clever?" "Who's creative?" "Who's good with numbers?" "Time is money." And so on.

Conversational intelligence, rooted in the reality of the disruptive era, requires us to leave our ego outside the room and bring our best selves to create transformational discussions with sensitivity and maturity. "Conversational intelligence is about advanced speaking and listening skills that lead to fair dialogue that respects multiple and sometimes conflicting perspectives; that fosters self-belief, progress and achievement," continues Lazarus. This approach is based on five key points that can help individuals to navigate complex or difficult conversations: "Rather than having this mindset of discomfort, we encourage clients to use the framework. This reframes the difficult conversation as not difficult, but complex with different components."

An example of such a framework would be:
- Here is the issue.
- This is my perception.
- What is your perception?
- How have I contributed?
- What other ways can I support?

This framework is based on the notion of building a culture of safety for potentially difficult conversations. The culture you have built in your team or your organisation intersects with leadership very significantly in this example. Both culture and leadership are based on relationships with people. Understanding the importance of fostering the right culture and the right relationships can be a significant learning for general counsel moving into leadership roles. Nilema Bhakta-Jones moved into a business leadership role at a legal technology company after 25 years as a lawyer, including 13 years in general counsel roles. The realisation that she was no longer an 'expert' also came with the realisation that new skills were needed:

In my new role, I was not prepared to have every assumption I made challenged or every single plan debated even on minor, innocuous decisions. But I learned to appreciate the true value of the debate, the challenge, and fostered a safe environment for this to occur... When you are a lawyer, you get used to being the expert on a given matter. The transition across to CEO requires a different approach – among other things, leadership, soft skills, people skills and experience.[12]

5. Outsight: more than me and what I do

Having a clearly defined sense of yourself as a leader and what individual strengths you bring to the table – essentially, knowing what works for you as a leader – when you start is key. But knowing what does not work can likewise be key, as Bhakta-Jones' quote above illustrates. It is also important not to become stultified in your sense of self when you start as a leader and allow yourself to develop further – in other words, to be aware of the need for continuous learning. This is also crucial to how other people see you. In the example of the CEO and general counsel relationship, moving beyond traditional expectations of your role and developing 'outsight' – as defined by Herminia Ibarra[13] – can be significant in determining how your journey as a business leader pans out.

Ibarra's work focuses on the fact that while we are exhorted to think like a leader, this is not an external epiphany, but rather an organic product of one's past experiences. But to really act like a leader, one must think differently and approach the role from something other than a purely functional viewpoint. In her 2015 book *Act Like A Leader Think Like A Leader*, Ibarra defines this as the 'outsight' principle. The paradox at the heart of leadership, suggests Ibarra, is that when we first get a leadership position, our internal mindset still has to play catch-up with our external reality. Given the demands of what we need to do day to day, there is generally not the time and opportunity for that to happen.

Ibarra proposes that leaders should use outsight to ensure that their mindset changes to match their new set of responsibilities: "The principle holds that the only way to think like a leader is to first act: to plunge yourself into new projects and activities, interact with very different kinds of people, and experiment with unfamiliar ways of getting things done."[14]

Ibarra believes that too much introspection and focus on what our core skills are and how we can use them in our leadership journey will inevitably anchor us in the past and not allow us to develop. For in-house counsel, this may involve an excessive focus on those attributes which are markers of success as technical legal specialists – but which may not be as valuable in the wider business role of general counsel. Peter Wexler, senior vice president and chief legal, risk management and compliance officer of Schneider Electric, certainly subscribes to this view:

> *One of the most critical things you can do is lose the lawyering. To make decisions, you have to understand the broader context and you have to think outside of the law – then you are three-quarters of the way there. You really have to understand not just the legal implications, but whether it's a strategic play, a defensive play: all those things are really important and have a huge impact on the bottom line of the corporation.[15]*

In the earlier examples cited by both Dimitrief at GE and Patel at Awaze, the desire expressed by their CEOs was very much for them to take this step outside their comfort zone of specialisation and take more general strategic opinions.

Similarly, focusing on the 'general' in general counsel and being wired into wider trends beyond the legal are becoming the defining markers of success for general counsel in moving into leadership. Sabine Chalmers, general counsel at BT, previously held the same role at global brewing company ABInBev. What struck me when visiting her at ABInBev's New York office was how she literally had a seat at the leadership table. The offices were open plan – even for leadership – and Chalmers sat at a three-person table with the CEO and CFO.

For Chalmers, what has come to define her success as an in-house leader is the ability to have outsight and think beyond the traditional parameters of the role. Ibarra's research reveals that successful leaders are those who develop a nose for emerging trends. This can also be defined as intellectual curiosity or – as Robertson at RBS defines it, using his favourite football analogy – "playing with your head up."

Chalmers thinks that this type of outsight will come to define the next generation of legal leaders: "At the end of the day, the folks who will rise to the top are, I believe, better described as generalists. They have a perspective on everything and are naturally intellectually curious, including with out-of-the-box areas like popular culture. They are constantly aware of the big picture – both within the company and in the world around us."[16]

This may sound easier said than done – particularly if you are moving from a culture such as a law firm, which focuses on a sense of the individual and the rewarding of specialist knowledge. Ibarra has researched what helps individuals to step up to leadership responsibilities, and one of the most consistently successful tactics is to take part in a business project outside of your normal responsibilities.

Devoting time and energy to projects which are outside your remit may seem counterintuitive to many, especially with regard to leadership – it's not called the career ladder for nothing! However, while many of us might assume that careers are linear and hierarchical, Ibarra advises that this is changing as the world of work changes. What is now needed is a 'jungle gym' career,[17] consisting of more lateral moves and hot projects. This produces a much more well-rounded knowledge base across organisations and industries.

This notion of broadening your expertise beyond a specialist area as you move into leadership is aligned to the notion of the T-shaped individual, as defined by McKinsey[18]: someone who has a base of specialist knowledge (the stem of the T), but who also has less specialised empathy and enthusiasms across different fields (the cross of the T).[19] Having broader knowledge and interests as you move into leadership can create greater trust across your organisation and allow for more ability to collaborate and build influence – both significant qualities for leaders. Bjarne Tellmann, in his book *Building an Outstanding Legal Team*, suggests that the role of the general counsel demands a number of strands of specialism joined by a general curiosity, not just one specialism; leading to models of pi and comb-shaped individuals. Pi-shaped individuals may have two key specialisms, with multiple general interests joining these two on the horizontal axis. Comb-shaped individuals have multiple areas of specialism joined by general interests on the horizontal axis, so that a diagrammatic representation would look like a hair comb.

Savvy general counsel also understand the need to think more broadly and to continuously learn and gain experience. Boggs has served in numerous general counsel roles and now advises boards and coaches general counsel in the United States. He suggests the key is to recognise and embrace the increasingly multi-dimensional nature of the role: "Today's successful general counsel are those who recognise that the job is multifaceted and has many different components, with which they need to engage and be involved in."[20]

For Boggs, this involves adopting a curious mindset, inspired by the recognition that your role is to help solve problems for the company, not necessarily confined to the legal sphere: "If you have the attitude that you are there to help the company broadly, then it makes more sense to embrace adjacent communities to traditional legal work."

As general counsel of Coors, Boggs was responsible for five departments, of which legal was just one: "The leadership there had the foresight to believe I could add value to corporate communication, government affairs, water and natural resources, and corporate and social responsibility, as well as legal. If you are there to solve a problem, you might solve it through a legal solution or through legislative solutions; or by influencing the court of public opinion irrespective of legal opinions."

Boggs' experience highlights the symbiotic relationship between the general counsel's view of what is needed when stepping into a business leader role and the CEO's view of what that role should be. As discussed in our case study with Maaike de Bie at EasyJet, her CEO' s expectation of what the general counsel needed to be and her view of what she herself was able to do had to be aligned for the relationship to run more smoothly: "I felt that the CEO at the time was looking for a litigator – a regulatory focused-style lawyer who would bang the table a lot, be dominant and argumentative. I personally couldn't be that and don't feel it is the right blueprint for any GC."[21]

Relationships with other business leaders – particularly those you report to – can be pivotal in determining whether you can develop as a leader in the way you wish. But influence is multi-directional, so approaching your role with an open mindset can help to shape your relationships with direct reports and peers, as well as those you report to. De Bie focused on developing her team and, through that, gained the confidence to assert to her CEO that she was the legal leader the organisation needed at that point. Boggs encourages newer general counsel he coaches to get out into the business early on and keep doing that:

> *I personally built it into my schedule to be out in the business in almost every role I have had: if that means I have to put a hard hat on or ride in a truck or stack shelves, then so be it. But stacking shelves and so forth: these are symbols that you care about what the business is doing. Business people remember when legal steps out of the office and show an interest in the business itself. Later you might deliver training to a business audience on a compliance topic, but when you say you went into a facility or they remember seeing you, then your training gains more resonance.*

This echoes ideas we will discuss in the next chapter and which are central to a group which probably has the best and the most focused leadership training in the world: the US military.

Notes

1   Interview with the author, October 2019.
2   Interview with the author, October 2019.
3   Interview with the author, April 2019.
4   Interview with the author, August 2019.
5   Natalie Reynolds, *We Have a Deal* (Icon Books 2017), pp18–21.
6   Interview with the author, September 2019.
7   Interview with the author, April 2019.
8   Interview with the author, June 2019.
9   Interview with the author, June 2019.
10   David Petraeus, "David Petraeus on Strategic Leadership", Belfer Center, 8 February 2016, www.belfercenter.org/publication/david-petraeus-strategic-leadership.
11   Interview with the author, November 2019.
12   Interview with the author, October 2018.
13   Herminia Ibarra, *Act Like A Leader, Think Like A Leader* (Harvard Business Review Press 2015).

14   *Ibid*, p5.
15   Catherine McGregor, "Act Like A Leader, Think Like A Leader: Skills in Management & Leadership", *GC Magazine*, Autumn 2016, p22.
16   *Ibid*, pp22–23.
17   Interview with the author, September 2016.
18   Wikipedia, "T-shaped skills", 19 May 2020.
19   Zenon Foltynowicz, "T-shaped Professionals", Researchgate.net, 16 September 2013, www.researchgate.net/publication/264419889_T-shaped_Professionals.
20   Interview with the author, November 2019.
21   Interview with the author, December 2019.

"Focusing on the 'general' in general counsel and being wired into wider trends beyond the legal are becoming the defining markers of success for general counsel in moving into leadership."

14. Servant leadership: lessons from the military

If there is one group that has a greater focus on the theory and effective practice of leadership than any other in the world, it is the US military. Simon Sinek's book about leaders and high-performing teams, *Leaders Eat Last*,[1] is inspired by the practice of leadership as defined in the training of officers in the US Marines.

How does this apply to lawyers? The role of military officers often requires high levels of technical expertise and very specific skills. But this technical expertise is never prioritised over leadership skills. It's not hard to see the correlation with the legal industry – and that lawyers can learn valuable lessons from the way things are done in the military.

David Petraeus, former commander of the multinational force in Iraq and of the Central Intelligence Agency, has described effective leadership in terms of what the priorities need to be. This prioritisation would apply equally well to any organisation and correlates with many of the ideas discussed in this book: "The first is to get the big ideas right.

The second is to communicate them effectively throughout the breadth and depth of the organization. The third is to oversee the implementation of the big ideas. And the fourth is to determine how the big ideas need to be refined, changed, augmented; and then repeat the process over again and again and again."[2]

Boggs' experience echoes Petraeus's quote. Boggs grew up in US military bases around Europe, following his mother's work with US Department of Defence schools. As an observer of this leadership machine in action, even from an early age he was intrigued: "Military structures were a fascinating experience. One thing is that there was such a sense of purpose and order and reason."[3]

1. Priorities – putting leadership first

Part of the reason why even a child can pick up on that sense of purpose, order and reason is because leadership is *the* crucial area of focus in the military and everything else follows from that.

Is this why there are issues in highly skilled professions such as law and medicine with regard to leadership, as identified earlier by management consultant Alex Lazarus of Lazarus & Maverick? Perhaps a key factor is that skills and leadership are considered as skills first, then leadership; whereas they need to be developed side by side. A compelling contrast can be made between how civilian professions and the military approach these concepts. Captain Andrew Eberhart is a former US Navy pilot (yes, as in *Top Gun*) and served as commanding officer of a US Navy carrier squadron. Since leaving full-time military service in 1994, he has held a variety of leadership positions in the financial services world. He sees a stark difference between how leadership is approached in the military and in the corporate world: "In most professions, it's all about professional expertise and then leadership; in the military, there's a complete inversion of priorities between being a technical expert and being a leader. The military starts with the leadership and then technical expertise is secondary; the view is you have to be a leader first, above all else."[4]

This is inculcated from day one – an important distinction from when you start thinking about leadership as a lawyer. In most professional roles, leadership is something that you focus on when you ascend to higher levels; it's something you work towards or aspire to. In the military, it is expected from day one, whether you are officer class or not. "Leadership is something that starts from junior ranks, not just officers; you can be a new recruit and after a few weeks you will be put in charge of some of the next round of newer recruits," Eberhart explains. This focus continues throughout your career, despite the often highly technical specialisms you might have – even if those specialisms are literally a matter of life and death. Despite flying fighter jets worth millions of dollars, Eberhart recalls that the main focus of every evaluation is leadership; in the list of what is important, technical war skills rank below that.

Some in-house lawyers also recognise the need to inculcate an awareness of the importance of leadership from very early on. At Royal Bank of Scotland, Kenny Robertson is encouraging younger lawyers in his team to view the world through this lens as early in their career as possible: "Thought leadership, fresh thinking – the concepts that transition from other industries or professions – are all examples of leadership to my mind; and the more these are able to create benefit or value for the team, the better."[5]

To be fair, the military does have the luxury of time, resources and budget to focus on developing leadership in a much more concerted and coherent way than any corporate realistically ever could. But what is replicable, believes Eberhart, is the unremitting focus on interpreting everything that is done through this lens. We saw an example of this in the first part of this book on purpose, in the story of Tony Meola, former head of US consumer operations at Bank of America. Meola's purpose was operational excellence. He realised that to achieve this, operational excellence needed to be the overarching focus of every meeting and interaction, so that it became part of every decision. Similarly, the case study on the Crown Estate's legal team showed how this laser focus on an idea can produce results. Leadership is no different.

2. What is servant leadership?

In the military, the overarching theme of leadership infuses all discussions and shapes the goal or mission and how you get there. The other aspect of this which has been popularised in recent years by books such as Sinek's *Leaders Eat Last* is the concept of 'servant leadership'. But what does this mean in practice and how can it be applied in legal teams?

At the heart of servant leadership is the notion that everything the leader does is about the team: getting the team to work together and developing the skills of individuals on the team. The leader is always secondary and is not thinking about himself or herself. The military – as portrayed in popular culture, at least – can seem incredibly hierarchical, with its focus on ranks and following orders. But Eberhart thinks this is a misconception: "Military leadership is not as hierarchical as people or Hollywood perceives it. No one says, 'Follow me, men!' In times of urgency or combat someone has to be in charge. And that is very clearly defined."

Similarly, says Eberhart, in the corporate world – particularly in times of crisis – there has to be a clear chain of command and someone who is making the decisions, in the interests of achieving the overarching goal or purpose. But the person who makes the decisions must do so with the aim of giving clarity to the team operationally and ensuring that there is cohesive action.

In the military, says Eberhart, "There is one person – the commanding officer – who is the decider, which is no different from what should happen in corporate settings. But the military always uses the word 'leader', not 'manager'. It's a subtle difference but an important one: the leader's role is to build the team." This is done is through delegating and giving responsibility; involving all members of the team; building up team members, often at the leader's expense; always being willing to do anything that you would ask your team members to do; and giving subtle but deliberate praise.

"Praise is much more effective than a raise," continues Eberhart. "It builds more loyalty." Here he echoes the views of various organisational behaviour experts that purpose, motivation and pride in what you do will always be more motivating than a monetary reward.

Another important facet of servant leadership is empathy: showing that you understand what your team is being asked to do and would be willing to do it yourself. Of course, for various operational reasons, you may not be able to do absolutely everything they will do; but showing that in general, you can and would is what matters. This really comes into play when we speak about 'tone from the top'. To be truly successful, the tone from the top must be authentic – actions as well as words. As Eberhart explains: "The fastest way to lose credibility is not to do what you ask others to do. We had a squadron commander who wouldn't fly at night (because it's scarier). He thought it was subtle – he created the roster and didn't make an issue of it – but people noticed. His call sign became 'Seagull' because you had to throw rocks at him to get him to fly!"

3. Tell me a story

Authenticity and connection with others as a leader are often achieved through storytelling. When this draws on lived experience, it can become very personal. The leader displays an aspect of his or her real authentic self, which resonates with the team, who feel inspired to follow him or her. One of the fundamental skills that Herminia Ibarra links to good leadership is the ability to tell stories.[6] As we saw in the chapters on purpose, this is fundamental in communicating your *why* and conveying what is important. Ibarra references the work of psychologist Jerome Bruner, who claims that a message is more likely to be remembered accurately and for longer when conveyed through a well-constructed story. She points out that it doesn't occur to many of us at work to reveal our personal sides, but this is a lost opportunity: "You probably already know which stories are your best ones. What you need to learn now is how and when to tell them in the service of your leadership."[7]

This is an interesting point for lawyers. On the one hand, many lawyers' fetishisation of their professionalism can potentially allow them to lose sight of the individual beneath the legalese. But on the other hand, lawyers as part of their skill set must be consummate storytellers, particularly in the context of litigation and trials. Successfully stating a case can obviously depend significantly on the ability to present a well-constructed narrative.

For some general counsel, telling stories and drawing on their personal narratives are seen as integral ways to enhance their leadership styles. Peter Beshar, general counsel of Marsh & McLennan, says: "The use of metaphors and analogies is great in breaking through the clutter. People's attention spans are not as extended as they used to be – it's best to jettison PowerPoints and dry treatises, and rely on tools like video, and within that tell a story that humanises the individuals."

For Beshar, this point was really driven home when he was asked to merge the legal and compliance divisions. To illustrate this, he told his entire legal team a story about his recently deceased father and his love of Stetson cowboy hats, although he did not hail from Texas:

> I distributed hats to the team to demonstrate the idea of many hats, one team. That involved using what is personal to me in a way that was relevant. What was fantastic was that members of the newly merged team from all over the world took photos of people, individually or in groups, wearing the hats. We had a town hall meeting around the merger and did a slideshow of these photos, which showed how that piece of authentic communication really resonated and got the message across.[8]

Sabine Chalmers, general counsel at BT, also cites the value of using stories based on personal experience: "One of the presentations that I most enjoy making is to our new hires and relates to career planning. I structure it around personal stories and experiences – my childhood, the role models in my life, people who have inspired me and how I have learned from successes and failures."[9] However, Chalmers adds the caveat that while personal stories are powerful, they must be delivered in the right way – and for leaders who are not truly comfortable with the idea of sharing of themselves honestly, the tactic can misfire. Authenticity is always key.

4. Listening in leadership

This may suggest that good leadership is about talking and telling the team about yourself to motivate them. But while this can be part of the good leader's toolkit, the other key aspect of communication – listening – is even more crucial. Eberhart says that this was the one overwhelming message from his training as a leader in the military: "While we might think that the focus is very much on talking about yourself as a leader, the thing your training actually emphasises the most is to just shut up and let people talk. It can be very hard to do that, as you are the leader. But it means when you do say something, it matters more and you pull in the team. It shows that you respect them and it's not just all about you."

A focus on listening also helps leaders to study the dynamics of the group and see who is doing what; get those who aren't participating to join in; give acknowledgement and praise when needed and so on.

This is a quality that really resonated with Alex Dimitrief during his various in-house roles at GE:

> I think that being a good listener right now is an important trait. I worked for John Krenicki as our CEO when I was general counsel of the energy business. We would sit through these detailed, lengthy reviews and John wouldn't interrupt. Unlike a lot of leaders, he just listened. He'd take it all in; then at the end of a one or two-hour session, he'd ask questions or give a couple of comments, and I was always struck by those comments because he really listened.[10]

You need to listen to understand your team – to know their strengths, their weaknesses and how they can develop. Listening is a building block for talent development and talent management. And as the legal profession faces increasing change, getting the right talent not just for now, but also for the future will be vital.

5. Inclusive leadership

When it comes to talent, it is increasingly recognised that diverse teams make better decisions, and are more likely to be innovative and thus ultimately to increase profitability for companies. But it is the tone at the top – the leadership – which often determines how inclusive a culture is, and therefore whether diverse individuals feel that they belong and can thrive in a particular setting.

We need more diverse leaders: globally, the statistics on diversity in leadership are not good. We regularly hear that there are more male CEOs called 'John' in the FTSE index than female CEOs. But to achieve greater representation, *all* leaders need to think about being inclusive leaders.

Boggs told me that his experience of growing up on US military bases in Europe was formative because it allowed him to see diverse leadership in action. This was incredibly powerful for him and his siblings, as young African American children. His older sister, Paula Boggs, served as general counsel of Starbucks from 2002 to 2012, but started her career as an officer in the army.

While the military is not immune to problems with inclusion, both Boggs and Eberhart point out that it is great at promoting diverse individuals and ingraining a sense that they deserve to be there in the wider structure. As Boggs explains: "I saw diverse leadership at an early age and in a way that wasn't questioned: if the military promotes a woman as colonel, then she is a colonel. We saw the military move ahead of other infrastructures in promoting and giving diverse communities opportunities to lead. When you see that as a child, you don't have the kind of inherent thought that it couldn't happen later in life as an adult."[11]

What is recognised in a range of situations pertaining to inclusion is that the involvement of white, cisgender male leaders is fundamental to success. When such men engage in diversity, it tangibly demonstrates that this is everybody's problem, not just someone else's. This is not without its dangers: there have been some well-documented examples of diversity discussions featuring only white, cisgender men that have ultimately missed their mark, smacking of 'mansplaining' or creating fear among diverse individuals that their safe space was being hijacked once again by the majority.

But like it or not, most leaders are still white, cisgender men; and without engaged leaders, real change won't happen. This is due in part to the fundamental fact that full-scale change needs resourcing and it is the leaders who control budgets.

Su Suh co-chairs the diversity and inclusion team in Intel's legal department. She also works as chief of staff to chief deputy general counsel Allon Stabinsky. The two roles are not mutually exclusive, as Suh explains:

> I was lucky enough to be chosen as Allon Stabinsky's chief of staff. One of the key reasons he chose me for that role is because of my experience in diversity and inclusion. Allon wanted to build an inclusive practice into all aspects of the way he manages the department. In order to build an encompassing inclusive culture, you need someone at the helm who believes in the business imperative of inclusion. More often than not, those who are at the helm are white cis-gendered men, so you need allies who wholeheartedly believe in inclusion and are ready to dedicate the necessary resources to build inclusive processes into business practices.[12]

When white cis-gendered men are deliberately engaged in gender inclusion programmes, 96% of organisations see progress – compared to only 30% of organisations when men are not engaged.[13] Discussing this effect of alliance on gender equality programmes, Johnson and Smith assert:

> Without the avid support of men, often the most powerful stakeholders in most large corporations, significant progress toward ending gender disparities is unlikely. What's at stake? A study by McKinsey projects that in a 'full potential' scenario in which women participate in the economy identically to men, $28 trillion (26%)

would be added to the annual global GDP when compared to the current business-as-usual scenario.[14]

This can be extrapolated out to include all minorities, as McKinsey's research again shows that the business advantages for ethnicity and gender inclusivity are almost double those for gender parity alone.

What is significant in considering the role of alliance in Intel's legal department is that efforts are being undertaken to engage with all diversities through everyday actions; and that there are allies and sponsors who are in the most influential positions of leadership. This is what is termed 'inclusive leadership'.

The Minority Corporate Counsel Association and executive search firm Russell Reynolds Associates (RRA) collaborated in 2018 on research that benchmarked inclusion in the legal profession and considered best practices to create an inclusive culture. RRA defines 'inclusive leadership' as: "A set of proactive behaviors that leverage the unique attributes of each person in the workplace with the goal of enhancing overall performance."[15]

While leaders' comprehensive recognition and support of an inclusive workplace are needed, it is ultimately the day-to-day experience of how a workplace feels for those who are in the minority that will determine whether its culture is truly inclusive:

> *Inclusion focuses on actively embracing diverse perspectives and changing the culture to reflect them, rather than simply hiring diverse employees and expecting them to fit into the existing culture. Importantly, any leader or employee can contribute to inclusion, regardless of background or demographic. Yet the measure of a culture's inclusivity ultimately lies with employees, and in particular, with those who have traditionally been marginalized.*[16]

6. It's all about the team

The definition of 'inclusive leadership' shows how a thoughtful focus on the team is needed for leaders (who may not themselves be diverse) to promote greater diversity and inclusion in their environments. But this is also a general prerequisite for all good leadership.

It is often said that the best leaders hire people who are smarter than them. This also proves Tomas Chamorro-Premuzic's thesis that hiring for perceived leadership qualities which may actually be narcissistic behaviours can lead to toxic outcomes, producing a cohort of leaders who are too focused on themselves, rather than on the development of others. Narcissists are unlikely to hire those smarter than themselves – or indeed, anyone who might not make them look good.

The proof of the pudding is in the eating, goes the old saying, and the proof of the leader is in the team. Do they have the ability to work together; to perform at their best; to grow professionally, both individually and collectively?

Eberhart agrees: "The difference between a manager and a leader is that a manager is more about the functional aspects – for example, making sure that things are done and browbeating people. Setting an aspirational goal and building a team – that's really leadership. Managers don't build teams; leaders do."[17]

Leadership is built on interactions between people, who are not homogenous and who all exist in changing circumstances: their own personal circumstances, those of the organisation and those of wider society. This means that leadership must likewise be dynamic. For Boggs, his main takeaway from his various leadership roles – which he now shares with other general counsel – is that it's better to be a smart follower where necessary than to get hung up on staying in control: "Good leaders are those who have continuous learning, including learning from your own team members and insights they gain from others outside of the corporation's walls... Continuous learning is key, as the role now involves topics that you wouldn't have seen five years ago, such as AI and predictive analytics."

Sinek also sums this up well: "Leadership takes work. It takes time and energy; the effects are not always easily measured and they are not always immediate. Leadership is always a commitment to other human beings."[18]

This commitment to helping other human beings become future-ready within an environment of continuous learning is discussed in the next part of the book, on talent.

Notes

1   Simon Sinek, *Leaders Eat Last* (Penguin Random House 2014).
2   David Petraeus, "David Petraeus on Strategic Leadership", Belfer Center, 8 February 2016, www.belfercenter.org/publication/david-petraeus-strategic-leadership.
3   Interview with the author, October 2019.
4   Interview with the author, November 2019.
5   Interview with the author, March 2019.
6   Herminia Ibarra, *Act Like a Leader, Think Like a Leader* (Harvard Business Review press 2015).
7   *Ibid*, pp64–65.
8   Catherine McGregor,"Act Like A Leader, Think Like A Leader", *GC Magazine*, Autumn 2016, www.legal500.com/assets/pages/gc/autumn-2016/act-like-a-leader-think-like-a-leader#sthash.TxT96MzQ.dpbs.
9   *Ibid*.
10 Interview with the author, April 2019.
11 Interview with the author October 2019.
12 Interview with the author, August 2019.
13 W Brad Johnson and David G Smith, "How Men Can Become Better Allies to Women", *Harvard Business Review*, 12 October 2018, https://hbr.org/2018/10/how-men-can-become-better-allies-to-women.
14 *Ibid*.
15 Minority Corporate Counsel Association and Russell Reynolds Associates, *Unleashing the Power of Diversity Through Inclusive Leadership* (2019), p19.
16 *Ibid*, p5.
17 Interview with the author, November 2019.
18 Sinek (n 1), p287.

15. Leadership case studies

In our discussion of leadership, we observed that in the modern world, leadership is much more complex and multifaceted than may have previously been considered by historical leadership theories such as the 'great man' theory. Reflecting this complexity, I am including here two case studies, comprising conversations with general counsel who have different experiences of and approaches to leadership.

1. Case study 1: leading with integrity and humility in a hyper-connected world[1] – Alex Dimitrief, General Electric

Alex Dimitrief's career trajectory shows the possibilities for general counsel when they embrace leadership. After positions as general counsel of GE Energy, GE Capital and GE, he became president and CEO of the company's Global Growth Organization.

When you started your CEO role did you feel underprepared? What was the steepest learning curve you encountered?

There wasn't a huge gap in my knowledge, with one glaring exception: the commercial and economic ramifications of given transactions and, in particular, the trade-off between market share and robust margins that business leaders face when closing transactions. As a lawyer, I never really wrestled with the implications of settling on a particular price point for a transaction on the long-term success of a business.

Business leaders constantly face trade-offs between the importance of share (market share as a sign of leadership in that market) versus strong margins (which investors gauge as a barometer of whether a business has its act together in terms of charging a significant price for its products). Robust margins signify that the products have value for customers and that you have your costs in order. When I moved to a business role, I found myself in constant discussions with other business leaders about how low to go on price or whether there was a particular larger strategic significance to a given transaction. But other than that, being a GC prepared me very well.

How so?

It can be transformative to understand and properly utilise the advantages that your training and experiences as a lawyer bring you in leadership.

First, there's a huge benefit to thinking like a lawyer. We're taught to evaluate the strengths and weaknesses of a position, but also to respect and hear out the other side. I've encountered a lot of leaders who don't want to hear bad news or contrary opinions. Our training as lawyers helps us identify and address weaknesses in our own arguments.

Second, lawyers – particularly litigators – by definition work with mistakes that businesses have made and, if they are smart, they learn from them. Having been involved in several transactions and commercial strategic relationships that had gone sour, I was able to learn from the mistakes that people made in those situations.

Third, I was able to see the importance of allowing other people to learn from mistakes. As a GC, trouble rolls downhill to you, and you're involved with people in the business who have made mistakes: sometimes honest mistakes, sometimes serious lapses in judgment. As a leader, it is fundamental to recognise the importance of second chances.

Are lawyers well-placed to hold a mirror up to the failings of their organisations?
All lawyers should take a hard look at how they communicate the importance of integrity, and the credibility and persuasiveness of those communications. One of my tests for whether a GC will be effective and able to make the transition is whether they can communicate judgment without being judgmental. Lawyers don't develop if they see themselves as above the fray, and simply sit on the sidelines talking about integrity and not making mistakes. They need to get their hands dirty.

The ultimate leadership goal is communicating the importance of integrity in a way that resonates with teams on the ground. This helps lawyers transition from a control function – where they're seen as criticising, preaching and second-guessing – to a leadership role where they're actually part of the team that's making decisions as they go, understanding that there are compromises to make at every turn.

How can general counsel develop as leaders while doing their day job?
I never really felt pigeonholed as a lawyer. Again, it's all about how you communicate: if you're always talking about the legal issues and risks, you're going to be seen as "just the lawyer." There are a couple of ways to break out of this mould.

Dive into the business. Understand your customers, the business model, and what's important for commercial success. Think of yourself as a member of the senior leadership team. Don't hesitate to express well-informed opinions on personnel, commercial, strategic and reputational matters. Don't limit yourself to the types of issues that lawyers are conventionally involved in.

Jeff Immelt, a former CEO of GE, gave me some great advice. He was frustrated with how I was limiting my comments at a particular series of reviews to legal issues. He said: "I really want to hear your opinion on some of these business issues. I have you at the senior leadership table because I like your judgment. I don't want you to always be the lawyer."

But the most damaging way in which lawyers reinforce the stereotype is by overstating risks and hedging the likelihood of a positive result. You need to pick carefully how you communicate and quantify risks.

When there's a 5% or 10% chance of a bad outcome, lawyers have a tendency to express it in ways that lead to business leaders thinking it's a 50-50 chance that something bad will happen.

When I was in private practice, I worked on a significant matter for a client facing bankruptcy. It was a company-defining moment. And I told that client that we should win a particular dispute 85%–90% of the time. The client was flabbergasted; he wasn't used to lawyers telling him that something's better than a 50-50 proposition. I just laughed, but came to realise over the years that he was right. Have the courage to express your views honestly, knowing that no prediction is guaranteed to be accurate.

What does authenticity mean for how you communicate as a leader?
Being honest and transparent is paramount. Authenticity means sharing your true views on something, rather than a view that protects you or always puts you in the best light. Business executives often get frustrated when they get a laundry list of problems that could happen, rather than an authentic communication that focuses on the true risks and issues of importance.

Authenticity is also having the self-confidence to admit when you don't have all the answers; when you need help. It is having the humility to listen to your team and leave them in no doubt that you value their input, which is an increasingly important trait for modern leaders.

Are there any particular leaders that helped you?
There are two leaders that stand out for me. The first is Mitch Daniels:

he was the head of intergovernmental affairs for President Reagan when I worked for him, and my very first boss. He went on to be the Governor of Indiana, and is now President of Purdue University.

Mitch taught me the importance of facts and evidence, of doing your homework and valuing expert advice. He's a lawyer who never practiced law for a day in his life – but he's a classic example of someone who was taught to think like a lawyer. I've always been impressed by how he takes an evidence-based approach towards things, coupled with common sense. And I've always admired how he is able to address incredibly complex and sometimes controversial issues in a way that inspires confidence in others.

The second is Jeff Immelt, whom I had the pleasure of working for at GE. As well as just being a brilliant guy, he exemplified the importance of being multicultural in today's world. Jeff led GE into 180 markets, and was fascinated by and respected the cultures and approaches that were taken in different countries. That fascination and eagerness to be multicultural is a strong skill for a leader.

Jeff is also a great example of the power of inclusion. I will never forget one occasion when he was speaking at a global diversity and inclusion meeting at GE. One of my colleagues asked Jeff why he had come to the meeting. He said, "Because I want to make sure that you know GE is everyone's company." That was such strong evidence of his approach towards inclusion and making sure that what mattered in GE was how good you were. I've seen the power of inclusion – particularly the power of including people who don't feel they're included elsewhere – drive a company to great things.

What traits define a good leader?
The first is what I call "integrity plus." That means integrity and a personal commitment to integrity that's so strong it seeps throughout the organisation. It's impossible to have a rulebook that covers every situation people are going to be in, so you need to have a baseline commitment to integrity. Leaders must embody that.

The second is self-confidence. Not just in your judgment and abilities, which is important for any leader. But as a leadership trait, I mean the self-confidence to bring in the very best talent, including people who might be smarter than you in certain areas. I highly recommend Doris Kearns Goodwin's *Team of Rivals: The Political Genius of Abraham Lincoln.*[2] Lincoln was self-confident enough to bring in the very best political rivals to advise him. The ability to do that, and not be worried about people outshining you, is a mark of a successful leader.

Third, you need to be willing to admit that you've made mistakes; that you're able to learn from them. I see many leaders who think that admitting a mistake is a sign of weakness. I view it as a sign of strength, because it gives teams confidence.

And following on from that, the fourth is humility: that you don't always have the answers, but have a willingness to ask questions and to listen. I worked for our CEO John Krenicki when I was GC of GE Energy. We would sit through these detailed, lengthy reviews, and John wouldn't interrupt. He'd take it all in, then at the end of a one- or two-hour session, he'd ask questions or give a couple of comments that showed he'd really listened.

The fifth, and last, leadership trait is something I say a lot to my teams: "I've got your back." You make sure to give the team credit for their ideas and advertise their success to the business. But you also let them learn from mistakes. If it's an honest mistake, I've got your back. I'm also going to make sure it's safe for you to learn and have a chance to try again, to grow as a person. This point is, to me, the ultimate test of a leader in today's environment. We're working in this hyper-connected world that's moving at warp speed. We don't have a lot of time to make decisions, and we're often acting on imperfect and incomplete information. So mistakes will happen.

Any final thoughts on leadership for law firms in particular?
From what I've seen over the past ten years, law firms need to do some soul searching about their missions and broader purposes. Whenever I took on a new job at GE, I'd go on a listening tour and summarise the

team's aspirations in a mission statement. When I became GC, the team identified our primary mission as "empowering GE to sell life-changing digital and high-technology products around the globe based on clear-eyed assessments or risks and rewards." Another aspect of our mission was to serve as "proud but humble advocates for the rule of law and to strive to serve as a trusted resource for governments and regulators around the world."

I suspect that most leaders at most law firms haven't taken their partnerships through exercises like this. But partners, associates and recruits want to be inspired by missions that are more meaningful and satisfying than simply winning cases and negotiating great deals for clients so that the firm can make a lot of money. Articulating these broader purposes is critical if law firms are to win the war for talent in the decades ahead.

2. Case study 2: people, purpose and curiosity – Maaike de Bie, EasyJet

Maaike de Bie is group general counsel and company secretary of FTSE 100 airline EasyJet. Prior to that, she was group general counsel at the Royal Mail Group. She is a leader who defines herself as empathetic and passionate about the human connections that make good leadership possible. De Bie started her career in private practice in New York, moving to London six years later, where she held a number of senior in-house legal roles at the European Bank for Reconstruction and Development, GE and EY. She has also trained as a coach – partly to assist her in being a truly effective, people-centred leader.

Today, de Bie operates on the principle that a key purpose of a leader is to create an environment for others to thrive; but she notes that it's also important to find a definition of leadership that works for you as a leader. She goes on to observe that her early career in private practice in the United States was formative for her as a leader:

I was lucky because when I started as lawyer in the US, I had a female partner who was my mentor and a really good role model, who showed to me what good leadership looked like. I also had plenty of examples of bad leadership! As a baby lawyer in a New York law firm in the 1990s, there were a lot of partners who would scream and shout at associates, and think that terrifying people was the way to get things done.[3]

De Bie acknowledges that there were significant differences in their leadership styles, as this partner was much more 'command and control' than she is: "There were associates who were terrified of this woman!" But de Bie got off to a great start with her by connecting with her as a person – something that has since become a hallmark of de Bie's own leadership style:

I joined this meeting with her and a senior associate as the junior associate for an upcoming big transaction and to hear about my first task on this deal. When I sat down, she and the senior associate were looking at pictures; she had just had a baby and so had the male senior associate. They insisted I first look at the pictures with them. It was a very human side of her, talking about her family, the arrival of her baby daughter, and that made a real impact and we hit it off. Having said that, she was also tough at times and didn't suffer fools gladly. Yet she was very protective of her team; she was thoughtful and worked as part of the team. For instance, she knew I had planned a trip to Toronto one weekend. It was a rarity to be given the weekend off – as was the way in New York law firms [in the 1990s], we worked seven days a week. On the Friday I was due to leave, we had been on a five-hour conference call and there were multiple edits to be made to the documentation. Surely, I was going to miss my weekend trip. Instead, the partner insisted that I go and said she would do it herself, as otherwise I would miss my flight. It showed me clearly that good leaders are in it together with you – you're a team.

Having a female role model was also significant in helping de Bie to cultivate her own style of authentic leadership:

The other thing I learned was it was OK to be a female leader, as she was very much a woman; she didn't try to mimic the men. She was always very much herself and was not intimidated by being one of the very few woman partners in the firm. She treated me as a peer and helped me improve. Rather than redlining a draft document, she would allow me to develop my own style, and she would only comment where substantially she wanted to add/change something – often in the form of questions rather than rewriting text. I was lucky to have her as a role model.

Beyond this early professional experience, de Bie feels that her passionate interest in people and her natural curiosity have served her well in developing as a leader: "I really like working with people and trying to get the best out of them, rather than telling them what to do." She was thrust into a leadership role sooner than she might have expected. When she joined her US law firm, it was in the midst of the early 1990s recession, which meant that a lot of mid-level associates who might naturally have left to move in-house did not have the opportunity to do so. However, once the economy began to recover, there was a sudden spate of departures. This left de Bie with a lot of control (and work!) as a junior associate, and she soon found herself running deals:

I was obviously not much older than many of the associates I was leading. What I found myself drawn to was always explaining the purpose of what we were doing and how a particular task fit into the bigger picture. I thought everyone did this, as I found that the work that was produced was far better than when I had not taken the time to explain. Turns out many partners did not bother, as they were "too busy" – yet they were continuously frustrated with associates not producing good enough work. I never understood why they did not provide better context and help the associates learn and grow – they treated them not as humans, but as units to deliver work.

2.1 Starting with why: the purpose-driven leader

For de Bie, having a sense of purpose or a sense of *why* is crucial for good leadership; but she feels that there is not enough of this sort of thinking in the law: "If you're going to bring a team of people along with you, you really need to have an intent and be able to clearly communicate that. Why do you do what you do and why that matters – it is something bigger than yourself."

This style of leadership is much more about what and how you are doing something, rather who you are. De Bie admits that many new leaders – including newly minted general counsel – can struggle with the misconception that there is only one perceived model of leadership. Like Marshall Goldsmith, she suggests that it is vital that you work on yourself. While at Royal Mail, de Bie was interim general counsel for seven months before she was appointed as general counsel: "I probably struggled myself then with the notion that there was just one template for a GC which I was trying to live up to when I was in the interim role. I struggled as I had a picture in my head of what a GC looked like and how they acted, and it was different from how I naturally was. I looked at my peers and saw that I was different."

De Bie believes that it is a challenge for all new leaders – whether lawyers or not – to figure out their own leadership style. This can be particularly hard for women and minorities, as if there are no leaders who look like you, developing your own template for leadership can involve a further leap of imagination. "It takes quite a bit of work and soul searching," she admits. "There is an element of understanding the picture of the GC that your predecessor may have built up, what that means and how far you feel from that picture."

This might involve redefining organisational expectations of the general counsel role – which is where relationships, influence and collaboration with other colleagues become central:

> When I was appointed interim GC first, my business colleagues were all very supportive and wanted me to become the next GC. Without that support, I probably would not have stayed. I felt that the CEO at the time was looking for a litigator – a regulatory focused-style lawyer who would bang the table a lot, be dominant and argumentative. I personally couldn't be that and don't feel it is the right blueprint for any GC. I had inherited a team who had been through a lot of change and upheaval – many worked long hours and were close to burn-out, and there was a lot to do with them; so I decided to throw myself into that.

I started with why, *creating the vision, the mission and the purpose to coalesce the team around. As the team came together, it started to change at so many levels and we had positive feedback about what I was doing as the catalyst for this change. This gave me confidence to go to the CEO, and say, 'I should have this GC job because...'. I think she wanted to see that hunger. It showed me that I didn't have to become someone else's template of a leader; I was just going to get on with it and do what I thought was right – even if that was completely different from my peers.*

This book began by considering purpose or *why*, and this is also how de Bie started on her leadership journey, considering the purpose of her legal team. She attributes this conviction of the importance of purpose to her natural curiosity as an avid reader and student of people:

I think the reason that why *is so important for me is that we are human, at the end of the day, and understanding why we do things is a key component of being human. Also, as humans, together we are far greater in our achievements than any individual on their own. I have always been curious as to why people show up differently at work than outside of work. I always try to treat people as individuals, as I would treat anyone, and take a personal interest. We may all be [lawyers], but we are all different – I think that difference is what makes us great too. What I saw when I took over the team at Royal Mail was that we were all very busy, but also very siloed. I had inherited a team that was working hard, was burned out, and engagement was low. I pushed the reset button and started by asking, "Why are we here? What are we here to do in this organisation and why?"*

This process began with a conversation around how the individuals on her team were connected to purpose: essentially, why they had chosen their careers, whether they were lawyers, compliance professionals or working in data governance. De Bie continues:

We were all trying to find out our own why, *and to connect that to the* why *of the broader function and then the company. What was amazing was how much people (also outside our function) were able to connect to that. We were able to articulate to our business colleagues why we were there. Initially, when I first started, many people in the business didn't know why we had lawyers, for instance, and therefore were not able to connect with us. We were very siloed. But figuring out a purpose helped us to begin to collaborate more as our purpose was, of course, tied to the business.*

And this collaboration really began to change the view both from legal and about legal: "Once we decided to connect and collaborate, it snowballed. The more we shared ideas, the more ideas came back. Business colleagues would engage with us earlier and the team felt it could add more value; and it was leading to more interesting work too."

In analysing her role as leader in creating this new atmosphere, de Bie recognises that this was an iterative process, involving lots of little things which gradually helped to establish a different culture in the team and therefore a different relationship with the wider business. One example was the establishment of a CSR programme for the function, together with the law firms it worked with. While this did not necessarily connect to the day-to-day business, it did allow the lawyers to connect back to what, for many, was their original purpose in becoming a lawyer; and it helped to build a true (legal) community, with different firms working alongside the in-house team.

One downside to connecting to purpose, cautions de Bie, is that it is often seen as a 'nice to have' – something that can be focused on only when times are good: "Often, this is seen as impossible when your team and your organisation are in crisis mode." Ironically, however, a crisis can become a catalyst for considering why the legal team exists and what its purpose is. De Bie has another tip for in-house leaders who are keen to reset their teams through thinking about purpose: "You have to be prepared to be vulnerable and say where your own failings are, and go through the journey with the team – we are all human."

2.2 Self-leadership and authenticity
Thinkers such as Marshall Goldsmith see an increasing need to develop self-leadership before one can successfully lead others; and de Bie would

agree that interrogating some of her own preconceptions about leadership and figuring out what worked for her as a leader were important learnings. The process essentially involves becoming an authentic leader yourself, rather than conforming to someone's else's blueprint of leadership.

However, today's fast-paced corporate environment does not allow much time to properly develop as a leader. This is why writers such as Herminia Ibarra suggest that those assuming leadership roles need to find ways to move through the process of developing self-leadership in the job.[4]

Again, de Bie agrees with this point of view, but suggests that the solution lies in continuous learning: "I really see leadership as a work in progress. For me, I do not stop reading – all sorts of books, not law books generally – and listening to podcasts and watching TED talks."

But she also recognises the validity of Ibarra's argument that it is challenging to find the time for this alongside your actual role, so you need to find ways to help you develop as a leader as quickly as you can while still doing the day job:

> When I read her book, the key message I took was that you cannot just look to what you have done in the past to get to where you want to go in the future. Considering the VUCA (volatile, uncertain, complex, ambiguous) world we live in, it is changing so fast that you cannot just keep doing what you have always done. You must constantly adjust, reflect and change. So to me, it's about trying out new skills and being curious.

The importance of connections also resonated with de Bie: "Another key message I took from Ibarra is that growing your network is very important as a leader, especially outside your normal network. You can use your network to learn from people who are very different from you. At Royal Mail, when I realised I just had to do it my way, it became about trying different things and giving it a go, not just staying in my comfort zone." However, she cautions that growth and development must still be rooted in your genuine self: "You can still be authentic in doing it – you are just extending yourself. What I wouldn't advocate is someone who appears to be caring, but isn't and is just going through the motions. People see through that in a heartbeat and you will lose credibility – it's a fine balance between extending yourself outside of your comfort zone and not being inauthentic".

2.3 Empathy and leadership

Unusually for a general counsel, de Bie has undertaken a coaching qualification: "Part of my inspiration was the desire to understand what makes people tick – how people work with each other and, if something doesn't work in teams or as between people, why it doesn't work."

This interest was triggered by her own experience of how leadership dynamics can vary so significantly: "I always got on with pretty much anyone I worked with. Then I got a boss who was a micro-manager and whom I just jarred with – whom everyone jarred with – so I wanted to figure out why it didn't flow with him."

A breakthrough came when de Bie was invited to go on a two-day communications course:

> When we came to analyse the communication styles of me and my then boss, I realised we were at completely the opposite ends of the map of communication styles. He was introverted and very analytical, and I was extroverted and a big-picture thinker. I was given some techniques to pivot my communication style to connect to him better. I couldn't believe how well it worked! All of a sudden, we connected; and I actually only needed to adapt my own natural communication style on one occasion to make a difference in the rest of our working relationship.

The technique being used was neuro-linguistic programming (NLP). This technique was developed in the 1970s and is based on the claim that there is a connection between neurological processes (neuro-), language (linguistic) and behavioural patterns learned through experience (programming), which can be changed to achieve specific goals in life. The programme suggests that its methodology can 'model' the skills of exceptional people, teaching their communication and behavioural styles to others. The objective credibility of NLP is doubtful and it has been dismissed as pseudoscientific – claims that de Bie was well aware of. But given that one of these techniques had produced results for her, she decided to research it further and found a very commercial, practical course coaching some of the techniques: "I was sceptical about the more outlandish, cultish-style aspects which NLP can definitely have. I see it more as a helpful tool that I use with many other tools I have acquired over the years. Two years ago, I also completed an executive coaching course."

Through her coaching training, de Bie realised that "good dialogue brings good outcomes. It's getting that relationship and dialogue going with individuals, understanding them and then being able to help them develop which I find really exciting".

All of these approaches are based on empathy with others – something that de Bie feels that leaders, and legal leaders in particular, should make part of their skill set: "Ultimately, I think I am a better lawyer because I care. I went to law school because I wanted to right wrongs and be a warrior for social justice. In the Netherlands, where I grew up, the study of law is not as celebrated as in the US."

However, de Bie also highlights the importance of remaining objective: "At times, I have found empathy to be a double-edged sword; I can take on a problem as if it were mine. I had to learn how to become disassociated, to some extent, without losing that connectivity." And empathy must always be genuine, she adds: "It's really something you can't fake; people immediately pick that up."

2.4 The CEO relationship

In addition to leading their legal departments, general counsel must report to the leaders in their organisations – namely the CEO, the board or, in some cases, the CFO. De Bie recognises the significance of this reporting line, and appreciates that any tensions in the relationship between the general counsel and the leadership can be an extra challenge. This was a crucial factor in her decision to take up her current role at EasyJet: "I had seen examples where the GC and CEO were working really well. When deciding on this new role, it was really important to me that the relationship with the CEO and the chairman was good, and that the relationship between the CEO and chairman was also good and built on trust."

When there are synergies between these stakeholders, de Bie feels, the general counsel role is brilliant. And there is an added dimension to her current position: "At EasyJet, I am both general counsel and company secretary, so I really have two bosses – the CEO and the chairman. As both general counsel and company secretary, it's about providing wise counsel and not involving yourself in the politics. I always used to say to my team, 'We are Switzerland: we are neutral and we give the same information to everyone.'"

If an apolitical approach is one key aspect of the role, discretion is another:

> *Discretion is important because you get involved in many issues and discussions that are confidential. It is critical to demonstrate calmness and willingness to listen, and give your views at the appropriate time. When colleagues see you have these skills – whether that be the CEO, your peers or your team – they will then come to you as a facilitator or wise counsel – someone able to provide impartial advice and viewpoints.*

It is also important to remember that the crucial relationship for the general counsel as a leader is with the company as a whole, and not primarily with the CEO. The way the role has developed – particularly in the United States – now positions the general counsel as something of a consigliere to the CEO; but it is important to keep in mind Ben Heineman's vision of the 'lawyer-statesman': "the General Counsel must operate effectively in the corporation but with an external view that helps define the vision of business in society."[5]

De Bie would concur with this view: "As GC, you are ultimately there to do the right thing for the company, including taking the wider stakeholder groups into account. It can be a tricky conversation when the CEO thinks you're there solely for them and you have to highlight you are there to do what is right for the company." Here again, an understanding of purpose and the why of your role – which is bigger than any one individual or relationship – can be helpful.

2.5 Servant leadership

For de Bie, connecting with purpose and leadership is also linked to the notion of servant leadership. She recalls that when she read Simon Sinek's *Leaders Eat Last*, she felt that "someone had at last written what I feel about leadership". Sinek's second book expands on his initial bestseller, *Start With Why*, examining the role of teams from the perspective of purpose and success in business. What brings a team together is its leader; but it is crucial to connect this leadership to a bigger vision or purpose.

De Bie believes that this focus on broader business skills, such as purpose and leadership, defines the role of the general counsel and fundamentally distinguishes it from the role of the private practitioner:

> *There is a big difference in the two roles; the only similarity between an in-house lawyer and a private practice lawyer is the word 'lawyer'! In law firms, there is room for people who are purely lawyers; ultimately, what the law firm sells is legal services. When you are in-house, you're in a supporting role and considered a business colleague first and a lawyer second. If you bring the notion of leadership into the equation, then it's really about working together with your team and with colleagues. That's my preferred way of working.*

> *When I became general counsel at Royal Mail, I decided I was going to be a completely different leader from everyone around me; many leaders around me preferred a 'command and control' leadership style. One of the things I noticed was that senior people would front/present their team's work as their own. I didn't do that and sometimes it harmed me, as people wondered, "What are you doing?" But I was coaching, supporting, mentoring and being the glue that held the team together. That, to me, is the essence of servant leadership: I was serving them to help them to do the great work that they were capable of doing.*

But while servant leadership produces great results because it puts the rest of the team at its heart, there are still occasions when you will need to lead from the front: "I agree that servant leadership is very powerful and strong, but there are times when as a leader you have to step up and take the decision. Sometimes you have to step up, take risks and go out there and be the first to do the right thing. That can also mean speaking truth to power when no one else will."

2.6 Courageous leadership

Courageous or ethical leadership is a quality which is increasingly gaining attention as the risk of crisis and the capital from CSR both increase. Business leaders at the top companies which comprise the Business Roundtable in the United States recently stated that the "purpose of a corporation is to serve all of its constituents, including employees, customers, investors and society at large".[6]

This changing ethos is reflected in the increasing value placed on courageous leadership. De Bie feels that this is fundamental to the role of modern leaders in general, but especially to that of legal leaders in a company:

> I did speak truth to power and it was difficult; yet I made sure it didn't flow through into a difficult position for the team. I have a very strong sense of what is the right thing to do and I will speak up if need be. That comes with integrity and the role of a GC – you need to be able to stand up for what you think is the right thing to do, no matter how difficult. But I am also of the view that ethics does not just sit with the GC; ethics sits with everyone.

For de Bie, the role of the general counsel as leader thus extends far beyond the letter of the law; it also encompasses whether something is right – taking into account not just the company's overall interests, but also those of wider stakeholders (including society at large and the environment).

Involvement in decision making at a sufficiently early stage to have these discussions before emotional or financial investment in a matter becomes too entrenched is a marker of success for the general counsel as business leader. "When you work closely with your colleagues, you have a much better opportunity to influence and to reflect all relevant stakeholders' views, and to get to the best outcomes for everyone," says de Bie.

The apolitical approach that de Bie mentioned earlier also serves in-house lawyers well when they need to display courage and deviate from the consensus, according to research by James Detert of the University of Virginia's Darden School of Business. In an article in the *Harvard Business Review*,[7] Detert reveals how to ensure that you make an impact when you speak up. It is crucial to amass 'idiosyncrasy credits' through everyday competency and conformity, which enables you to challenge the norm when needed:

My research shows that employees whose workplace courage produces good results have often spent months or years establishing that they excel at their jobs, that they are invested in the organization, and that they're even-handed. They've demonstrated that they're able to stand both apart from and with those whose support they need. In doing so, they've accumulated what psychologists call idiosyncrasy credits – a stock of goodwill derived from their history of competence and conformity – which they can cash in when challenging norms or those with more power.

This quote sums up much of what modern general counsel such as de Bie demonstrate as leaders. It is based on competency, but also displays a sense of a greater purpose aligned with that of the company. It is also reflective of collaborative leadership – again based on the shared goal of the company's success, but also encompassing the ability to work with and understand the viewpoints of other business stakeholders.

Notes

1   Originally published as part of DLA Piper's *WIN (What In-House Lawyers Need) Insights*, 28 August 2019, www.dlapiperwin.com/win-insights/. This text is reprinted here with permission.

2   Doris Kearns Goodwin, *Team of Rivals: The Political Genius of Abraham Lincoln* (Penguin 2009).

3   Interview with the author, December 2019.

4   Herminia Ibarra, *Act Like A Leader Think Like A Leader* (Harvard Business Review Press 2015).

5   Ben Heineman, *The Inside Counsel Revolution* (Ankerwycke 2016), p24.

6   Anders Melin and Jeff Green, "JPMorgan's Dimon among CEOs rejecting investor-centric model", Bloomberg, 19 August 2019, www.bloomberg.com/news/articles/2019-08-19/jpmorgan-s-dimon-among-ceos-rejecting-shareholder-centric-model.

7   James Detert, "Cultivating Everyday Courage", *Harvard Business Review*, November-December 2018, https://hbr.org/2018/11/cultivating-everyday-courage.

Part IV: Talent

....

When you were small, you were always the last one picked for the team and put out in right field. The years passed, and then you were putting guys in right field. You learned one thing as you got older: You picked the best players and you won.

Jack Welch, CEO, General Electric

16. The need for talent

If artificial intelligence (AI) and robots will redefine the future of work, what will be the place for human talent? Advances in technology could change the workplace forever: according to a 2017 McKinsey report, at least 30% of activities associated with the majority of occupations in the United States could be ripe for automation.[1] This includes tasks that are primarily knowledge driven, such as law. Humans now need to think about the value they can add in the workplace and what their purpose is for being there. Yet at the same time, we hear about a 'war for talent'. This is certainly a factor that remains front of mind for many business leaders. Surveys of CEOs constantly highlight talent as the issue that they think most about, but feel they have done least about. As Dominic Barton, then managing partner of McKinsey, shared in a podcast from May 2018, not focusing enough on talent is a regret that many leaders share:

I have this rule of meeting two CEOs or government leaders or social-sector leaders a day, which I've done for the last nine years. One of the questions I ask, particularly CEOs, is, "If there are three things that you could teach your younger self, what would they be?" What I've found consistently across countries and sectors is that CEOs say, "I would have spent more time on people. I would have removed people faster. I would have pulled people up faster. And I would have spent more time with people." It was consistent. The most scarce resource is talent. We are awash in capital. It's talent that you need to drive it.[2]

It may seem contradictory that, as we start to seriously consider machines and even robots doing more for us and gradually replacing jobs, we also see that human talent is becoming even more highly valued. But what that talent might be and how it is deployed are changing.

For lawyers, managing talent is not a skill that their training prepares them for. This is an issue both in private practice and in-house. Arguably, though, the very structured and hierarchical model of progression in law firms means that historically, active management of talent has been less of an issue in private practice. This is beginning to change as the legal industry develops and what 'good' looks like in terms of career outcomes morphs into something different. The options available to lawyers are more diverse than previously. In-house is no longer seen as the poor relation to law firm success or a fall-back position. Indeed, some young lawyers now look to start their careers in-house. This is particularly true in newer business sectors such as technology, where some of the legal challenges may be more strategically significant and the law may be untested in how it can be applied.

In recent years, yet another path has opened up in the form of the burgeoning industry of alternative legal services. This includes everything from legal tech start-ups to the rapidly growing law companies such as UnitedLex and Elevate, which aim to act as a 'one-stop shop' encompassing technology, outsourcing, flexible staffing and consulting, in addition to traditional law. It can also encompass the addition of legal to the roster of services offered by the Big Four accounting firms. Alternative solutions for legal services also present an opportunity for lawyers to set up and run their own companies, and are proving an attractive option for some lawyers from both the private practice and in-house sides of the profession.

The premise of this is book is that the in-house lawyer's role has shifted from a predominantly legal focus to more of a business focus. This means that increasingly, the areas of focus and interest for in-house lawyers are becoming the same as or similar to those of their corporate peers. As lawyers become more senior, some will be more attracted to the prospect of an enhanced business focus as a career aspiration – either as an in-house lawyer or in the alternative services market – rather than equity partnership in a law firm.

These changes in the legal profession sit within the context of larger macro-dynamics which are changing the nature of work more generally. They include increased digitisation in business; an increased focus on efficiency in business; globalisation; and the shifting demographics of work – all of which are affecting how lawyers function throughout the whole of the legal industry.

The effects of these macro-dynamics in business are perhaps felt more strongly in legal departments than in law firms. This is also coupled with the ongoing need to demonstrate purpose (or value, in more reductive terms) for in-house teams.

Traditional solutions to increased volumes of work, such as more permanent hires, may no longer be viable or desired. Amid this maelstrom of change, general counsel must consider the best talent solutions for their needs. In a world of uncertainty around hiring, how are new hires justified? As industries change quickly, how can general counsel hire for the future, as well as the present? With more work and fewer people, how do you find the right people and use them in the smartest way possible?

1. Work shifts

So, what are some of the macro dynamics in terms of how we define work and therefore on what the talent we might need will be?

Professor Lynda Gratton of London Business School, in her book *The Shift: The Future of Work is Already Here*,[3] predicts that the changes we are undergoing in the world of work will be considered as momentous as those in the Industrial Revolution. During that period, the world moved from economies which were driven by more artisanal occupations, undertaken mostly in or close to the home, to increased manufacturing and subsequently increased urbanisation.

Gratton acknowledges the difficulty of accurately predicting the future; however, she identifies five forces that are currently reshaping our world and will continue to do over the coming decades. These five forces will also have a significant impact on how we work and how it is considered best to perform that work. The five forces are:
- technology;
- globalisation;
- demography and longevity;
- society; and
- the future of energy resources.

2. Technology

Technology has already been the focus of much discussion in the legal profession, particularly with regard to how legal technology solutions will change how lawyers work. But in a broader sense, technology has already made a significant difference to how people work. It is helping to drive economic growth and longevity. Indeed, the second major force that Gratton identifies – globalisation – has largely been facilitated by technology, which makes the movement of goods and services much easier and communication across jurisdictions almost instantaneous. However, there are also subtler shifts, from our increased reliance on technology to more emotional aspects, such as how technology is changing the way we think and how – and whom – we trust. These are discussed by Gratton and by commentators such as Rachel Botsman, whose work considers how trust has shifted due to the increased digitisation of the economy.[4]

Technology is also increasing exponentially. One need only look at Moore's Law: the observation made in 1965 by Gordon Moore, co-founder of Intel, that the number of transistors per square inch on integrated circuits had doubled every year since the integrated circuit was invented. This means that the power of computers and their ability to process and hold more data are continually increasing. That this is a reality is clear: while the earliest computers took up whole rooms, similar processing power is today contained in the average smart phone. Moore predicted that this trend would continue for the foreseeable future. In recent years, the pace of increase has slowed down somewhat; but data density has still doubled approximately every 18 months – this is the current definition of Moore's Law. The current rate of increase is likely to continue until between 2020 and 2025.

With regard to how we work, the growth of technology has made global dialogue much easier and faster. It has also allowed for work to be conducted remotely and on the go, dispelling the need to be tied to an office or a nine-to-five routine.

Specifically, in the legal sector, technology is increasingly used to deal with a range of issues that previously relied on human interaction, such as contract reviews and document searches. The revolution for many legal departments has been striating their work to focus lawyers on more complex and strategic work, and using technology either to complete routine tasks or to assist non-lawyers in completing these tasks, including business clients themselves.

The shift to replace human talent with technology obviously comes with costs as well as savings – the loss of workers and colleagues. Indeed, much commentary on the future of law has predicted dystopian possibilities for lawyers. Some writers, such as Richard Susskind, anticipate reduced demand for lawyers: "Looking to the longer term, then, the future of legal services is unlikely to look like John Grisham or Rumpole of the Bailey. More probably, our research suggests that traditional lawyers will in large part be 'replaced by advanced systems, or by less costly workers supported by technology or standard processes, or by lay people armed with online self-help tools'."[5]

However, the advent of more sophisticated technology may also transform the role of the lawyer in a much more positive way. It may be that the focus or the skills needed may shift; but the demand for talent in the profession is going nowhere.

The case study for this part of the book examines how global oilfield company Schlumberger has integrated talent acquisition, talent development, the use of process efficiency, the use of technology and the development of a diverse global workforce. This shows that the future for lawyers with regard to technology can actually be a 'both/and', not an 'either/or'. This is reflected in the attitude of Tunji Williams, a lawyer who was pitted against a computer running a program to review two non-disclosure agreements by legal tech company LawGeex for HBO's *Vice News*. Williams took over an hour to review the contracts, with 83%–85% accuracy; whereas the LawGeex programme took only 18 minutes and achieved 95% accuracy on both contracts. When asked how he felt, Williams responded: "I wasn't disappointed when the iPhone came out and I could do more things with this piece of technology, so this is exciting to me."[6]

As a millennial, Williams is also innately more comfortable with technology than some older generations, having grown up with it. Indeed, at Schlumberger, one key advantage of hiring a younger demographic of lawyers was the ability to tap into a pool of digital natives, for whom working with technology would be much more seamless as a process than for older generations.

Technology will remain 'the great disruptor', with innovations such as AI processing much of the 'grunt' work of law. More roles are likely to be near-shored (where, instead of outsourcing to distant hubs, companies and law firms use lawyers or non-legal professionals in nearby jurisdictions which are cheaper to operate in). Law firms will increasingly seek to employ not just lawyers, but legal managers and specialists in areas other than law – such as project innovation technology and project management – as well as supplementing full-time personnel with contract workers. In-house teams may find their lawyers integrated into teams with these differing roles; in this way, the legal function may become less discrete and more embedded alongside other functions in the business. Law firms are already developing software and online products to assist their clients and selling these rather than just legal advice. This trend is likely to increase and will require both new roles (eg, technologists) and new skills.

3. Globalisation

Globalisation presents both opportunities and challenges when it comes to talent. For companies of all sorts, the marketplace has increased – but so too has the competition. Gratton identifies the phenomenon as starting after the end of the Second World War, when many trade agreements were ratified, allowing for greater movement of goods, services and people around the world. Add in technology and the movement has lately accelerated even further.

What globalisation and technology mean in practical terms is that individuals can work smarter and be more connected across time zones than ever before. But for many, the downside of this can mean never switching off. Work can creep into every aspect of life and every moment of the day. The pressures on lawyers to be responsive are leading to increased reports of mental health issues, both in law firms and in-house, with technology and the greater ease of doing business across time zones often leading to unrealistic expectations. This is also reframing how talent is managed, both internally and externally – for example, with the introduction in 2018 of the Mindful Business Charter by Barclays (in conjunction with Pinsent Masons and Addleshaw Goddard).

Some law firms continue to increase their global footprint through expansion and mergers. But the globalisation of many law firms is dwarfed by that of many of their clients – we need only look at Schlumberger, which operates in 81 countries worldwide. A significant practical challenge for many in-house legal leaders is thus how to manage individuals across time zones and locations, and create a sense of belonging, shared purpose and career development for the employees from vastly different cultures who make up their talent pool.

4. Changing demographics and longevity

Much has been written about the effects of millennials and Generation Z on the marketplace. The reality is perhaps less dramatic than some might have imagined. But managers who may be baby boomers or Gen Xers certainly need to take into account the different expectations of, and drivers for, their current and future talent.

Thinking about how future generations of lawyers will wish to work links to many of the other issues that general counsel need to think about, such as operational efficiency and the use of technology. Strategic and prepared thinking about these issues can be an important factor in the war for talent, suggests Mastercard general counsel Tim Murphy: "I do think many GCs still aren't thinking about, 'What's my technology stack and how do I invest in it for the future?' It's something you have to do for your talent management, because those entering the workforce today want to work and interact on the kinds of tools they are used to using. If you can't provide that, they'll go work someplace that can."[7]

But what are millennials and Generation Z looking for from their workplaces? Technology that mirrors the usability and ubiquity of the technology in their personal lives is likely to be a key priority for these digital natives. The use of technology to work differently will be matched by a desire to create a mode of working which may likewise differ from what work has traditionally looked like.

Expectations are changing among those who will become the talent of the future.

A 2018 survey of law students at BPP Law School found that when applying for training contracts, quality of training, salary and the chance of retention after training were the key factors considered in choosing firms. Only 17% said that the opportunity for flexible working once qualified affected their decision – although, perhaps tellingly, around 70% of respondents *expected* their employer to offer flexibility as regards hours and location (and the technology to support it) once qualified. This could suggest that, for millennials/Generation Z, this is seen less as a differentiator between firms than as an expected aspect of employment. Some 73% saw the option to work from home as a positive.

Notes

1   James Manyika, Michael Chui, Mehdi Miremadi, Jacques Bughin, Katy George, Paul Willmott and Martin Dewhurst, "Harnessing Automation for a Future That Works", *McKinsey Featured Insights*, January 2017, www.mckinsey.com/featured-insights/digital-disruption/harnessing-automation-for-a-future-that-works?cid=soc-ap.

2   *Ibid.*

3   Lynda Gratton, *The Shift: The Future of Work is Already Here* (William Collins 2011).

4   Rachel Botsman, *Who Can You Trust?* (Portfolio Penguin 2017).

5   Richard Susskind, *The End of Lawyers Rethinking the Nature of Legal Services* (Oxford University Press 2010), p2.

6   "HBO's Vice News features LawGeex in 'The Future of Work' – and LawGeex beats human lawyer again", LawGeex blog, 23 May 2019, https://blog.lawgeex.com/hbos-vice-news-features-lawgeex-in-the-future-of-work-and-lawgeex-beats-human-lawyer-again/.

7   Interview with the author, November 2018.

"*Many lawyers actively seek out the challenges and commercial focus of working in-house. The ability to apply their legal skills much more broadly and to focus directly on business issues is a major draw.*"

17. In-house lawyers and the definition of talent

Twenty or 30 years ago, in-house legal roles were often seen – at least by those still in private practice, if not by in-house lawyers themselves – as a consolation prize for not having had a successful career in a law firm, specifically as an equity partner. Many chose in-house roles because they offered shorter hours and a better work/life balance. The trade-off for this balance was financial.

In many industries, in-house legal roles are still not as lucrative as those in private practice. However, lots of the old ideas about in-house roles are now being turned on their heads. Many lawyers actively seek out the challenges and commercial focus of working in-house. The ability to apply their legal skills much more broadly and to focus directly on business issues is a major draw. The way in which many companies – especially technology companies – have redefined work means that some are seen as aspirational brands to work for, whether in a legal capacity or otherwise. I remember five years ago meeting a young lawyer in the United States who had just joined Google directly after graduating law school; all he had ever wanted to do, he told me, was be a lawyer at

Google. The power of Google's brand and its associations with cutting-edge technology, its mission and its different style of working eclipsed the traditional prestige of top law firms for this young lawyer. And it's clear that he is not alone – Google receives millions of CVs each year. This phenomenon is also in evidence at other companies in Silicon Valley. Many young lawyers seek to become the first lawyer of the next hip start-up to go big; stock options in a company that turns out to be the next Google will dwarf even what the best-paying law firms can offer.

For most who move in-house, though, it's not the money that motivates, but rather the evolving challenge of what being an in-house lawyer actually means. But the corollary of the growing prestige of in-house roles is that there are more general counsel candidates than there are positions available. That said, to some extent this has always been the case, suggests Christopher Hurst, who oversees in-house recruitment at global search firm Carlyle Kingswood Global.[1]

Career progression and keeping talent happy are often significant areas of focus for incumbent general counsel. Most in-house departments are fairly flat structures and their progression routes and pay grades can be very opaque. To achieve the coveted title of general counsel or chief legal officer, a significant amount of lateral movement may be needed, rather than assuming internal succession as a given. A range of experience and perspectives from different geographies and different industries may also be a distinct advantage, allowing a prospective general counsel to collate ideas from across industries and cultures.

The skills needed to become a successful general counsel are rarely those taught at law school, so they must be developed on the job. As we discussed in the last part of the book, leadership and people management skills can often be a significant part of that requirement. This can produce a Catch-22 for many ambitious in-house lawyers. Getting the experience may require you to secure a role that offers this; but you may be unable to land such a role without the experience. Howard Harris, North American general counsel at the BMW Group, has faced this challenge when recruiting for roles and recognises that it can be a challenge for both the recruiter and candidate to overcome:

You find a lot of people with the credentials. You find a lot of people with the experience. You find a lot of people with the accomplishments and a lot of people that interview incredibly well; but then if you boil down to the leadership piece – a lot of people can talk about what their vision is, but it's the managing and leading people component where I don't know that people focus so much. For example, you can have a GC of a company where they're the only lawyer. Well, one of their challenges in getting their next role is: will somebody give them the opportunity if they haven't led other lawyers? And I can tell you, people who are not lawyers really don't count managing outside counsel or project teams. They are really looking for evidence of: how do you develop talent; how do you get the most out of your people? So somebody who's on their own has a challenge in terms of how they get that type of experience.[2]

Recruiter Hurst agrees with this assessment that leadership experience – and, he would add, global experience – is now a prerequisite. He advises prospective general counsel to look for departmental head roles to prepare them to get a general counsel job, as a key is being able to say you have run appraisals. Hurst's advice is that if you love being a technical lawyer, you will hate being a general counsel now because it skews so much towards other skills such as leadership and strategy: "It's much more about multi-function business management. From that perspective it's not about law as much as broadly managing risk and managing a team."[3]

1. The getting of wisdom: training lawyers

The 1910 Australian novel *The Getting of Wisdom* was written by Henry Handel Richardson (a pseudonym of Ethel Florence Lindesay Richardson). It tells the story of a clever and imaginative young girl, Laura, who goes away to boarding school. The experience turns out to be more about the desire to fit in and preconceived notions of what young women at the beginning of the twentieth century should be like, and less about actual education or wisdom. At the end of the novel, Laura literally runs away to distance herself from this stifling environment. The 'wisdom' of the title is ironic – her teaching does not imbue anything useful. In considering legal education today, many general counsel, lawyers and other commentators similarly query its utility and fitness for purpose.

Much legal education is still focused on the requirements of being a lawyer in private practice. In the United Kingdom, many see the training contract as a stumbling block to progress because of how it starts to structure the journey for young lawyers. The preferred route to ensure that they are not saddled with debt is for aspiring solicitors to secure a training contract with a firm prior to starting postgraduate study in law, which the firm will usually pay for. This means that much postgraduate study in law is being funded by large law firms, which have little reason to change the status quo.

Historically, working as a trainee in a law firm meant lots of mundane, admin-related work. It involved lots of checking contracts and due diligence – the very tasks which are currently being disrupted by technology. Therefore, an oft-heard protest around the digitisation of law is, "How will we train young lawyers?" This assumes that the current means of doing so is fit for purpose – which many argue it isn't.

Deutsche Bank made headlines in the United Kingdom in 2017 when, as part of its panel review, it declared that it would no longer pay for trainee solicitors or newly qualified solicitors. Similarly, in the United States, as early as 2011 an Association of Corporate Counsel survey of 366 general counsel showed that 20% had refused at some point to pay for work by very junior lawyers.

The angst around training young lawyers and the advance of technology is often predicated on a human versus machine binary: if one, then not the other. But as our case study on Schlumberger shows, the two can co-exist and complement each other even more when it comes to training.

However, many general counsel feel that the current routes to qualification are still not preparing lawyers for the range of challenges in the profession now, particularly in-house. As Chris Fox at Kambi explains:

The issue is that most top firms in London, while attracting high-quality, high-calibre talent, aren't training people for what you need in-house. The thinking in some law firms is rigid with respect to problem solving and advice can go through multiple layers of lawyers before being issued to clients. When you're in-house, you can't work like that. I need people who think outside the box, are proactive, curious, responsible and able to work in a collegiate, supportive environment. So I think that's the issue with the status quo – the fact that one of the major sources of supply isn't actually prepping lawyers for one of the greatest growth areas there is: in-house demand.[4]

Veteran general counsel and change advocate Jeff Carr, now at Univar, agrees that fundamental change is needed in how lawyers are trained: "Change has to start in the academy. Statistically, it's astounding as to how few law graduates actually have jobs when they exit law school and of the 50% or so that do, only a small slice is going to Big Law. Lots of folks are spending a lot of money and are employed in jobs that need not be done by lawyers and at relatively low wages – where do they get the return on investment?"

Return on investment for talent is also increasingly a consideration for clients – as shown by Deutsche Bank's move – but it's long overdue, according to Carr:

We are in the midst of major transitions as to how talent is viewed; what that means is the customers do not want to pay for the trainees that are not useful to us. Increasing numbers of GCs are simply not willing to pay for on-the-job training... Still, there has to be more action at the buyer level from the in-house community: there's a lot of talk about this stuff, but I question how many people actually do something about it? I believe it is because we all come from the same tribe. I have been trying to drive change for 25 years because I know we need to think differently.[5]

This echoes the views of some who work in legal education, and particularly those who are proactively considering the future of law with regard to innovation, such as Cat Moon at Vanderbilt University in

Nashville, Tennessee. Part of the issue, she feels, is the way the legal profession cognitively organises itself into lawyers and non-lawyers:

> *Too much discourse reinforces the world view of lawyers and non-lawyers, and the way we educate lawyers could go a long way to dispelling that mindset. We need to engage in exposing them early and often to experiences that show that multidisciplinary, cognitively diverse teams get better solutions. A group of people who are trained to see things and solve problems in the exact same way won't get to the best solution specifically in an innovation context.*[6]

This danger of specialisation and fetishisation of a particular type of knowledge or world view is also in evidence in the parts of this book on leadership and creativity. Understanding the value of cognitive diversity – most of which comes from actual diversity – is a significant aspect of the talent strategies that are needed for all businesses. Matthew Syed's book *Rebel Ideas: The Power of Diverse Thinking* explores why this is in relation to a number of real-life events – why a lack of diverse viewpoints produces bad outcomes and why diverse viewpoints can often produce great outcomes against the odds:

> *The first step for any group seeking to tackle a tough challenge, then, is not to learn more about the problems itself. It is not to probe deeper into is various dimensions. Rather, it is to take a step back and ask: where are the gaps in our collective understanding? Are we beset by cognitive blinkers? ... We need to address cognitive diversity before tracking our toughest challenges. It is only then that team deliberation can lead not to mirroring but to enlightenment.*[7]

But is this diversity and broadening of perspective being supported by legal education? Traditionally not. The cost of postgraduate legal qualifications has soared in recent years. In the United States, the cost of a Juris Doctor degree after paid-for undergraduate degrees puts legal qualifications beyond the reach of most of the population. And in many cases, legal education has remained relatively static compared to changes in the wider profession. As legal commentator Mark Cohen wrote in *Forbes Magazine* in 2017, US legal education "is crazy costly, outdated in its curriculum, out of touch with the marketplace, and seemingly indifferent to a majority of graduates that lack practice skills, confront bleak job prospects, and are saddled with six figure debt".[8]

But changes are afoot. In 2017 the Solicitors Regulation Authority (SRA) in the United Kingdom announced an overhaul of legal training and licensing, coming into effect in 2020. The Solicitors Qualification Exam offers a number of routes to qualification, not just a law degree and training contract.

One of the schemes being offered as part of this overhaul is the Trailblazer scheme: essentially an apprenticeship scheme – developed by UK firms in conjunction with the Chartered Institute of Legal Executives and the SRA – where prospective lawyers can work as an apprentice in a law firm or an in-house department and study part time to gain a law degree over six years while working.

The legal team at ITV thought this was a perfect solution both to acquire future talent who would be well equipped to understand the needs of a global legal function, and to ensure a more diverse talent pool by opening opportunities up to students who might have traditionally been put off by the cost of an undergraduate degree plus postgraduate qualification to practise as a solicitor. Barry Matthews, the former legal director at ITV who instituted the scheme, feels it is a better solution to the talent needs of in-house teams than the traditional conception of legal training:

When I became aware of the Trailblazer scheme I thought, "Why aren't we doing this?" The key to being a great in-house lawyer is understanding the business as well as the law; hence the qualification is a natural fit for in-house. [Our apprentice] Holly will work as part of each divisional legal team while studying, and will obtain an LLB and the equivalent of an LPC/PSC qualification after six years. Year one of Holly's studies focuses on contract law, and Holly has just started drafting contracts for us this week as part of the Commercial and Group Marketing legal team. The experience will really be from the cradle to the grave in terms of what ITV does: Holly will have experience of everything. So, she really should be the next GC! It's a real opportunity for us, as we will have someone who, on qualification, lives and breathes our business, and can link the businesses. As with any large group, communication between divisions is a constant challenge. Holly will have a great ability to look across all areas.[9]

This diversity of perspectives in the broadest sense is what is lacking from the current configuration of legal education, suggests Moon; and this has serious ramifications, as the future of the profession will be driven by the talent we access and train now: "The traditional conception of lawyers is inadequate to serve the needs we have. The framework has to be reconfigured and we need to move the ball to get a more diverse profession and we need more people and more skill sets to help us."

In our case study, one key aspect of Schlumberger's talent programme is utilising the perceptions and skill sets of digital natives. Training these younger lawyers to have a business and technology mindset, not just a legal one, is producing better results and feedback from business clients than hiring more experienced lawyers whose skills are centred very much on their expertise as lawyers.

Notes

1   Interview with the author, November 2018.
2   Interview with the author, November 2017.
3   Interview with the author, November 2019.
4   Interview with the author, August 2019.
5   Interview with the author, August 2019.
6   Interview with the author, November 2018.
7   Matthew Syed, *Rebel Talent* (John Murray 2019) p55.
8   Mark A Cohen, "A British Reboot Of Legal Education – Law School Optional", *Forbes*, 1 May 2017, www.forbes.com/sites/markcohen1/2017/05/01/a-british-reboot-of-legal-education-law-school-optional/.
9   Interview with the author, May 2020.

18. Putting talent to work: how lawyers work and how that is changing

The traditional model of legal training is beginning to be overhauled; but so too is how lawyers work once they are trained. This is occurring within the context of a broader global trend of changing work patterns, which in turn can affect the talent pool. Different ways of working may retain, attract or open the door to previously untapped or lost pools of talent. This may help to address the need for more diverse perspectives, as the traditional model of office work is replaced by new ways of working and new industries in which the traditional model is not the norm. Experts such as Rita Gunther McGrath[1] and Lynda Gratton[2] – who have both researched the workplace of the future – argue that the traditional fixed, salaried job in an office may soon be a thing of the past. This may well change what we value as talent and how we define excellence of talent. Working differently may also open up more opportunities for diverse talent, particularly as regards progressing in the profession both in-house and in private practice. The traditional 'jacket on the seat' culture of presenteeism may have benefited certain identity groups more than others; as a result, talent and successful talent have been coded in ways that inherently privilege certain groups over others.

While flexible and agile working has become more popular due to the forces of technology and globalisation, its adoption can still be fraught with issues. Although these different ways of working are gradually being adopted, there are concerns that many workplaces are merely paying lip service to the new models. Many organisations may still expect successful talent to fit a certain blueprint of working, which privileges certain groups over others. Although many employers offer flexibility of working, for cultural or practical reasons, this approach may not extend to the hiring or retention of talent. A 2017 study by Catalyst – a global think-tank which advocates for gender progression in the workplace – revealed that in the United States, while 80% of employers offer flexible working, only 30% of employees take up this offer.[3]

The mismatch is due to the fact that employees believe – often with good reason – that to take advantage of these opportunities would result in negative career outcomes. In law, this perception is a handicap to progress. When introducing a flexible return to work policy for associates coming back from maternity leave, US-based law firm Proskauer made this mandatory, to try to change the perceptions of both employees and managers that this would limit career advancement or that those working flexibly did not take work seriously.

For many years, it has been argued that current working practices in much of the legal profession are not conducive to everyone. As clients increasingly demand greater diversity of thought from their external counsel, law firms are beginning to reconsider how, when and by whom work is done, to try to secure a competitive advantage in this regard.

Other forces are also influencing this debate, including the increase in legal operations, the need for greater efficiencies in law, and the rise of alternative legal providers that utilise both new technology and alternative staffing.

The outcomes-based business structures of many newer players on the legal market have produced new ways of looking at working models, and at what success means and thus who can achieve that. John Croft

– president and founder of Elevate, a global law company which provides technology, consulting and staffing solutions to law departments and firms – suggests that players in the legal market that can imagine what 'different' looks like enjoy a significant advantage:

> *We don't care who does the work – lots of junior lawyers or some artificial intelligence technology and then one senior lawyer or any other combination. We don't care where you do it – in London in a big, marble-clad office block or on your laptop at the kitchen table while your kids are eating their supper next to you; or in India. We don't care what you are wearing. We don't care if you are young or old. We don't care if you are male or female. We don't care if you are black or white; gay or straight; disabled or able... You are either capable of doing the work, or you are not.*[4]

This attitude yields considerable dividends for companies such as Elevate, Croft believes, as inclusivity is built into their DNA: "The flexibility of a law company (where, how, who, when etc) is helpful for a more inclusive workforce – as against the old way, where you had to be in the office from 9:00am to 5:00pm; you had to charge by the hour; and you were likely to be a straight, white, middle-aged bloke wearing a dark suit and a tie."

Working practices can limit the view of what talent looks like and what is considered normal and acceptable in the workplace. In-house legal departments have long had a reputation for better gender equality than law firms, due to more predictable hours and a better work-life balance. Many female lawyers – particularly mothers and would-be mothers – move in-house because of these perceived benefits; although not all legal departments are created equal, and some may expect a fairly fixed or even demanding schedule. However, while the increasing mobilisation and digitisation of work mean that there is greater flexibility in-house as to how work is completed, this can also erode the boundaries between working and not working, which in turn can threaten employees' wellbeing.

1. The dark side of the 'work anywhere, anytime' utopia

So the downside of this greater flexibility in the workplace can be the creation of a culture where workers are never off duty. A 2008 study of 477 Dutch freelancers who worked from home revealed increased levels of stress and ill health due to their inability to switch off from work.[5] Research conducted in 2015 by Harvard Business School and Stanford University found that $48 billion on average was spent every year in the United States due to stress-related illness caused by overwork.[6]

As digitisation and agile working have increased exponentially since this research was carried out, so too have the mental and physical tolls. In a profession such as law, where responsiveness is prized, are some lawyers in danger of killing themselves through overwork? Sadly, this is all too possible. While greater connectivity means potentially greater flexibility, it can also lead to the danger of never being off work. The implications of this for workplace health, stress levels and overall productivity are massive. In 2017, this prompted the enactment of new legislation in France requiring companies with more than 50 employees to set expected working hours and not send emails or contact employees outside those hours.

In law, the discussions on wellbeing and mental health are gradually becoming louder, both in-house and in private practice. Traditionally, when moving in-house, lawyers expected shorter hours and a better work-life balance. While it is still true that in-house lawyers – unlike, say, corporate lawyers at the top-tier firms – are not routinely expected to pull all-nighters, their workloads have increased, in no small part due to the forces of globalisation and digitisation. Connecting team members who may be scattered across the globe will generally involve unsociable hours for some. When you then layer in the types of industries in which lawyers work and the stages that such companies are generally at, this can add further demands: start-up and high-growth companies will generally be very time-intensive for everyone, including their lawyers. A better work-life balance is no longer guaranteed in-house.

That said, one big difference which has made in-house more appealing to working parents – particularly working mothers – is that fact that there is generally less pressure to be present in the office for all hours worked. But flexibility of location can still lead to heavy demands on time; and some experts argue that it can even create more stress, as there is insufficient demarcation between work and down time. As a result, some general counsel feel that it is part of their remit to push back on demands for ultra-responsiveness from their team. Chris Fox of Kambi, for example, feels strongly that it is the responsibility of general counsel as leaders to ensure that their talent do not end up burned out by unacceptable demands from the business.

And Fox is not alone here. The Barclays in-house legal team was central to the creation of the Mindful Business Charter, which aims to promote greater vigilance regarding working practices on both the client and supplier sides.

Mental health has become a significant issue in many professions in recent years, but particularly in the legal profession. In 2017 the UK government commissioned the Stevenson/Farmer Review to examine the issue of mental health and employment. It concluded that there was a potential mental health crisis among UK employees, who were found to be "surviving, not thriving": "The UK is facing a mental health challenge at work that is much larger than we had thought. Not only is there a big human cost of poor mental health at work, there are also knock on impacts for society, the economy and Government. Employers are losing billions of pounds because employers are less productive, less effective, or off sick."[7]

The demands of law can trigger mental health issues in several different ways. The foundations of most law firms – a focus on the individual and the metrics of billable hours connected to individual output – are associated with poor work-life balance, due to the perceived requirement to work long hours. This is exacerbated by a competitive culture and a focus on perfectionism, which are initially internalised during a lawyer's education – with its focus on academic strength and perfection, and competition for training opportunities –

and then consolidated in private practice. The flipside of perfectionism can be imposter syndrome, where one feels that nothing is ever good enough and that success is undeserved. This again can prompt individuals to push themselves to extreme lengths to try to prove their worthiness.

By extension, this focus on individual productivity and a perceived need for perfection can create a cultural stigma around mental health problems in the law. Key personnel, such as line managers, often lack awareness of such problems and training on how to deal with them; and when such issues are raised, they are often mishandled or ignored altogether, leaving the individual unsupported.

Since the advent of #MeToo and #TimesUp, there is greater recognition of bullying and sexual harassment in the workplace. The recent focus on #BlackLivesMatter has also shone a spotlight on racism, discriminatory behaviour and micro-aggressions within organisations. A recent International Bar Association report based on a comprehensive survey across the profession revealed that uncivil and corrosive workplace cultures, bullying, harassment and discrimination have a significant impact on lawyers' wellbeing.[8] While much of the focus has been on the corrosive cultures and mental health dangers in private practice, in-house departments are not without their issues and have a fundamental role to play in promoting change in the working practices and attitudes that contribute to mental health issues.

2. The Mindful Business Charter – making a change

The desire to start a dialogue and make a change inspired the legal team at UK bank Barclays to institute conversations with in-house lawyers in London, and with lawyers from a handful of law firms, on the topic of mental health and wellbeing. The aim was to identify how collaboration between legal teams and their suppliers could minimise avoidable stress through a set of mindful working principles.

On 10 October 2018 – World Mental Health Day – in conjunction with other leading banks and law firms, Barclays launched the Mindful

Business Charter to help reduce workplace stress. The Mindful Business Charter is a set of principles focused on four pillars:

- openness and respect;
- smart meetings and emails;
- respect for rest periods; and
- mindful delegation.

The charter is not intended as a set of rules; rather, its principles are designed to encourage everyone to make small adjustments to how they work which could help to reduce instances of avoidable stress. By making small adjustments to our behaviour together, suggests the charter, we can sustain the long-term mental wellbeing of our colleagues. The charter's real power comes from its collaborative approach: working together to do things differently.

The charter aims to remove unnecessary sources of workplace stress and promote better mental health and wellbeing in the legal community. Its introductory statement acknowledges that this will not always be achievable; but a recognition of the need for a baseline of practice which prioritises mental health and wellness can start to produce cultural and behavioural change both in individual organisations and in the profession as a whole.

The pillars highlighted by the Mindful Business Charter are mostly focused on communication and empathy. The first pillar – openness and respect – aims to build trust and effective communication. Action points include:

- discussing upfront with colleagues, clients and contacts their preferred method of communication, and ensuring that the relevant implications of individual working patterns are taken into account;
- treating internal colleagues and external contacts with the appropriate level of respect and courtesy; and
- asking for and providing feedback to others on a regular basis.

The second pillar focuses on the delivery of interactions through smart meetings and email protocols. Action points for smart meetings include:

- allowing people to join meetings in the way they deem suitable;

- providing dial-in details as default on meeting invites, unless it is imperative that everyone attends in person;
- being respectful of others' time by planning meetings properly (considering who needs to attend, giving appropriate notice and setting clear agendas and objectives); and
- avoiding last-minute cancellations.

Action points for email protocols include:
- avoiding overuse of email and not copying people into emails that they do not need to receive; and
- making use of subject lines in emails and ensuring that these are reflective of the email's content.

The third pillar aims to promote respect for work-life balance through consideration for rest periods and the need to 'switch off'. Action points include:
- where support is required outside of someone's core working hours, giving him or her the option to choose when that could be (eg, early morning, in the evening or at the weekend);
- when sending emails outside business hours, being clear in the title as to whether they need to be read or actioned promptly, or sending pre-timed emails so that emails are not received late at night and at weekends;
- including working hours or availability in email signatures, so that people are aware of each other's working patterns;
- respecting people's right to take annual leave without expecting them to check emails or be on call; and
- role modelling the same behaviours where possible (particularly by leaders).

The fifth pillar aims to promote mindful delegation by implementing a best practice approach to collaboration, instruction and delegation – a particularly pertinent consideration for clients when instructing law firms. Action points here include:
- respecting the need to provide sufficient context and information for a piece of work, ideally including the purpose and ultimate recipient;

- when instructing on a task, negotiating rather than imposing a deadline;
- being transparent on the wider timetable where possible;
- promptly communicating timing changes that impact on others; and
- when being instructed on a task, being confident enough to flag when a deadline is unrealistic or unachievable.

Notes

1   Rita Gunther McGrath, *Seeing Around Corners: How to Spot Inflection Points in Business Before They Happen* (Houghton Mifflin 2019).
2   Lynda Gratton, *The Shift: The Future of Work is Already Here* (Harper Collins 2014).
3   Liz Mulligan-Ferry, "How Workplace Flexibility Can Promote Inclusion and Prioritize Talent", Catalyst blog, 10 August 2017, www.catalyst.org/2017/08/10/how-workplace-flexibility-can-promote-inclusion-and-prioritize-talent/.
4   Interview with the author, April 2019.
5   Toon W Taris, Sabine AE Geurts, Wilmar B Schaufeli, Roland WB Blonk and Suzanne E Lagerveld (2008), "All day and all of the night: The relative contribution of two dimensions of workaholism to well-being in self-employed workers", *Work & Stress*, 22:2, 153–165, DOI: 10.1080/02678370701758074.
6   Joel Goh, Jeffrey Pfeffer and Stefanos A Zenios, "The Relationship Between Workplace Stressors and Mortality and Health Costs in the United States", *Institute for Operations Research and the Management Sciences* Issue 2 Volume 62 2016).
7   Paul Farmer and Dennis Stevenson, *Thriving At Work: The Independent Review Of Mental Health And Employers* (2017) p5; www.gov.uk/government/uploads/system/uploads/attachment_data/file/658145/thriving-at-work-stevenson-farmer-review.pdf.
8   Kieran Pender, *Us Too? Bullying and Sexual Harassment in the Legal Profession* (International Bar Association, 2019), www.ibanet.org/bullying-and-sexual-harassment.asp.

"Greater awareness of inclusivity is slowly beginning to change the models of how lawyers work. And in the wider business world, other forces are aligning to ensure that traditional modes of working are being reconsidered in ways that can help to create a more diverse workforce."

19. Whose talent is it anyway? Diversifying the workforce

How the professions view work – and success at work – affects how people view their roles and, as discussed in the previous chapter, their mental and physical health. However, as also mentioned previously, how success at work and talent are categorised in the legal profession – that is, predominantly by billable hours and time worked – also has a significant effect on how talent is valued and whose talent is valued.

Historically, minorities faced the stark choice of either adopting the traits and behaviours of the successful majority in order to succeed or not progressing at all. So, for example, women avoided discussing their families at work; lesbian, gay, bisexual, trans and queer employees stayed in the closet; and ethnic minorities played down their ethnicity at work. In a report on how to use talent management to drive inclusion, Catalyst – a non-profit that works with CEOs and industry leaders to drive greater use of female talent – suggests that companies should begin by deconstructing what is meant by 'talent' in their own organisations, asking questions to determine what success looks like and why, and whether common traits are shared by the firm's talent:

How is TALENT defined in the organization and who does talent look like (eg, gender, age, race/ethnicity, region, educational institution, etc.)?

What are the key COMPONENTS of the talent management system?

How are they connected (eg, goal-setting, key competencies, performance appraisal, feedback loop, etc.)?

How are different levels of employees held ACCOUNTABLE for effective talent management (eg, performance rating, compensation, bonus, goals and evaluation criteria, etc.)?

What MESSAGES do senior leaders convey about leadership competencies and promotion opportunities (eg, key leadership behaviors, written and oral communication regarding key competencies, etc.)?[1]

But in many professions, including law, the 'jacket on the seat' mentality is still alive and well: you are only considered to be working if you are seen to be working. This means that those with fewer caring responsibilities – particularly for children – are more likely to progress up the ladder. Thus, opportunities are skewed towards men, who are generally less likely to be the primary carers for children or elders.

In professions such as law, this leads to the acceptance of what Professor Joan Williams of the Center for WorkLife Law has termed the 'maternal wall'. Many commentators on diversity in the workplace cite this as a defining factor in continuing gender inequality, including the gender pay gap. Williams highlights the maternal wall as a factor which stalls women's progression and even inclusion in the workplace: "Women who have been very successful may suddenly find their proficiency questioned once they become pregnant, take maternity leave, or adopt flexible work schedules. Their performance evaluations may plummet and their political support evaporate. The 'family gap' yawns: An increasing percentage of the wage gap between men and women is attributable to motherhood."[2]

Once triggered, the maternal wall can be the strongest form of bias. More than 20 years of studies show that motherhood can trigger negative competency and commitment assumptions. In addition, mothers walk a precarious tightrope: if they work too much, they may be seen as bad mothers; if they work too little, they may be seen as bad workers.

Greater awareness of inclusivity is slowly beginning to change the models of how lawyers work. And in the wider business world, other forces are aligning to ensure that traditional modes of working are being reconsidered in ways that can help to create a more diverse workforce – which in turn is changing how we think about and manage talent.

But for women and diverse lawyers in law firms, the traditional law firm model – where success is calculated through the number of hours billed and key client relationships owned by individuals – continues to perpetuate prejudicial working practices and mindsets. This influences how success is defined at work: if this definition hinges on attributes and behaviours that are predominant among one demographic, then diversity and inclusion cannot be achieved. Further work is also needed around the semantics of success in the profession, which may skew towards a white, cisgender, heterosexual, male definition.

Arguably, the supplier side of the industry faces the greatest challenges here. The billable hour model is being questioned on many fronts as no longer fit for purpose. While most law firms offer alternative billing models, the basic calculus used for those is still how much time each lawyer spends on a matter. This structure means that those who can work longest and more consistently are the most successful.

But time is not the only factor at play here: many female lawyers – both partners and associates – report difficulties in accessing key client relationships. The same is true for lawyers of colour, both male and female. Given that valuable relationships, both internally and externally, can be formed at social gatherings, it is important that leaders in the profession consider whether such events are truly inclusive or find ways to make them more so.

It is thus clear that the traditional model of success in law firms is often based on privilege and a definition of talent that benefits those who are already systematically advantaged. Some clients proactively try to mitigate this by insisting on diversity in client relationship partners. Walmart's legal team, for example, demands that a second diverse relationship partner be appointed if the incumbent relationship partner is not diverse.

1. Defining talent

One key question that comes up regarding inclusion is whether it is clear, when discussing talent, how the term is being both used and defined. A broad definition of 'talent' refers to both current and future employees. A narrower definition of 'talent' refers to those with exceptional talent or high potential. Ideally, these should overlap significantly. The legal profession must grapple with the fact that the definition of 'good', in relation to talent, will need to change substantially; otherwise, lawyers will end up conforming to a notion of talent which is no longer fit for purpose. This will also inform how the profession as a whole both predicts and attracts the talent it needs.

As the definition of a 'lawyer' evolves, driven by technological advances and new service delivery options, the definition of a 'good lawyer' will also change. There will also be a need for greater contextual variations going forward, as the business world and the legal world face increasingly more complex and faster-changing problems. Many of these will be augmented by the drive towards greater innovation and digitisation, which will both provide solutions and throw up new legal and regulatory issues – many of which have not yet been considered or even thought of. We need only look at the current state of laws pertaining to the Internet: most are still jurisdictional in basis, whereas the Internet is by nature multi-jurisdictional. Much of the legal world still lives in analogue, and its definitions of 'talent' and 'merit' are also often outdated.

When considering talent, a significant challenge for many organisations is considering what is meant by talent and how that maps with different identities. Talent and merit are often spoken of and used as if they are objective traits which lie outside of any context. However, that is very much not the case. What talent means is defined, more often than not, by those who are in the majority or who have control in an organisation. Having merit in these terms is not just about academic achievements, but a whole raft of other assumed associations. The problem is not with diversity, but with the supposedly objective, non-values-based concept of merit, which is actually subjective and values based. Merit and diversity are often cited in conjunction with one another. The assumption is that merit will ultimately prove the solution to diversity: if people are talented, they will succeed no matter what. In practice, this definition of 'merit' and its application result in an assumption that if there are not enough diverse people who meet the definition, this is obviously a fault on their part, rather than in how merit is defined and applied.

Writing in the *Financial Times*, Andy Haldane, chief economist of the Bank of England, defines the conundrum as follows: "[W]hile people believe that workplace diversity is valuable, they also think recruiters should choose the best person for the job. The problem is that these propositions have a nasty habit of jarring. How many times have you heard an organisation say they would have loved to close their diversity deficit, but selected 'on merit'?"[3]

Haldane offers an interesting analogy based on investment returns. When choosing between shares which might offer the same return, but where one has a higher volatility or risk than the other, it might seem that the lower-risk option is the logical choice. Not so, counters Haldane, who suggests that always going with the obvious choice is the result of a mindset which does not consider the bigger picture. How does the choice of share A versus share B map out as a decision across your whole investment portfolio?

Similarly, hiring decisions in law often use very safe metrics without a sense of the bigger picture at play.

2. Putting talent in perspective – different paths to success

By relying on narrow definitions of 'talent', the legal profession is setting itself up for failure with regard to innovation and the changes needed to keep pace with the broader forces affecting business. More diverse talent is needed to address these, as well as a recognition that there are now myriad paths to success.

One of the new tools being used to try to balance definitions of 'success' in the pipeline to law is contextual recruiting. Here, exam results are analysed in relation to the wider context. For example, is the applicant the first generation in his or her family to go to university? What was the average A-level attainment at his or her school? A fairly average A-level result can suddenly be redefined as outperforming the average if considered in this context.

Pirical is a data analysis company which uses artificial intelligence to analyse data around hiring and HR trends, and increasingly has been using this to deconstruct some perceived 'truths' around diverse hiring. In a 2019 blog, founder Jason Ku posits that the outperformance of candidates who attended the lowest-performing schools in the United Kingdom is a very strong predictor of outperformance in the workplace: "An R-squared of .328 for the bottom 20% of schools suggests that for candidates who attended a low-performing school, the more they outperformed their school peers, the better they performed as a lawyer."[4]

As discussed in the chapters on creativity and leadership, there is a significant focus in the legal profession on the acquisition of knowledge and the enhancement of this through further specialist knowledge. Accordingly, 'merit' with regard to talent in the profession is still often defined as expertise in, and the ability to apply, a particular knowledge base. This is also how 'merit' is defined in most legal training. And often, this 'merit' is perceived to exist only where the knowledge has been acquired at a school deemed 'worthy'. Many working in the diversity space report that diverse candidates from leading schools do not experience problems being hired; the blind spot of the legal profession lies in its inability to look beyond these narrow parameters. Admittedly, this is truer of law firms than of legal departments; but given that most legal teams recruit from law firms, they are also affected by this problem, albeit at a remove.

Structurally, if merit is still being defined in one way, this also suggests that those who cannot meet this definition are not talented. Merit is often touted as the ultimate leveller: those who have talent will rise to the top regardless of their circumstances. There are similarities here with the outdated theory of the 'great man' that was previously discussed in the chapters on leadership: the concept that someone is destined for leadership no matter what. Both theories tend to privilege certain people over others – generally white, cisgender men. Those who ascend to leadership and are not part of this group – although they might be few and far between – are often used as examples to shore up the prejudices that this theory masks: namely, that most diverse people are not sufficiently talented to make it. Those who do succeed often feel that they need to hide intrinsic aspects of their identity to do so. This is ultimately symptomatic of a broken system. As legal scholar and professor at New York University School of Law Kenji Yoshino writes in his landmark text *Covering*, this is:

> *[a] hidden assault on our civil rights. We have not been able to see it as such because it has swaddled itself in the benign language of assimilation. But if we look closely, we will see that covering is the way many groups are being held back today. The reason racial minorities are pressured to 'act white' is because of white supremacy. The reason women are told to downplay their childcare responsibilities in the workplace is because of patriarchy. And the reason gays are asked not to 'flaunt' is because of homophobia.*[5]

As Kimberlé Crenshaw's theory of intersectionality defines it, focusing on diverse groups is always doomed to failure, as it suggests that the problem lies with them.[6] Rather, the problem lies in the system itself and how it defines 'talent'. Addressing this problem requires a recognition of the power systems inherent in the definition and application of a seemingly neutral term such as 'talent'. This redefinition is a key issue for many general counsel – as regards both their own teams and those of outside advisers. Striking the right balance of diverse ideas and experience is central to effective collaboration, creativity and innovation. In our case study, a significant aim of the rationale behind the talent programme at Schlumberger was to stimulate greater diversity in the legal team – in part, by creating a new playing field.

In many companies, a more considered focus on talent development and how it relates to diversity and inclusion has been playing out over the last 15 years. But there are still challenges and some way to go, as Boehringer Ingelheim USA's chief diversity and inclusion officer, Nancy Di Dia, explains:

> *I think we are still focusing on the best candidate for the position, and overall, we tend to buy talent more than we build it – specifically for certain areas – and I don't think that sits well with some employees. We often hire for the position today and not for the potential tomorrow. What we need to do is make sure that our talent can grow, so we don't find ourselves in these conundrums where we have talent that might not be able to take us where we want to be in the future.*[7]

This conundrum can be a challenge for all businesses, particularly in fast-changing industries. For most companies, what got you here won't get you there; but how can you balance talent needs with strategy when you may not yet know your strategic roadmap for the future? A big question for general counsel and law firm leaders now is: how can we futureproof our talent?

Notes

1   Catalyst, "Using Talent Management to Support Inclusion; A How-To Guide for Organisations", 4 January 2012, www.catalyst.org/system/files/using_talent_management_to_support_inclusion_a_how_to_guide_for_organisations.pdf.
2   Joan C Williams, "The Maternal Wall", *Harvard Business Review*, October 2004.
3   Andy Haldane, "Diversity versus merit is a false choice for recruiters", *Financial Times*, 22 July 2018, www.ft.com/content/e01b4bc0-8c31-11e8-affd-da9960227309.
4   Jason Ku, "Do privileged children who attended the best schools become better performing employees?", Pirical, 1 January 2019, https://pirical.com/blog/socialmobility.
5   Kenji Yoshino, *Covering* (Random House 2007) pxi.
6   Sumi Cho, Kimberlé Crenshaw and Leslie McCall, "Intersectionality Studies: Introduction", in "Special Issue on Intersectionality", 38 *Signs: J Women in Culture & Soc'y* 785 (2013).
7   Catherine McGregor, "Case Study 01 Boehringer Ingelheim", *Minority Corporate Counsel Association & Paul Hastings Case Study Series* (2019) www.mcca.com/wp-content/uploads/2019/10/MCCA_CaseStudy_Spread_R2.pdf, p15.

20. Futureproofing: redefining talent and redefining expertise

One of the most significant aspects of innovation in law is a questioning of the skill sets and specialisations needed to successfully deliver legal services.

Increasingly, it seems that there is a bifurcation between the skills needed in-house and those taught in legal education and valued in private practice. Structuring work allocation differently and using paralegals rather than fully qualified lawyers were key factors in some of the early innovations in legal services pioneered in the 1990s and 2000s by companies such as DuPont and FMC Technologies.

The logical corollaries to these initial innovations are today's alternative legal providers – many of which are as reliant on different staffing models as they are on technology to devise new solutions.

When we look at talent, we once again see many of the strands discussed elsewhere in this book come together:
- Why are we doing this (purpose)?

- Is there a different way of doing this (creativity)?
- What problem is the client hiring the innovation to solve (innovation)?
- How can we work together more effectively to solve this problem in the right way (collaboration)?

Certainly in the case of most large corporate law firms, the legal profession has become a profession that worships at the temple of specialisation and expertise. This seems natural, given that law firms are selling their expertise in law: honing and refining that expertise would therefore seem a logical aim. But is this always the best way to develop talent? And is it the best way to develop the right sort of talent, thinking in the right way to address the challenges that their clients are increasingly dealing with?

More and more people – and particularly general counsel – would say no. There is a clue in the job title: 'general'. Yet the training and expertise of most general counsel are highly specialised. For many, moving into their first in-house position involves both a steep learning curve and a process of unlearning some behaviours. By its very nature, the in-house counsel role is one where an understanding of the law must be broadly applied. Increasingly, the discussions I have with in-house counsel show that they are much more business advisers who happen to be lawyers than lawyers who happen to work in a business.

Mastercard's general counsel, Tim Murphy, says that CEO Ajay Banga frequently tells him: "Don't just give me a lawyer's answer – put it in context."[1] This might be an increasingly popular refrain. Murphy suggests that the fact lawyers train so hard and become so specialised sometimes makes it hard for them not to 'show their workings' and all the brilliant thought that has led to a recommendation. Deconstructing Banga's request, it is really saying, "Don't get so overspecialised; focus on the problem and how to solve it, and communicate that to me in plain terms." Many of the other key ideas influencing business, and thus influencing in-house teams, likewise involve an ability to understand both the macro level and the micro level, and to put changes in the broadest possible context.

There is also a significant issue with the definition of a 'lawyer' as an expert who solves problems. Increasingly, what is valued in the new digital economy is the ability to proactively spot problems and manage a wide variety of risk situations. In our case study, the hiring impetus is to look for T-shaped individuals who have a level of specialisation, but can apply that more generally and think much more broadly than in just that one area.

In her book *Rebel Talent*,[2] Harvard Business School Professor Francesca Gino analyses the connection between talent and rule breaking – that is, harnessing the forces of creativity and innovation to look differently at the status quo. As Gino defines it, rebel talent is about breaking the rules that are holding you back: questioning assumptions and beliefs, as well as the widely accepted norms around them, to identify more creative, effective ways of doing work that will be transformative. Or to put it even more succinctly, it champions "People who are 'deviants,' but in a positive and constructive way".[3]

From both her own research and the findings of others across a range of disciplines, Gino has discovered that too much expertise can hamper problem-solving abilities. Indeed, it is often non-experts who delve deeply into a new field that come up with the most effective and creative solutions.

One example cited by Gino is that of InnoCentive, a pioneer in crowdsourced innovation, which enables companies to post problems and experts to provide ideas and solutions via an open source network. The companies, called 'seekers', post their challenges on the InnoCentive website; the 'solvers' are those who try to come up with answers. Solvers can win cash prizes offered by the seekers. InnoCentive believes that this approach of posting challenges and inviting solutions via open source can work for a range of problems across many fields – from engineering, chemistry and computer science to life sciences, business and even economic development. InnoCentive defines solvers thus: "If your mind sees solutions everywhere, challenge yourself to change the world." While the solvers might include experts from within an organisation's industry,

InnoCentive suggests that more important are those experts from outside that industry who can offer diverse perspectives and fresh insights.

In her discussion of InnoCentive, Gino cites the research of her Harvard Business School colleague Karim Lakhani, who has analysed four years of data from InnoCentive around problems that have been successfully solved. The results that Lakhani and his researchers came up with back up InnoCentive's own assertion that it is the external perspectives that are most useful. Lakhani and his team found that solvers whose domain of expertise was at least six times removed from the problem were more likely to solve it than those whose expertise was up to three times removed. The research also found that experts had more success when they looked for ideas and solutions outside of their own area of expertise; and that those who were not experts, but who delved deeply into understanding a new field also had better odds of solving the problem. This echoes some of the ideas discussed in the chapters on creativity.

So what does this mean for law, and specifically for in-house teams, with regard to talent?

In our case study on Schlumberger, Kevin van Tonder highlights the advantages gained by the company completely changing its talent strategy and moving away from hiring mid-career lawyers from law firms to hiring recent graduates trained by the company. One key advantage that Van Tonder outlines is that the new legal talent has grown up within Schlumberger in the same way as much of the company's other talent, and can therefore approach problems with a mindset that is much more aligned to the holistic needs of the business, rather than being focused primarily on their legal subject-matter expertise.

More broadly, this echoes the idea of agility and broader knowledge – informed by law, but not completely defined by it – which is now part of the specific nature of the in-house role. Particularly in the senior echelons, these roles are not at all about technical legal expertise.

Frequently, the in-house lawyers I speak to – across jurisdictions and sectors – mention the ability to think on one's feet and craft solutions in areas where you might have limited specialist knowledge, but are a quick study. As Gino writes of the advantages of non-expert talent:

> *It can be easier to approach problems from fresh perspectives when we are not experts. Unfamiliar or unpleasant arguments, opposing views, information that disproves rather than affirms our beliefs, and counterintuitive findings – rather than familiar arguments and evidence that confirms our views – cause us to think more deeply and come to creative and complex conclusions. And that's where outsiders have an advantage over experts: They are less rooted in, and defensive of, existing viewpoints.*[4]

When it comes to applying for senior in-house roles, you can demonstrate this ability by focusing less on what qualifications you have and more on how you work. As our earlier conversation with recruiter Christopher Hurst pointed out, the general counsel role of today is not a great fit for those who want to demonstrate their expertise as a technical lawyer. This can be even truer for in-house legal teams in industries where they may be facing newer or untested legal issues, or in start-ups. Google can certainly take its pick of personnel: it receives floods of applications each year from candidates who think they meet the criteria that make them 'Googley'. This has been well documented both in the press and in Google's former chief people officer Laszlo Bock's book, *Work Rules!*.[5] For Catherine Lacavera, vice president legal at Google, a lot of work is done before interview by researching candidates' background and collecting references. But as in other companies, it's not "the exact things you've done [that matters], but more how adaptable are you to new scenarios. You can deal with the known, but how are you going to deal with the totally unknown?"[6]

Lawyers are generally at their best when dealing with tangibles and where there are precedents; but companies such as Google – which work in areas where the law may be playing catch-up with their strategies – must consider different metrics to find the right people to cope with this. At Google, candidates are given a number of hypothetical scenarios during the extensive interviewing process. Says Lacavera: "We do these hypotheticals that really have no answers to watch the person think through that and see how they are on their feet. Sometimes they are legal scenarios; sometimes they are some weird things that happened to us that week. Other questions will focus more on management style."[7]

In *Work Rules!*, Bock describes how Google's interviewing process has developed and continues to develop. Bock observes that most traditional interview processes are predicated on a framework that privileges first impressions and 'gut instinct' over techniques, which can be more solid predictors of how interviewees might perform. These include work sample tests, general tests of cognitive ability and structured interviews where candidates are asked a consistent set of questions with clear criteria, which may be behavioural or situational in their focus.

This echoes the experiences of lawyers at another company that is redefining the rules of industry and therefore the workplace: Amazon. Like Google, Amazon bases its interviews on behavioural questions that test how applicants might behave in hypothetical situations. These questions are based on Amazon's leadership principles, which are seen as fundamental to the hiring process.

When hiring for in-house roles, general counsel now must think about the needs of the business and how the talent they are hiring can adapt and change. Increasingly, this may mean that the people who are hired and the merits they are judged on will also need to change. This is a conundrum facing all companies, as Eric Schmidt, co-founder of Google, attests:

Favoring specialization over intelligence is exactly wrong, especially in high tech. The world is changing so fast across every industry and endeavor that it's a given the role for which you're hiring is going to change. Yesterday's widget will be obsolete tomorrow and hiring a specialist in such a dynamic environment can backfire. A specialist brings an inherent bias to solving problems that spawns from the very expertise that is his putative advantage and may be threatened by a new type of solution that requires new expertise. A smart generalist doesn't have bias, so is free to survey the wide range of solutions and gravitate to the best one.[8]

Schmidt's quote echoes the ideas of Gino and Matthew Syed,[9] showing that – as Marshall Goldsmith defined the journey to leadership – what got you here won't get you there. The talent journey in law must be redefined; the career path of only ever being a technical specialist in black-letter law will become increasingly obsolete. Considering the purpose of the legal department may well lead legal teams to become more digitised and look to outsourcing solutions as they start to dig into the question: what is the purpose of the legal department? But will this be the end of the world? Could it actually make the in-house lawyer roles that are left much more exciting?

In the next part of the book, on collaboration, we will examine some radical in-house solutions which take as their starting point the purpose of the legal team and how it can be optimised to provide more future-ready solutions for companies. This is not just about process or technology, but really starts with people. As Jeff Carr, general counsel and adviser to the CEO of Univar, states: "This is breaking down everything a law department does, which is essentially four things: advocacy, counsel, process and content. Only counsel and advocacy need legal judgement."[10]

Disruptors such as Carr feel that making radical change will ultimately redefine the lawyer's role in a way that takes it to much more interesting places. But change is hard – particularly when those being asked to make the change are products of the existing talent system. Carr does not even define himself as a lawyer: "When I say, 'I am not a lawyer; in fact, I am an executive in a company who happened to be tasked with providing legal services to that company,' that is unusual, as most people still define themselves as lawyers. We have to get outside of our tribe, outside Law Land and live in the real business world."

In our case study over the following pages, we see an approach which has redefined talent and what it means to be a lawyer in a company. This approach blends people, process and technology – but with people placed firmly as the first consideration.

Notes
1   Interview with the author, March 2020.
2   Francesca Gino, *Rebel Talent: Why it Pays to Break the Rules at Work and in Life* (Pan Books e-book 2018).
3   *Ibid*, location 100.
4   *Ibid*, p102.
5   Laszlo Bock, *Work Rules!* (John Murray, 2016).
6   Catherine McGregor, "In-House Got Talent?: Bay Area GCs on Hiring", *GC Magazine*, Summer 2015 www.legal500.com/gc-magazine/feature/in-house-got-talent-bay-area-gcs-on-hiring/.
7   *Ibid.*
8   Eric Schmidt and Jonathan Rosenberg, *How Google Works* (John Murray 2015), p104.
9   Francesca Gino, *Rebel Talent: Why it Pays to Break the Rules at Work and in Life* (Pan Books e-book 2018). Matthew Syed, *Rebel Ideas* (John Murray 2019).
10   Interview with the author, August 2019.

21. Future talent: Schlumberger's marriage of people, process and technology

Kevin van Tonder is the former general counsel, legal shared services at global oilfield services company Schlumberger. He was responsible for driving innovation in the company's legal department, including employing technology, metrics and data analytics to drive performance.

What is revolutionary about Schlumberger's approach, spearheaded by Van Tonder, is that it combines people, process and technology, with the people (or talent) piece the leading part of this equation. Van Tonder believes that an understanding of the importance of talent is fundamental to the future of the profession: "This is what we were thinking – it has to be everything working together. Too often, when people in legal think about innovation, all they ever think about is technology. But to get that working, you have to have the right people and process. Our journey started with people and process – getting that right first – which was why we established the legal support centres [LSCs] in 2017."[1]

The LSCs were inspired by the team's use of some basic workflows linked to an internally built matter management tool. Although that tool is now being phased out in favour of third-party provision from Onit, those initial workflows acted as a prototype to figure out what might work and what might not.

Van Tonder's personal journey into how the future of legal talent could map onto other aspects such as process and technology began in 2010, when he took over the contracts function in Schlumberger. At that point, legal contracts were owned not only by legal, but also by sales and marketing and a procurement function, which was separate from the legal department. One of Van Tonder's first moves was to merge the two external pillars of contracts and bring these into the legal function. He then started looking at efficiencies such as using legal process outsourcing (LPO) for overflow work, instead of adding internal headcount.

Another potential solution that presented itself was moving some of legal's functions into a shared services organisation such as that which the HR and finance functions at Schlumberger were already using. Van Tonder was still looking for the right solution for the contracts function in 2013:

> *Part of my initial thinking was to create a legal support system – not just contracts, but like UnitedLex is doing now with the HP and DXC lawyers; basically to rebadge a bunch of lawyers and stick them under the LPO model. Could we take some Schlumberger contract people and rebadge them under the LPO? Or could we use LPO people for most of the work and use Schlumberger lawyers to manage them and run the function?*

1. Driven by disaster – how the oil crisis wrought changes

Some of that initial work was put on hold due to a move back to Africa for personal reasons in 2013. While Van Tonder was still employed by Schlumberger, providing legal advice for its operations in Angola, the whole project of looking at efficiencies, processes and better use of people would not be resuscitated until 2015. This was driven by pressing concerns which were much bigger than the legal department, wreaking fundamental changes on the whole oil industry. From 2014 to 2016, oil prices suffered their biggest slump in history. This was partly due to new supplies being accessed via shale drilling in the United

States and increased efficiencies in the traditional industry. The world had a glut of oil and demand was beginning to fall. Additionally, traditional oil-importing countries, such as the United States and China, were not enjoying as much economic growth as previously.

For a company such as Schlumberger, which supplies oilfield services and equipment, this was catastrophic. Its share price slumped, leading to the lay-off of 15% of its global workforce. All departments now had to reduce costs, including legal. Schlumberger's general counsel was given an ultimatum by the CEO to reduce structural costs or face the business making the necessary changes with little or no input from legal. What was needed was a transformation programme. Van Tonder was approached in 2016 to return to the company's headquarters in Paris and run with this.

On his return, Van Tonder started looking again at the notion of LSCs. The proposal this time was that they would be used not just for contracts, but for a whole range of high-volume, low-complexity, day-to-day legal work. However, what proved truly transformative was when the concept of talent and how to make legal talent more future ready was factored into the mix.

The inspiration for this was a consideration of Schlumberger's traditional methods of recruitment and management of high-potential talent in other functions. In most other key areas, such as engineering and sales, Schlumberger followed a model of recruiting promising graduates directly from university and training them in the Schlumberger way throughout their career. Legal bucked the trend by hiring mid-career, generally from law firms. But did it have to be this way? Could a revolution in hiring be coupled with a wholesale change in how high-volume work, such as contracts and other non-complex matters, was handled?

2. T-shaped talent

When considering the type of talent that the legal department needed, and the type of future talent that the use of process efficiency and technology might help to create, Van Tonder focused on the notion of the 'T-shaped individual'. This concept has been used for a number of years in recruitment and HR to describe the mix of specialist and generalist skills needed to succeed in a modern organisation. The vertical bar on the letter T represents the depth of related skills and expertise in a single field; whereas the horizontal bar represents the ability to collaborate across disciplines with experts in other areas and to apply knowledge from areas of expertise other than one's own. For Van Tonder, this was a key concept both in developing the concept of the LSCs and in determining how these might be most successfully staffed:

> *In our focus on people, we were first using the T-shaped lawyer analogy. Being in-house and having that viewpoint helped a lot, in the sense of seeing what finance or what HR were doing and being able to think more broadly about what we did. It's that cross-silo viewpoint: instead of the inside-out mentality, in that everything has to be unique to legal, it's outside-in, looking at ideas and best practices from other functions within the organisation.*

The Schlumberger HR and finance departments had created hubs in Kuala Lumpur, Bucharest and Bogota, staffed mainly by locals. Those hubs dealt with high-volume issues such as payroll, relocations and accounts payable. While the legal team was inspired by this, it wanted to take things one step further – particularly in the deployment of talent. As Van Tonder explains: "As a legal function, we want to develop a pipeline and make it diverse."

The three LSCs would also become a conduit for this talent pipeline. About 50% of staff would be citizens of the relevant jurisdiction; but the other 50% would be high-potential international hires straight out of law school or university, who would learn about the legal function and the company by working in the three shared LSC locations.

Explains Van Tonder: "These were people coming in quite green. Traditionally, Schlumberger has recruited engineers right out of university and put them through a rigid and fixed training programme, so we took a lesson from that example."

The idea had been discussed for some time, but had never been actualised. It needed what was literally a shock to the system to force action, recalls Van Tonder:

> *I had been talking to people internally about what would work from 2010 to 2013. Then there were three to four years of this idea percolating; the only way it came to the surface quickly was external circumstances driving wholesale corporate changes. Lawyers are resistant to change. People would think, "If it ain't broke then why fix it?" It's like an internal ego thing: you keep your headcount and you add, but don't lose any. The challenge from our CEO was: "Either you change yourselves or someone else will do it for you." And the last thing you want is finance coming in and taking charge of it.*

3. Blending technology and talent

So what resulted from this process? Shared services generally were used across functions in the business more widely. And as Van Tonder mentions, a key factor in the journey was a collaborative approach: looking from the outside in at what had worked for other functions and learning from that.

The initial work that went to the LSCs for functions such as HR and finance was very transactional, such as payroll. This then moved completely to an outsourcing model, with Accenture taking over many of these functions.

As time progressed, the work conducted by the LSCs evolved from the purely transactional to increased layers of complexity. But when it came to talent, it was still a case of business process insourcing: hiring local people who would not progress. However, as the use of the LSCs continued, things became more complex, particularly with regard to the deployment of talent. Some functions began to create centres of excellence and transferred in different nationalities to staff them. This talent would come in and help to develop the centre, and then move out after a certain period. Legal decided to adopt a hybrid approach to talent and staffing from day one, as Van Tonder explains:

Half the team would be local; they would not necessarily be fixed. So high-potential local nationals could move to other international opportunities if they wished and could. About 40% to 50% would be high-potential talent from target nationalities recruited as graduates. This was where we wanted more high-potential talent to bring more diversity to our operations. It was also interesting to see how, globally, the ease of bringing in talent differed – compared to the United Kingdom or the United States, for example, where it would be a long and time-consuming visa process and work period in their home jurisdiction. In places such as Kuala Lumpur and Bucharest, we could recruit people and start immediately in the hub.

Diversity – having a workforce that reflects the global diversity of Schlumberger, which operates in 81 countries – was a significant driver for the legal team. But with the more pressing goal of cutting costs in mind, the recruitment of younger talent was also significantly cheaper than the mid-career hires that the team had traditionally relied upon.

There was also another key advantage to attracting younger workers: millennials and Generation Z are digital natives. At Schlumberger, as in many other companies, a driving force of corporate strategy generally is increased digitisation, so having a tech-savvy workforce for whom a digital workplace was natural was a significant benefit. Digital natives could also be more seamlessly integrated into the process and technology-driven ways of working needed by the legal team to cut costs and produce greater efficiency.

A further advantage of this new talent pool was that they were to all intents and purposes a blank slate, given that this was generally their first full-time job. Past experiences of hiring lawyers mid-career were often mixed, as Van Tonder attests: "Recruiting from law firms could be hit or miss, as the lawyers still often acted like law firm lawyers in-house. As a legal team, our model is to place lawyers with the management teams in country. That is why our lawyers are spread all over the world, and we tend to place them in our functions to develop them."

This geographical placement of lawyers means that their value comes much less from their technical knowledge of the law than from their business awareness, as Van Tonder explains: "When in-house, lawyers move into a local business unit, it's not their knowledge of the law that's valuable – it's their knowledge of the issues for the company and their ability to translate legal knowledge into business needs. We have local law firms for the local law. Our lawyers need to be able to take a 10-page opinion and turn this into three or four succinct points for the business they work with."

The legal team found that while mid-career hires typically had 10 to 12 years' post-qualification experience, their credibility in Schlumberger as lawyers was zero: "Particularly when you consider that the rest of the business team will likely have been in the company for their whole career. This meant that lawyers often found it hard to get traction with local management teams. This challenge is something that the new way of bringing talent in via the LSCs is explicitly addressing."

4. How it works

4.1 Path for future talent at Schlumberger

- Eight months on a selected legal focus such as contracting and a regional focus (eg, sub-Saharan Africa).
- Eight months on the next legal and geographic focus.
- Ten months on the next legal and geographic focus.
- At the end of the first stint in the LSC, exposure to three different business/legal pillars and three different geographies.
- A 12 to 24-month role on the ground, working with a business unit in a specific geography.
- A move back to the LSC for about a year in a team leadership role, managing seven to 10 people; this factors leadership and management experience into talent development.
- A move back into a geography role, usually managing a few lawyers.
- Finally, for talent destined for senior legal management roles, a two to three-year stint managing an LSC of 25 to 30 people.

High-potential talent work in the LSCs for about three years. During that time, they don't just do the work that comes in, as in the traditional service centre approach, where work tickets are generated on a first come, first served basis. Instead, Schlumberger allocates them to a particular pillar, such as contracts or sales support, and a geographic focus. For example, a new hire might start with eight months covering sales contracts in sub-Saharan Africa, followed by eight months focused on supplier contracts in Europe. That might be followed by 10 months focusing on North Africa covering day-to-day legal for a business unit.

Van Tonder explains the benefits of this approach:

> When our talent come out of LSCs, they have covered three different functionalities and three different geographies. This means they are knowledgeable and flexible for a move into business unit support. This summer, we moved nearly one-third of our function globally and people came out of the LSCs to plug the gaps on the ground. So, their next experience will be on the ground covering legal for a geography of a cluster of countries: usually about $1 billion of revenue, with two or three people in the geography working with them.

But the first move out of the LSC does not mark the end of the journey: "The talent works in a geo-specific legal support role for about two years, getting exposure to day-to-day legal work and working directly in situ with the business. But then we move you back to a legal support centre as a team leader, so you get exposure to leadership. (Although if you're less high potential, we might leave you in geography.)" He continues: "If you think about the LSC managers, these are legal counsel who might have had two or three people under them in geo-specific roles; now they are managing 28 or 30 people back in the LSCs."

The programme therefore gives talent exposure to specific business areas, working initially in the LSCs – where process and use of technology are core to how work is approached – and then layering in leadership.

4.2 Process centred

The way that talent is trained and the way work is structured are centred on new methods of working that foreground process, so that everyone is thinking about how they work as well as what they work on. From day one, new recruits are thinking about process, efficiency, project management, task-based technology, understanding data, using dashboards and so forth. Taking its cue from new ways of working and leading, the overall management of the process is designed to be one of co-creation, not the imposition of how to do things from on high.

Van Tonder explains:

> *What we have done with the LSCs is to empower team managers to work together to figure out what process works best for what issues. I can sit here and draw the high-level processes and then others can follow that. But there are some very specific steps you need to take on the ground and realistically it's only ever those working through this who can choose the right way to approach them. That democratic way of working enhances what we do, as does the understanding which is created through that approach to the process.*

What was also needed to arrive at a more process-driven way of working were processes for introducing those processes! One fundamental aspect of this – for the lawyers in the service centres, the talent in development and the rest of the legal team – was an appreciation of the purpose and the *why*. This in turn shifted attention to other aspects, such as collaboration, creativity and thinking differently. Collaboration became key in ensuring that the new incarnation of legal could work effectively across the business, as Van Tonder explains: "Showing our guys, 'You have to sit with the other functions' was important. You have to work things out when there are, say, conflicts in our processes versus sales."

One of the significant aspects in understanding, working out and finding solutions to potential conflicts between different functions is the ability to present to others and state your position. Lawyers have traditionally not had to focus so much on public presentation and this is a skill that many are sorely lacking – so a key aspect of the training process at Schlumberger is how to present, as Van Tonder elaborates: "One of the key things all the lawyers do is simply present. It's not only to more senior members of the team or when they are in senior roles. They have a training target in the hub; they create their presentations as part of that, and are not just presenting to senior managers, but presenting to their peers and making them feel much more comfortable in presenting to their team."

5. Finding tomorrow's talent

So how does the team source future talent? Like other processes, Schlumberger's recruitment process was ripe for reinvention. Previously, new recruits were identified through CVs and then invited for multiple rounds of interviews, which took months to complete. Recruiting into the LSCs had to be more scientific and efficient, as Van Tonder explains:

> Initially, a pool of talent is identified through traditional graduate recruitment paths such as career fairs at law schools. Once this pool is identified, the focus becomes much more on their individual qualities, rather than grades attained or the prestige of the law school or university. We developed some tests using CEB [Corporate Executive Board, now Gartner]. This initial test is based on a contracting exercise which contains a range of legal and risk issues. The purpose is not to test for 100% accuracy, but rather to identify candidates who have the right instincts in both legal and business terms.

Those who progress move to another round of online testing, this time focused on deductive reasoning and the potential for professional development. This generates a report which identifies each candidate's strengths and weaknesses. Once these reports have been assessed, a cohort is selected to go through to interview, with a specific focus on commercial skills. "Looking at the commercial side forms part of that," says Van Tonder. "It's a key driver: do they have the commercial skills and can they adapt in the commercial organisation?"

Whereas previously selection was based on academic and professional qualifications, it is now much more aligned to the skills and processes actually needed in the role; indeed, according to Van Tonder, "Law schools don't really feature in our reasoning."

Overall, the process aims to identify the sort of talent needed both now and in the future at Schlumberger. Futureproofing its recruitment strategy in this way has meant that the focus has become increasingly generalist, as Van Tonder explains: "It's seldom we recruit specifically now. How we recruit is informed by the types of challenges we are looking at long term and we feel people development will need to match those. So when we recruit someone, it's for the long term. Could they be the next GC – or certainly the next GC in a particular geo-market?"

And when the time comes to step into this geo-market position, the successful appointees have already built up significant traction in the wider business – unlike the mid-career legal hires who preceded them, as Van Tonder explains:

> With the LSC model, by the time our talent get to that legal counsel geo-market role, they have been with Schlumberger for a number of years and know a range of key challenges the business is facing; suddenly their credibility is very different and they can engage with peers as peers. This has already solved a lot of issues we may have previously faced in-country. Some of those people are moving out of the LSCs to in-country roles and the business leaders now report they are seeing the difference. Just by the feedback we're getting, it seems to be working and developing the right kind of profile.

Given the specific locations of the LSCs in Bogota, Bucharest and Kuala Lumpur, the decisions on where to place future talent are driven by factors including language skills and where work is coming in from – for example, the Bucharest LSC might need Portuguese speakers because of work coming from Angola.

Those who have been progressing through this talent development model are already enjoying the benefits, in terms of both how it embeds them in the business and the exposure it gives them to a broad range of legal work, operational processes and technology solutions. Van Tonder recounts the story of a young US-qualified lawyer who worked with him in Paris, but was prepared to take a pay cut to move to the LSC in Bucharest, as he recognised this as an invaluable opportunity to immerse himself in a broad spectrum of business areas and the new ways in which they are being serviced.

When it comes to talent progression, the leaders of the legal function meet once a year for a week in Houston or London and work through the entire function to identify the top talent. Van Tonder explains: "Whoever has a team comes and presents their team. We finish at the end of the week with a list of 20 high potentials who will move up. We now do most of our recruiting through the LSCs (although IP attorneys follow a different route) and move up from there."

And the type of talent they are seeking to identify comes in many different forms, as Van Tonder elaborates: "We also identify the foot soldiers who might not be managers, but rather subject-matter experts. It's a project of constant evaluation. All senior leaders in the legal team know who the high potentials are and get to meet them and take them out for dinner when we visit their jurisdiction, so we get to know them as people too."

While the high potential talent may be on a different track from the other support staff in the LSCs, in general they do the same work as their peers – although Van Tonder notes, "We may also involve them in the occasional department project, so people get a feel of what it's like to work with them." But the overarching priority is to avoid creating an 'us and them' mentality in the LSCs – the local staff are considered just as important and are valued and treated accordingly: "The local talent are the keepers of the knowledge, who know how things get done. So it's key to keep them motivated. And if local talent are high potential, but not geographically mobile, they can still become very key and involved in substantive projects."

6. People, process and technology

One of the most interesting features of Schlumberger's approach to talent development is its seamless integration of people, process and technology.

When Harold Leavitt coined the phrase "people, process and technology" in his 1962 paper *Applied Organization Changes in Industry*,[2] he likely never imagined how often it would be used to identify the key components of business success. However, numerous studies have shown that many companies still place too much focus on the process and technology components, and neglect the people component.

In the legal profession, meanwhile, some have predicted that as a result of advances in process and technology, lawyers may no longer be relevant or needed – perhaps rendering the people component completely obsolete. Some of these predictions – such as those of Richard Susskind[3] – have been selectively sampled to suggest that the end is nigh for highly skilled people in legal services. But as real-life examples such as Schlumberger's bear out, the reality will more likely be a shift in focus and deeper integration of talent and technology.

These trends are not unique to law, but reflect wider shifts being driven by major forces such as digitisation, globalisation and changing working patterns. What is clear, however, is that the talent of the future will need to be different and more adaptable. Schlumberger has adapted by making talent a fundamental pillar of its response to this new constellation, and then by recruiting and developing talent to match the realities of the business.

Notes
1   Interview with the author, July 2019.
2   Harold Leavitt, *Applied Organizational Change in Industry: Structural, Technological and Humanistic Approaches* (Carnegie Institute of Technology, Graduate School of Industrial Administration 1962).
3   Richard Susskind, *The End of Lawyers* (Oxford University Press 2010); and Richard Susskind and Daniel Susskind, *How Technology Will Transform the Work of Human Experts* (Oxford University Press 2015).

Part V: Creativity

· ·

Creativity is the most practical thing a businessman can employ.

Bill Bernbach

22. Business, creativity and the competitive edge

The reason we need creativity in business is simple: most ground-breaking business success is built on creativity and the linked skill of innovation, which essentially involves putting creativity into practice.

Why has creativity lately become a hot topic in relation to business? Arguably, it has always been part of business: what is any new idea, such as Thomas Edison's lightbulb, but an example of creativity in action? But in recent years, creativity has increasingly been recognised as something that should be actively sought out and embraced. I would argue that this is a direct result of factors that are seemingly discrete, but in fact are interlinked: the growing importance of innovation and a willingness to redefine working culture – both of which have been inspired to a significant extent by start-up culture.

Creativity and its application are also increasingly seen as key differentiators – essential tools for sharpening competitive edge.

1. My journey back to creativity – from theatre to law

I started my professional career in theatre, a sphere that is inarguably 'creative': performing, directing and teaching. When I moved into legal journalism, it felt as though my background would be a handicap. I would often underplay it, suffering badly from imposter syndrome – a square peg in a round hole.

However, my experiences in the legal sector have since changed my mind. I now take pride in my creative background and I return to many of the ideas I previously used, both explicitly and implicitly, in my current work. While this may be partly due simply to growing older and becoming more comfortable with myself, it is also the result of my experiences in starting my own business, which forced me to think about my unique selling proposition and to recognise my creative background as a strength that marks me out from my peers, rather than a weakness.

This change has also been informed by my increasing focus on the business of law, particularly as experienced by general counsel and their teams. I realised that many in-house lawyers were hungry for ideas that went beyond what was considered 'standard thinking' for the industry. As I started to explore the future of law and innovation, it became clear that thinking differently and being creative come with the territory; but that these are areas where the traditional behaviours and practice of law have left many woefully underprepared for the challenges of the future.

So what do we mean by 'bringing creativity' to law and how can this be achieved? You may notice as you read this chapter that there is a lot of synergy and overlap with innovation, which is discussed in greater depth later. It is inevitable and only right that the two concepts bleed into each other, as they are symbiotically linked. The difference between them is often summarised as follows: creativity is the idea, while innovation is making the idea work.

Despite this synergy, I think it is important to consider each concept separately within a broader discussion of the legal profession, as the thought processes and ability to formulate and reformulate new ideas (creativity) are needed before full-scale implementation of those ideas (innovation) can take place. Lots of time and money are often wasted by rushing into solutions simply to tick the 'innovation' box. Creativity is a key part of the innovation process, bringing different thinking and different viewpoints to the table to ensure that problems are understood completely and to identify a range of potential solutions. Collaboration, culture and leadership are also significant ingredients in this process. And purpose obviously feeds into this too; as does your talent and how you empower and inspire that talent.

2. Why do we need creativity in business?

Adam Brandenburger, writing in the *Harvard Business Review*,[1] explores the essential link between creativity and business strategy. While most business students are still taught strategy through rigorous analytical tools such as the 'five forces' theory, Brandenburger has noticed that many students now feel that something is missing: "Game-changing strategies, they know, are born of creative thinking: a spark of intuition, a connection between different ways of thinking, a leap into the unexpected."[2]

Balder Onarheim, who co-founded the Copenhagen Institute of Neurocreativity, has researched creativity for many years, particularly from a neurological perspective. His research has led him to conclude that creativity is fundamental to success: "In a work-related context, I would go as far as to say that creativity is a competitive advantage. If you're competing with someone else and you are working in the same area or in the same circumstances, creativity that can give one idea the competitive edge over another."[3]

This is true even in law, suggests Onarheim – for example, in a lawsuit, both sides often have access to the same information and legal precedents. "The way I see it, there are very few places where creativity isn't a strong competitive factor – even in dating, creative profiles are more successful!" he adds.

Creativity can also help to futureproof your business, continues Onarheim:

> *Creativity should definitely be a significant area of focus for all organisations. One of the biggest concerns for me with creativity and education is that we have more and more machines and artificial intelligence (AI), and there are more and more repetitive tasks at which computers excel. What we are left with is being creative: there's not even a strong hypothesis on how we can develop AI creativity. So humans will be useful as long as we can be creative.*

This is echoed by Penn State University's Roger Beaty, who has been exploring how our brains may make connections differently when working on creative tasks:

> *There's an element where the focus on this in business can be faddish, echoing the way 'innovation' has become a buzzword. But it also taps into the fact that people are realising the importance of creativity when you compare it to what computers and AI can do. Creativity is something that humans do really well and it sets us apart. In the future, as the workplace and society change because of technology, what we can leverage is our creativity. Increasingly, you see in industrial organisational psychology that there's a lot of value placed on creativity in leaders in organisations. To some extent, this plays into how much creativity is valued – what the message from the top is in organisations.*[4]

3. Creativity and the business of law

Creativity is also increasingly important in the legal profession. As business becomes more innovative and new industries and radically different business models throw up brand new legal issues, creativity may offer surprising solutions on how best to navigate these changes.

Annabelle Newman is assistant general counsel at Syneos Health and runs its legal team across Europe and the Middle East. Newman started out in the creative industries, managing bands and DJs and writing music herself. She believes that in the new business and legal landscape, creative thinking is vital:

The dictionary definition is "the use of imagination or original ideas to create something; inventiveness" and I think this is key, having worked in areas of law where there isn't yet any case law or where there is no precedent. One of my strengths, I believe, is the ability to communicate and explain these solutions to others. I believe creativity means that one must be brave, open-minded and prepared to take managed risks; ignore doubt; and face fears like a pioneer, in order to find a better way of achieving solutions.[5]

This is echoed by Royal Bank of Scotland's Kenny Robertson, who likewise characterises the approach and thinking needed to bring creativity to the profession as "being brave" or – to use his favourite football analogy – "playing with your head up".[6]

Notes

1   Adam Brandenburger, "Why Strategy Needs Creativity", *Harvard Business Review* March–April 2019, pp58–65.
2   *Ibid*, p60.
3   Interview with the author, April 2019.
4   Interview with the author, April 2019.
5   Catherine McGregor and Annabelle Newman, "The Show Must Go On: Creativity and Thinking Differently in Law" in *Carlyle Kingswood Global Insights*, January 2020, www.ckgsearch.com/blog/2020/01/the-show-must-go-on-creativity-and-thinking-differently-in-law.
6   Interview with the author, September 2019.

"As business becomes more innovative and new industries and radically different business models throw up brand new legal issues, creativity may offer surprising solutions on how best to navigate these changes."

23. Creative cultures: freedom and discipline

Creativity (and its close relative, innovation) involves a constant dance between freedom and discipline to create the optimal conditions for it to flourish. This concept dates all the way back to the Ancient Greeks, who viewed creativity as a blend of practicality and spirituality; this can be translated into modern business terms as a mixture of freedom and discipline. My experiences working and teaching drama and performance also bear this out: the process involves continuous practice and improvement, while also allowing space for ideas to bubble up which will lift the technique beyond the ordinary.

Recent research likewise suggests that creativity involves a complex interplay between spontaneous and controlled thinking – the ability both to brainstorm ideas and to evaluate them to determine whether they might be workable in practice.[1]

This may well resonate with the experiences of those who have been through the process of transforming legal departments, such as legal operations professionals and general counsel. To successfully implement this process, you need to know what you are doing and be open to ideas from outside; but you also need the freedom and the right conditions in which to do it. This is also perhaps why some of the successful law firm innovators are separating out their more creative and innovative enterprises from their main business: they need the freedom to grow, and their people need structures that give them the confidence to stray outside their normal boundaries and question what is accepted. As the research on successful cultures teaches us, this safety to explore and – perhaps even more crucially – to fail is vital to truly foster creativity.

The notion of inspiring creativity goes hand in hand with creating an outstanding organisational culture. Many of the examples cited in business thinking on creativity embody what can be defined as a culture of freedom and responsibility. Two companies which are often highlighted in this regard are entertainment giants Netflix and Pixar.

Former Netflix chief talent officer Patty McCord describes the company culture as a mix of freedom and discipline – not unlike how creative professionals approach the way they work. What is interesting in McCord's book *Powerful*,[2] (and other writing around creativity) is the interplay between allowing the freedom that encourages divergent thinking while also providing guidance and structure to give people the confidence to do this. Sometimes, this is as simple as ensuring that everyone's ideas are heard and valued, and that people feel secure in speaking up.

Similarly, in *Creativity Inc*,[3] Pixar co-founder Ed Catmull suggests that leaders play a crucial role in establishing an environment that is conducive to creativity. In most cases, this hinges on affording greater freedom and trust to employees, rather than imposing more restrictions on them: "I believe that managers must loosen the controls, not tighten them. They must accept risk; they must trust the people they work with and strive to clear the path for them; and always, they must pay attention to and engage with anything that creates fear."[4] That said, Catmull also recommends that certain constraints – such as tight deadlines and budget – be built into the creative process, to help maintain focus; this is discussed further in Chapter 25.

What is most significant in what is being described here is the importance of creating a whole culture that generates ideas, responses to those ideas and ways of working collaboratively for everyone. Culture and collaboration are fundamental to creativity – as is leadership, which can be instrumental in actualising both culture and collaboration. This means that everyone can be empowered to be creative, as Catmull explains: "In a healthy, creative culture, the people in the trenches feel free to speak up and bring to light differing views that can help give us clarity."[5]

1. The general counsel's role in changing legal culture

Catmull's thoughts on the need to create a culture in which creativity can thrive align with many of the ideas that underpin the definition of a good organisational culture more generally, such as psychological safety and the ability to fail. As discussed earlier in this book, the notion of cultural engineering in terms of creating an optimal culture is increasingly part of the general counsel's remit. With the legal industry on the cusp of major disruption, this aspect has become especially significant. This disruption is in large part motivated by the needs and demands of in-house lawyers for different ways of working, whether internally or externally; and is a direct response both to limited resources and to the growing need to demonstrate strategic thinking and value.

For the general counsel, establishing a culture is often linked to ethics and corporate social responsibility. It goes further and is much more aspirational than mere legal and regulatory compliance. It also involves creating an environment in which risks can be taken in the right way, and which recognises that to be creative, there has to be an openness to ideas that lie outside the status quo or that even challenge the status quo. To my mind, this is one of the key areas of development for the modern general counsel, which will only become more important, while also providing synergies with the role of the CEO.

Leadership is therefore a crucial building block in establishing the conditions for creativity, and ultimately for innovation. In *Collective Genius*, Linda Hill *et al*[6] distinguish between leaders who create organisations that are *willing* to innovate and those who ensure that their organisations are *able* to innovate. Ideas can only go so far; and arguably, what has hindered traditional law firms in this regard is the absence of both the willingness and the ability to create and innovate. Hill *et al* argue that leaders first need to establish a desire for creativity and innovation in their organisations before these can be actualised. However, efforts around creativity in the legal profession tend to be more reactive and inspired by commercial opportunity, rather than truly organic and inspired by a real desire to establish a more creatively fertile culture.

2. Space for creativity – physical and temporal

Space for creativity can refer to both physical space (eg, breakout hubs in an office) and temporal space (ie, time put aside to think about ideas outside of day-to-day work). Companies that rely on creativity try to design workspaces and working practices that align with the purpose and vision to be creative and innovative.

However, it's important to remember that once again, the *why, what, who* and how must be aligned. In *Work Rules!* Google's former chief people officer Laszlo Bock, relates an anecdote about an executive who came to the Google campus with the aim of reproducing some of the company's culture successes at her own organisation. She was very focused on the quirky communal spaces, filled with bean bags and lava lamps. When Bock tried to suggest that the key in fact lay in more intangible elements, such as openness between management and employees, workforce empowerment and psychological safety, his visitor wasn't listening. Instead, she thought that the symptoms of that culture – the unusual spatial accoutrements – would establish the context for creativity and innovation.

Physical and temporal space are doubtless important, but they must be aligned with the other crucial forces of purpose, culture, leadership and collaboration. Google has devoted itself to designing workplaces that fuel creativity and innovation, as Bock writes in *Work Rules!*: "The most salient one is the way we use our benefits and also our environment to increase the number of 'moments of serendipity' that spark creativity." One way in which this has been achieved is through the creation of 'micro-kitchens', which serve as places where people can gather. Google drew inspiration from the mission statement of Starbucks, as defined by former CEO Howard Schultz as a 'third place'.[8]

The micro-kitchens are designed to gather people away from their desks in a space that looks and feels different from Google's designated meeting rooms, and to organically bring together people from different teams to exchange ideas and viewpoints. This yields exactly the kind of divergent thinking that many researchers have identified as crucial to stimulate creativity.

Another inspiration for Google's unique configuration of its working space was Steve Jobs' famous redesign of the working space at Pixar. This aimed to bring different teams together to promote greater collaboration and encourage the cross-pollination of ideas through more spontaneous encounters. That ethos was subsequently reflected in Jobs' final focus point, Apple's new ring-shaped campus at Cupertino. As Apple's chief designer Jonathan Ive told *Wired Magazine*, the aim was to design "a building where so many people can connect and collaborate and walk and talk".[9]

Increasingly, and particularly in-house, more open working spaces are a feature of legal workplaces – although this is often driven by the need to save money on real estate costs. Whether such spaces are conducive to creativity remains open to debate: it is not entirely certain that open-plan workplaces are more collaborative and creative. Recent studies examined in *Philosophical Transactions of The Royal Society* by Ethan S Bernstein of Harvard Business School and Stephen Turban of Harvard University question whether open work spaces are actually more creative and collaborative: "Like social insects which swarm within functionally-determined zones 'partitioned' by spatial boundaries (eg, hives, nests or schools)... human beings – despite their greater cognitive abilities – may also require boundaries to constrain their interactions, thereby reducing the potential for overload, distraction, bias, myopia and other symptoms of bounded rationality."[10]

As with the bean bags and lava lamps at Google, it is likely that creating a certain type of physical space will not automatically make people creative; rather, spatial considerations should be built into a portfolio of creative catalysts. It may be that a truly creative space must be designed by people themselves – not just in terms of the actual architecture, but also in their freedom to use and interact with that architecture.

3. Open-plan offices and flexible working – a boost to creative thinking?

Space is certainly an issue for many in-house teams and the need to maximise the use of office real estate is one driver of the move towards more flexible working. Many in-house lawyers no longer have desks; they might variously work from home, at a different office or on site with a supplier, and be 'in the office' for just one day a week. Indeed, increased real estate costs mean that some companies are now insisting on flexible working. The lack of a billable-hour model and a focus on outcomes, rather than time make this more readily achievable for legal departments than for law firms. But does flexible working in itself help to promote creativity?

One significant advantage of not being tied to an office is a greater focus on outcome-based thinking. In other words, the focus is on delivering a particular outcome, with the freedom to achieve that in whatever way makes most sense, rather than being tethered to billable hours and law firm protocols. But this focus on outcomes may increasingly come to define all service professions, as Richard Susskind has argued: "The disconcerting message here for all professionals is that our clients don't want us. They want the outcomes we bring. And when these outcomes can be reliably delivered in new ways that are demonstrably cheaper, better, quicker, or more convenient than the current offering, we can expect the market to switch to the alternatives."[11] Certainly, outcome thinking now defines the business models of many of the most successful law companies, which have thrown out the rulebook on *who, where* and *how*, instead focusing on the *what* and how to get this done.

In one of the most extreme examples, Univar's general counsel Jeff Carr has outsourced much of his legal department to law company Elevate. As the legal team's work is outcome focused, this helps it to secure the best outcomes at the best price and the greatest efficiency. This frees up the general counsel and internal lawyers from much of the day-to-day management of the team, allowing them to focus on strategic decisions and play more of an executive role. This is discussed in more detail later in this part of the book, and in the epilogue; but Carr's thinking illustrates that creativity is sometimes a corollary of simply focusing on outcomes and how they are best achieved for the business.

4. Different spaces, different ideas – why getting out of the office can boost creativity

In day-to-day terms, it is often true that the more we try to solve a problem, the more the answer can elude us. Sometimes a different space and a distraction are needed. This can also help to bring different perspectives to the issue: literally – to use a hackneyed phrase – 'thinking outside the box.'

This may strike horror into the hearts of many lawyers who are trained to focus on rationality. But if rationality is envisioned as linear in its flow, then creativity is seen as much more lateral in its conception.

Rob Booth at the Crown Estate, whom we spoke to in detail in the part of this book on purpose, knows the importance of allowing himself thinking time. He finds conferences very useful for this, as they take him outside the office and expose him to new ideas and perspectives. This viewpoint is shared by Kenny Robertson at Royal Bank of Scotland: "I wrote our 2017 team plan in a five-minute period at a conference in London at the end of 2016 and much of that content is still in the team plans. The environment just worked to unlock the necessary thought process."[12]

Their experiences confirm that conferences present a perfect opportunity to shift to a different space, both physically and mentally; engage with new ideas and perspectives; meet new people; and make new connections – whether that be by connecting ideas or expanding your network. New mental connections can literally establish new connections between different parts of our brains and enable us to view problems from a different perspective; while a broader network can likewise promote creative thinking and innovation. So those who find themselves contemplating cancelling conferences due to work pressures might want to reconsider.

Shorter stints outside the office can also prove invaluable for in-house lawyers. Many teams schedule away-days to carve out time to think differently and work together in a different way. One general counsel I spoke to reported that he likes to take his team out of the office for half-days or full days, not just for team-building exercises, but also to work together on key business of law issues. They don't travel to any exotic locations – just a conference room in the offices of one of their law firms – but the physical journey to a different environment can disrupt conventional ways of thinking. Similarly, Robertson's team – which now uses design thinking (see Chapter 26) to unlock creative ways of exploring problems – generally does this off-site: "It really makes a difference to the mindset and approach."

That said, while some large law firms are now giving staff time away from their normal duties to become more creative or innovative, the research and experiences of Hill *et al*, Catmull and McCord suggest that this can sometimes end up being counterproductive. Constraints – including temporal constraints (eg, strict deadlines) – can sometimes prove more stimulating. I will discuss this in more detail – particularly with regard to how I think constraints have made in-house legal teams the driving force behind true change in the legal industry – in Chapter 25.

Notes

1   www.scientificamerican.com/article/why-are-some-people-more-creative-than-others/.
2   Patty McCord, *Powerful: Building a Culture of Freedom and Responsibility* (Silicon Guild 2018).
3   Ed Catmull, *Creativity Inc* (Transworld Digital 2014, Amazon Kindle e-book).
4   *Ibid*, location 167.
5   *Ibid*, location 2623.

6   Linda A Hill *et al*, *Collective Genius: The Art and Practice of Leading Innovation* (Harvard Business Review Press 2014).
7   Laszlo Bock, *Work Rules!* (John Murray 2015).
8   Starbucks, "Our Heritage", www.starbucks.co.uk/about-us%2Four-heritage.
9   Steven Levy, "One More Thing: Inside Apple's Insanely Great (Or Just Insane) New Mothership", *WIRED*, 16 May 2017, www.wired.com/2017/05/apple-park-new-silicon-valley-campus/.
10 Ethan S Bernstein and Stephen Turban, "The impact of the 'open' workspace on human collaboration", *Philosophical Transactions of The Royal Society*, 2 July 2018, https://royalsocietypublishing.org/doi/full/10.1098/rstb.2017.0239.
11 Richard Susskind, "AI, Work and 'Outcome Thinking", *British Academy Review No 34* (Autumn 2018), p30.
12 Interview with the author, September 2019.

"By the time most of us reach adulthood, creativity has been buried under rules and regulations. So creativity is therefore not so much about learning creative behaviours as about unlearning non-creative behaviours."

24. Debunking the myths of creativity – or why anyone can be creative

One constant challenge, when thinking about bringing more creativity to what you and your team do, is the myth that creativity is a gift bestowed upon a lucky few. I firmly believe that anyone can be creative in one form or another. We can't all be Emily Brontë or Michelangelo, but creativity can take many forms and can be incremental.

As Tim Brown, founder of IDEO, writes in the *Harvard Business Review*:

> *The myth of creative genius is resilient: We believe that great ideas pop fully formed out of brilliant minds, in feats of imagination well beyond the abilities of mere mortals. But what the Kaiser nursing team accomplished was neither a sudden breakthrough nor the lightning strike of genius; it was the result of hard work augmented by a creative human-centered discovery process and followed by iterative cycles of prototyping, testing, and refinement.*[1]

Another myth is that creativity is often seen as something divorced from work – a flash of inspiration. Those who never experience this bolt from the blue might think, "I'm just not creative." But neurological and behavioural research shows that this is not strictly true. The science confirms that some people do enjoy distinct neurological advantages, but this is not down to the right brain/left brain divide or to gender; rather, what is key is the ability to make connections between different parts of the brain. Further research reveals that the most creative individuals have a smaller area of connective tissue between the two halves of their brain. Some experts believe that our brains can be trained to be more creative through techniques that help to make these connections and encourage greater divergence in how we think. Others suggest that the secret lies in the conditions and cultures within which we operate – and leaders play an important role in developing these. But the consistent message is that everyone can be creative.

1. Lawyers – logic versus creativity

Interestingly, some of the academic experts with whom I discussed the issue of creativity were not surprised that lawyers tend not to see themselves as creative; but suggested that in fact, what lawyers actually do is often very creative. Even the traditional sense of 'lawyering' involves interpreting law, regulations and precedents in ways that – although bounded by what is legal – are indicative of creative thinking.

The very mention of creativity can produce a knee-jerk reaction in many lawyers who have primarily focused on the logic and reason-based study of law throughout their careers. It can inspire fear or feelings of inadequacy; and many lawyers believe that 'being creative' is beyond them. But this isn't necessarily the case. In our conversations,[2] assistant general counsel at Syneos Health Annabelle Newman directed me to the work of George Land – an author, speaker, consultant and general systems scientist who founded a research and consulting institute to study the enhancement of creative performance. Land devised a creativity test for NASA to help select innovative engineers and scientists. The assessment worked so well that he decided to try it on children. In 1968, Land conducted a research study to test the creativity of 1,600 children aged from three to five who were enrolled on a Head Start programme. The test encouraged participants to come up with new, different and innovative ideas to problems. He re-tested the same children at the age of 10 and again at the age of 15. The results were astounding:

- Five-year-olds: 98% showed creative behaviours.
- 10-year-olds: 30% showed creative behaviours.
- 15-year-olds: 12% showed creative behaviours.
- Same test given to 280,000 adults: 2% showed creative behaviours.

The results confirm that by the time most of us reach adulthood, creativity has been buried under rules and regulations. So creativity is therefore not so much about learning creative behaviours as about unlearning non-creative behaviours.

Newman agrees with this and suggests that lawyers (and indeed businesses) need to find ways to reconnect with their creativity. Creativity is essentially the basis for innovation, and innovation will not spring fully formed from minds that cannot embrace creativity:

> *I think that in current businesses, employees need to be encouraged and supported to reconnect with their creativity. It's about peeling back the layers of conformity: helping employees to fight incapacitating self-criticism, perfectionism and the fear of failure that lead to creative blocks. Time needs to be made available for employees to collaborate and shares ideas freely, with the opportunity to receive and offer constructive feedback, and to learn from people who may have more experience or different ideas.*[3]

In thinking about how she has balanced her own creative and more logical ways of thinking, Newman sees this as a symbiotic relationship – neither logic or creativity need be a zero-sum game: "My progression has been about finding the balance of the realms of the law, with the ability to think without boundaries, to find solutions to issues. Nothing to me is impossible; there might just be adjustments to methods or a compromise to the objective in order to operate within regulatory or legal requirements."[4]

Notes

1   Tim Brown, "Design Thinking", *Harvard Business Review*, June 2008, https://hbr.org/2008/06/design-thinking.
2   Catherine McGregor and Annabelle Newman, "The Show Must Go On: Creativity and Thinking Differently in Law" in *Carlyle Kingswood Global Insights*, January 2020, www.ckgsearch.com/blog/2020/01/the-show-must-go-on-creativity-and-thinking-differently-in-law.
3   *Ibid.*
4   *Ibid.*

"*Merely replicating what has come before is a guaranteed path to mediocrity. The desire to be safe – to succeed with minimal risk – can infect not just individuals, but entire companies.*"

25. Divergent thinking

George Land's creativity study, cited in the previous chapter, presented problems to subjects and tested how different and innovative their solutions were. The more different the ideas they came up with, the higher they scored. The results confirm that, at its heart, creativity requires individuals to think differently. One method that can encourage them to do so is through divergent thinking.

Divergent thinking is a method used to generate creative ideas by exploring as many potential solutions as possible. This is done by brainstorming in a spontaneous, free-flowing, non-linear manner, which generates myriad ideas through an emergent cognitive process. In neurological terms, this means that the more cognitive aspects of the brain are connecting with the more emotional parts of the brain. As Roger Beaty's research discussed later in this chapter also shows, more creative brains generate more neurological connections. This echoes the lived experience of creativity:

Creativity is just connecting things. When you ask creative people how they did something, they feel a little guilty because they didn't really do it, they just saw something. It seemed obvious to them after a while. That's because they were able to connect experiences they've had and synthesize new things. And the reason they were able to do that was that they've had more experiences or they have thought more about their experiences than other people. Unfortunately, that's too rare a commodity. A lot of people in our industry haven't had very diverse experiences. So they don't have enough dots to connect, and they end up with very linear solutions without a broad perspective on the problem. The broader one's understanding of the human experience, the better design we will have.[1]

This 1996 quote from Steve Jobs is still relevant today, as it shows how thinking differently is fundamental to creativity in business. If we consider the notion of creativity in the business of law, much of this involves thinking differently about how certain legal functions have traditionally been approached. As Tom Sager said with regard to the creation of the DuPont Legal Model, "Nothing was sacrosanct."[2]

It may have become a hackneyed business term, but 'thinking outside of the box' is still a relevant concept. Taking risks and thinking differently are skills that are increasingly valued in the business of law. As assistant general counsel at Syneos Health Annabelle Newman explains, her creative background has set her up well for practical problem solving: "As I have moved through my career, the ability to think not just outside the box, but without any constraints of a box has been my success. Having worked in the music industry, where you have to think on your feet and where very haphazard and unique problems often arise, I realised that if you don't find a solution, then you don't progress – the show must go on."[3]

Merely replicating what has come before is a guaranteed path to mediocrity. The desire to be safe – to succeed with minimal risk – can infect not just individuals, but entire companies. Law firms are particularly at risk here, as for many, their financial returns suggest that there is nothing wrong with how they currently do things. But increasingly, it would appear that this is no longer the right course of (in)action. The study of creative thinking in business suggests that if we sense that our structures are rigid, inflexible or bureaucratic, we should bust them open. The question of how to do this must continually be addressed; there is no single answer, because conditions and people are constantly in flux.

Strategy expert Adam Brandenburger[4] has defined four types of thinking which he feels bring creativity to strategy:
- Contrast: What pieces of conventional wisdom are ripe for contradiction?
- Combination: How can you connect products or services that have traditionally been separate?
- Constraint: How can you turn limitations or liabilities into opportunities?
- Context: How can far-flung industries, ideas or disciplines shed light on your most pressing problems?

1. Contrast: questioning norms

Considering contrast first, it is clear that many examples of creativity and innovation that are today being adopted wholesale are the result of questioning accepted norms. A reluctance to do this may also be why, in many metrics, the legal profession lags behind others with regard to innovation.

One significant example of thinking differently that has opened the door to a number of innovations in the legal industry is challenging the assumption that law is solely the provenance of fully qualified lawyers. New models that jettison this assumption – such as legal process outsourcing, temporary and alternative staffing structures, and the increasing use of technology for certain routine functions – have blown open the future of the legal profession.

An early illustration of this is the DuPont Legal Model, which in 1992 was an outlier for the strategic application of vision, creativity, innovative thinking and collaboration. It was inspired by what former DuPont general counsel Sager has described as a "tsunami of torts". Litigation – and therefore spending on outside counsel – was spiralling out of control. Sager recalls that this was affecting the entire culture: "We saw that the legal department was bumping along really as a B minus department. Costs were going through the roof and there was a lack of discipline in dealing with law firms."

Something clearly needed to be done, so the legal team started to think differently in its approach to practical problem solving: "Other corporations were suffering, but no one was willing to invest like we were in time, thinking differently and instituting the importance of operational efficiency process."[5]

In starting work on the legal model, the team forensically analysed everything that was being done and questioned why it needed to be done that way. "Nothing was sacrosanct," recalls Sager.

The success of the new model was predicated on reliance on data-driven analytics rather than relationships; collaboration with a smaller group of legal suppliers; and the allocation of significant volumes of legal work to non-lawyer legal professionals, to drive down costs. In many ways, this foreshadowed the subsequent boom in legal process outsourcing, which in turn paved the way for the legal technology and alternative staffing providers that are currently redefining the legal industry. DuPont's 'eureka' realisation that legal work need not be the sole purview of lawyers is a classic example of contrast thinking. By identifying capable paralegals and tasking them with leading various practice areas throughout the process, the DuPont legal team was able to save millions – not to mention empowering talented professionals to take a greater stake in the business.

1.1 Always ask why

For Jeff Carr at Univar, contrast thinking involves continually challenging the accepted way of doing things and always asking why: "Unpicking how we do the work and who does the work has been a function of asking why we are here and essentially deconstructing many of the assumptions about what that looks like."[6] As a result of this process, most commoditised work at Univar has now been shifted from the legal team to law company Elevate:

We don't think of it as outsourcing; rather, we think of Elevate as part of our legal team. The concept is to send the work to whomever can do the work as well as necessary, and so is a better value proposition. But going back to the initial concept, part of it was getting the lawyers to understand that they do not need to do everything. The concept used comes out of manufacturing and of the Lean Six Sigma disciples – there are people who design and own those processes and those who operate and deliver those processes. Lawyers are traditionally both the process owner and the operator. I think that the best use of their time is as the process designer and owner. They should only operate processes that require a lawyer's judgement – and in actuality, that's precious few steps in the continuum of legal process management.[7]

Tellingly, this positions the lawyer at the creative end of the process. In many ways, it resembles the creative efficiencies in the art world, where the artist – particularly once he or she has achieved a significant level of acclaim – is the owner of the process, but not always the operator. This model has been successfully applied by many giants of the art world throughout the centuries, from Michelangelo and Caravaggio to Andy Warhol and Damien Hirst. But perhaps the best analogy is with architecture, where the architect designs and owns the process, but generally does not do the building work.

Carr goes on to explain that his willingness to challenge and upend the status quo is rooted in his own creative background: "I always had a very deep creative side and started out as a music major and a painter. When I finished law school and worked for a law firm in DC, what amazed me was how much administrative stuff I had to do as a baby lawyer. It irritated me to some extent that the industry was being run on these very inefficient lines and was not allowing me to work where I was most needed."

The logical extension of what innovators such as Sager and Carr pioneered in the 1990s and early 2000s was the advent of the various alternative legal service providers and law companies that are reshaping today's legal profession. This is now recognised as a credible and sustainable means of providing legal services, unfettered by seemingly unassailable tenets such as the billable hour and the need to work from an office. In turn, this is supporting diversity and inclusivity by allowing working parents and anyone with additional responsibilities (and even those without) to work hours that suit them better.

2. Combination: connecting what has traditionally been separate

As the Jobs quote cited earlier bears out, a significant aspect of creativity is the ability to make connections between different ideas – especially ideas which may not previously have been connected. Connection is thus fundamental to creativity and innovation.

Nathan Furr – a professor at INSEAD and an expert on innovation – has shown in his research that innovators generally tend to come up with more ideas from outside their industry and discipline. They often arrive at these ideas through their networks, which likewise tend to be much broader and less confined to one industry group than those of others. If we consider many of the major innovations that are driving the legal industry forward – artificial intelligence, project management, operational thinking – their initial applications were all outside the law. Much of the creativity in law has resulted from combination thinking: the application of ideas that had their genesis elsewhere and the application of different types of thinking to what lawyers have traditionally done. This may not quite be 'bolt from the blue' inspiration, as it is traditionally defined; but it still reflects an openness to ideas from outside your comfort zone.

Some lawyers have embraced design thinking, such as LEGO Serious Play, to help them think differently about business of law problems (this is discussed further in Chapter 26). This may be a catalyst for creative problem solving because it is based not on overthinking, but rather on brainstorming – that is, thinking more freely and suggesting as many new ideas as possible in as short a time as possible.

2.1 Your brain and creativity
This process reflects what goes on in the brain when thinking

creatively. A group of researchers in the United States, led by Roger Beaty at Penn State University, discovered that connected thinking is literally a factor of creativity: the different areas of the brain become physically more connected when people come up with creative ideas. They discovered this by setting volunteers a series of tasks and measuring their brain activity as they completed them. The tasks asked the volunteers to take an everyday object and think of a variety of different uses for it. Those who came up with responses that diverged most from the accepted use of the object were rated most creative.

The researchers observed that in the brains of these highly creative individuals, more connections than usual were made between three specific networks: the default network, the executive control network and the salience network.

The default network is the area of the brain used when people are engaged in spontaneous thinking, such as mind-wandering, daydreaming and imagining. It plays a key role in idea generation and brainstorming – thinking of several possible solutions to a problem. The executive control network is activated when people need to focus or control their thought processes. It is likely to play a role in idea evaluation: determining whether ideas will actually work and modifying them to fit the goal. The salience network acts as a switching mechanism between the default and executive networks, and may play a key role in alternating between idea generation and evaluation.

Beaty *et al*'s research revealed that the most creative individuals had a greater capacity to switch between these networks:

> *An interesting feature of these three networks is that they typically don't get activated at the same time. For example, when the executive network is activated, the default network is usually deactivated. Our results suggest that creative people are better able to co-activate brain networks that usually work separately.*
>
> *Our findings indicate that the creative brain is 'wired' differently and that creative people are better able to engage brain systems that don't*

typically work together. Interestingly, the results are consistent with recent fMRI studies of professional artists, including jazz musicians improvising melodies, poets writing new lines of poetry and visual artists sketching ideas for a book cover.[8]

Similarly, Balder Onarheim and the team at the Copenhagen Institute of Neurocreativity are exploring how to help people become more creative. Onarheim suggests that those seeking to tap into their creativity should embrace randomness and make connections between things which might seem unrelated. Even something as simple as taking a different route to work allows our brains to be stimulated by different variables. He also advises using the Wikipedia 'Random' button the next time you are researching a problem. What it throws up can be very random (I have tried this!), but Onarheim says that forcing our brains to try to make a connection engenders a more creative mode of thinking.

This could explain why senior general counsel are increasingly seeking out content and events which might not be directly related to the day-to-day activities of their legal departments. Many report that ideas from outside their usual knowledge base and frame of reference are more useful in solving the significant problems that they now face – possibly because many of these issues are not straight legal issues, and because 'technical' legal now represents just a fraction of what takes up a general counsel's time.

Making connections and thinking beyond what has traditionally been done have driven many of the innovations which are transforming the legal industry. For example, an increasingly significant play for the most successful new entrants to the industry – such as UnitedLex and Elevate, as well as the Big Four accountants – is connecting services that go beyond the practice of law. By thinking differently, ideas that have revitalised other areas of business have been imported into law; so too have concepts and skill sets from outside traditional legal training. This connection of different ideas and expanded networks of ideas and experiences is a classic example of combination thinking.

3. Constraints: the 'more for less' conundrum

I would argue that most, if not all, of the significant advances of creativity and innovation in the legal industry have been driven by in-house legal departments. I would further suggest that this is largely due to the constraints under which they operate in terms of time, cost and personnel. This reflects the 'make, do and mend' side of creativity.

Reflecting on the early days of Pixar, Ed Catmull concludes that limits can be incredibly valuable in stimulating creative thinking and practices.[9] Deployed correctly, they can force people to adapt how they are working and sometimes to invent completely new ways of working. The limitations within which most in-house departments operate often prompt them to adopt new approaches and find smarter ways of working. Catmull believes that the external imposition of constraints – usually cost, resources, time or a combination of all three – forces us to rethink how we work and can push us to new heights of creativity.

This is also borne out by broader studies of leaders who have successfully fostered creativity and innovation, as outlined by Linda Hill *et al* in *Collective Genius*:

> *Many of the leaders interviewed in this research considered necessity the mother of invention. What happened was that constraints would spur innovation. Indeed, the research in the book confirms that part of the role of a leader in a creative and innovative culture is to confront the group with critical deadlines or budget realities, which could foster creative thinking by forcing the evaluation of key assumptions and the reframing of opportunities. As one leader said, "Our creative process will go on forever unless there's a hard stop. Constraints seem to sharpen thinking because they force the team to find ways to get around them."*[10]

Indeed, much of the genesis of what we now call legal operations was driven not by a desire to be innovative or creative *per se*, but simply by the bottom line. The experiences of Sager and Carr reflect this: the sheer cost of external legal services led to a need to rethink the *what, how, who* and *why* for their legal departments.

4. Context: looking beyond the law for ideas

Brandenburger asks: how can far-flung industries, ideas or disciplines shed light on your most pressing problems? Many of the innovations in the legal industry originated in other industries, and many of those who have pioneered these new ways of thinking and doing have imported ideas from outside of law.

In conjunction with Professor Cat Moon from Vanderbilt University in Nashville, Kenny Robertson and his team at Royal Bank of Scotland (RBS) have been pioneering a concept called 'Failure Camp', which involves structured diagnosis of and learning from failures (discussed in more detail in Chapter 8). As part of this initiative, the technology, outsourcing and IP legal team at RBS received training from a pilot and a surgeon, who shared insights on how they deal with failure in more immediate, high-stakes contexts than those which most in-house legal teams will ever face.

This stems from Robertson's belief that law must look beyond its traditional boundaries to be fit for purpose in the modern business environment:

> It's one of the things I ask the team to focus on, like being brave. There is an absolute place for technical specialists; but in an increasingly competitive environment, when you want to progress, you've got to accept that you have a God-given set of skills and weaknesses. Holding a mirror up to yourself, self-managing around doing things and figuring out where you don't have all the knowledge of the best ideas are fundamental.[11]

Robertson recommends Michael Watkins'[12] idea of upending the traditional SWOT analysis and foregrounding the threats first in a 'TOWS' analysis. From running the SWOT exercise multiple times with different groups, Watkins found that beginning by focusing on their strengths led to a conversation that was excessively inward-looking and ultimately reductive. As an experiment, he turned the order of the analysis on its head and began by looking externally rather than internally. The results were transformative:

Teams were able to have focused, productive discussions about what was going on in the external environment, and to rapidly identify emerging threats and opportunities. This provided a solid foundation for talking about weaknesses and strengths. Do we have weaknesses that leave us vulnerable to emerging threats? Do we have (or can we acquire) strengths that enable us to pursue emerging opportunities?[13]

Robertson's experience echoes Watkins' findings: "Look at threats, opportunities, weaknesses, strengths. Do that on yourself and think about what you need to do to mitigate the threats and maximise the opportunities. Have that degree of discipline to expand your own repertoire and put different tools in your toolbox." What is key to this approach is starting with an outward-looking mindset, rather than being hemmed in by the constraints of one's own experience and industry norms.

Rob Booth of the Crown Estate has also found this approach transformative:

A big personal learning has been trying to make sure I leave significant thinking time in my diary – I'd aim for about 20%, to allow time to be strategic and creative. It might not be for everybody, but going to conferences is a great way to help me to get dedicated time to be creative. Hearing from different perspectives – sometimes wildly different from those within our industry – aids diversity of thought and is a very positive challenge to our ways of thinking and problem solving.[14]

Notes
1 Steve Jobs, quoted in Gary Wolf, "Steve Jobs: The Next Insanely Great Thing", *Wired*, 1 February 1996, www.wired.com/1996/02/jobs-2/.
2 Interview with the author, October 2019.
3 Catherine McGregor and Annabelle Newman, "The Show Must Go On: Creativity and Thinking Differently in Law" in *Carlyle Kingswood Global Insights*, January 2020, www.ckgsearch.com/blog/2020/01/the-show-must-go-on-creativity-and-thinking-differently-in-law.
4 Adam Brandenburger, "Strategy Needs Creativity", *Harvard Business Review*, March-April 2019, pp58–65.
5 Interview with the author, October 2019.
6 Interview with the author, September 2019.
7 Interview with the author, September 2019.
8 Roger Beaty "Why Are Some People More Creative Than Others" in *Scientific American*, 16 January 2018, www.scientificamerican.com/article/why-are-some-people-more-creative-than-others/.
9 Ed Catmull, *Creativity Inc: Overcoming the Unseen Forces That Stand in the Way of True Inspiration* (Transworld Digital 2014), location 2937.

10   Linda Hill, Greg Brandeau, Emily Truelove and Kent Lineback, *Collective Genius: The Art and Practice of Leading Innovation* (Harvard Business Review Press, Kindle Edition 2014), location 892.

11   Interview with the author, September 2019.

12   A professor at IMB Business School and the author of *The First 90 Days* (Harvard Business Review 2013).

13   Michael D Watkins, "From SWOT to TOWS: Answering a Reader's Strategy Question", *Harvard Business Review*, 27 March 2007, https://hbr.org/2007/03/from-swot-to-tows-answering-a-readers-strategy-question.

14   Interview with the author, September 2018.

26. A framework for thinking differently: legal design thinking

The best-known writers who brought design thinking to prominence include IDEO CEO Tim Brown and Roger Martin of the Rotman School of Business at University of Toronto. Since Martin popularised design thinking both in the business academy and in management consulting in the mid-2000s, it has been introduced as a tool in many professions, including medicine and law.

Lucy Kimbell's 2011 article "Rethinking Design Thinking: Part I"[1] proposes three different definitions of 'design thinking':
- a cognitive style that designers use in solving problems;
- a general theory of design used in solving wicked problems; and
- creative and innovative approaches for organisations that need them.

"Inspiration, ideation, implementation," is how Brown defines 'design thinking'. It is a methodology that has come to infuse a number of different processes and industries. For Brown, it is essentially "a methodology that imbues the full spectrum of innovation activities with a human-centered design ethos. By this, I mean that innovation is powered by a thorough understanding, through direct observation, of what people want and need in their lives and what they like or dislike about the way particular products are made, packaged, marketed, sold, and supported".[2]

The main elements of design thinking are:
- focusing on the user experience;
- bringing different ideas together, often from different disciplines;
- prototyping what solutions might look like; and
- using the efficacy of these prototypes to advance workable solutions.

While design thinking is an important part of the innovation process, the inspiration aspect and the different ways of thinking this stimulates arguably fall within the sphere of creativity.

Design thinking is particularly effective in ensuring that there are as many different sources of creativity from within a team as possible, and that everyone is involved in the change process. Mo Zain Ajaz heads up legal operations at National Grid and has pioneered the use of design thinking and Lean Six Sigma in how he approaches this. "Creativity is a tool that gets people out of their comfort zones. It's getting people who are, say, blue on the Myers Briggs spectrum and are very reflective to open up; design thinking techniques are a really good way of getting these guys to share ideas. Design thinking is not about the person who shouts loudest; it's Post-it Notes and writing on the wall. It's a tool to generate new ways of thinking and doing things."[3]

Ajaz came to design thinking via the application of Lean Six Sigma from a more general project management focus in businesses. Lean is about simplifying processes: reducing the number of steps, maximising process speed and improving productivity. Six Sigma is focused on reducing and controlling variation. Put together, Lean Six Sigma is about deciding the best way to do something and then always doing it that way. Initially, experts on design thinking such as Brown were sceptical as to whether design thinking and Lean were compatible or were more likely to conflict. However, Brown changed his mind after seeing organisations such as Toyota successfully use both. As he wrote in 2009: "I have realized that high quality (the goal of Six Sigma) is a great platform for new ideas (the goal of design thinking)... Perhaps we should think of design thinking and Six Sigma being part of a cycle, each feeding the other to create new and improved products, services and experiences. Of course, the biggest challenge will be to build business cultures that are agile enough to incorporate both."[4]

While Lean Six Sigma effectively allows you to take a step back from what you do day to day and examine it critically to identify potential improvements, design thinking allows you to creatively brainstorm and think bigger. As Ajaz defines it, design thinking is "a tool that takes you from your current state to a future state and imagining a future state that's bigger than what you currently do".

Ajaz created his own model based on design thinking theories, which essentially seeks to solve key problems by taking a creative view and considering a range of different approaches. As he explains:

We take the problem statement, brainstorm what has caused it and brainstorm potential solutions. We divide these into options, then into results and then into project management. So it takes project management and combines it with a creative approach. It's more beneficial because those who are impacted by the issues are also co-creating the results and helping with change adoption.

This co-creation aspect is key for Ajaz: "That helps with change adoption and gets you to a place where you can achieve these sustained results."

Ajaz has also applied design thinking to the National Grid law firm panel review: "We did the 'three Cs' exercise from Lean process improvement, looking at commitment, communication and collaboration. We used the results to identify internal and external concerns. Breaking down what we identified were lots of issues around the process for on-boarding panel firms and around ways of working together."

Brainstorming and thinking creatively together with the law firms yielded positive results: "On an away-day together, we were able to come up with tangible ideas that the law firms could collaborate with us on. This was sustained over a period of time and was important in linking the internal team and the external suppliers."

For Ajaz, creative thinking techniques such as design thinking have revolutionised how he and his colleagues approach what they do:

> *Another project is with law firm DWF, where we are looking at redefining the contract lifecycle, as it doesn't work for both GCs and law firms. Can we come up with a new definition and solve the key problems? What's key is that we are using a multidisciplinary approach: law firms, in-house, technology, new law providers all coming together and trying to solve this problem in creative ways. What happens when you bring these different constituents together is that creativity sparks ideas off each other: people can take the outputs from creative sessions like these and run with them from their angle. But it's also educational.*

1. Prototyping – or why it doesn't have to be right first time

A significant aspect of design thinking is prototyping. This can take various forms – for example, building a model, creating a flowchart or drawing a picture of what a solution might look like. This move from "physical to abstract and back again is one of the most fundamental processes by which we explore the universe, unlock our imaginations, and open our minds to new possibilities".[5]

Design thinking experts such as Brown acknowledge that prototyping takes time, but it ultimately produces faster results. Brown debunks many of the myths around prototyping in his book *Change by Design*. While many think of a prototype as something created just before implementation, which is therefore close to perfect, Brown argues that this undercuts the importance of the creative thought process in considering solutions. Often, it is not until something is prototyped that you can truly evaluate it and zero in on what works and what doesn't.

Design thinking is an iterative process, rather than a linear process; and this is how creativity generally works. When I was directing plays, the rehearsal period was one constant iterative design thinking process – though we might not have known to call it that. Even in a one-person show, it's best not to have just one vision!

The kiss of death for any kind of theatre performance can be too much thinking and talking in rehearsals, rather than getting on your feet and doing. Those who use design thinking as a creative process to drive innovation similarly apply tangible brainstorming techniques – even if this is just writing ideas on Post-it Notes and sticking these on a whiteboard to start generating ideas.

A key feature for many in-house legal teams in using design thinking is the fact that it is built on empathy with the client and encourages co-creation as part of the process. However, it is important to progress beyond merely thinking and actually create something which can be tested accordingly. It is also important that, in the application of design thinking in legal, the 'design' aspect is respected and prototyping takes place early on in the process, to allow for multiple iterations. This will help in determining what works and what doesn't.

Notes

1   Lucy Kimbell, "Rethinking Design Thinking: Part I", *Design and Culture: The Journal of The Design Studies Forum*, Volume 3 2011, Issue 3 pp285–306.
2   Tim Brown, "Design Thinking", *Harvard Business Review*, June 2008, https://hbr.org/2008/06/design-thinking.
3   Interview with the author, May 2019.
4   Tim Brown, "Six Sigma and Design Thinking", IDEO Design Thinking blog, 10 September 2009, https://designthinking.ideo.com/blog/six-sigma-and-design-thinking.
5   Tim Brown, *Change by Design: How Design Thinking Transforms Organizations and Inspires Innovation* (Harper Collins 2009), p87.

"Does the overspecialisation that characterises the legal profession preclude a recognition of what other disciplines can bring to the table, in terms of complementary skill sets and ideas?"

27. Tears in the rain: the lawyer/non-lawyer conundrum

One significant theme highlighted by many of the lawyers I spoke to who are interested in creative thinking was their recognition of the value of non-lawyers and subject-matter experts, and how this can redefine the role of the lawyer into something potentially more exciting. (Perhaps unsurprisingly, many of these interviewees came from a non-law background.) However, too often in the legal profession, there remains a stubborn focus on elevating the qualifications, experience and viewpoints of lawyers over those of non-lawyers. This has ramifications for both creativity and innovation in the legal sector.

1. Not a negative: what does it mean to be a non-lawyer?

Let's start by deconstructing the term 'non-lawyer'. First, the term implicitly elevates the primacy of the lawyer; the prefix 'non-' suggests that everything else is somehow lacking or sub-par. I use the 'tears in the rain' quote from *Blade Runner* because it sprang to mind during a discussion with a group of lawyers and non-lawyer colleagues on the future of the profession. The irony was that from looking at us and listening to us, you would have been unable to tell which of us were qualified or practising lawyers and which were not.

The lawyer/non-lawyer dichotomy is primarily a semantic distinction used in law firms, whose business model is defined and owned by lawyers. But in reality, especially in Big Law, the success of a firm can depend on many non-lawyers. And this is increasingly the case – not least due to the heightened focus in business on innovation and digitisation. From the client perspective, moreover, lawyers are generally not considered the best people to run, plan or impose process on legal projects. Many lawyers are not used to thinking in a process-driven way. Big-picture thinking about a project can seem at odds with the practice of time-based billing.

In many science fiction works – such as *Blade Runner* and its source novel, Philip K Dick's *Do Androids Dream of Electric Sheep?* – the question of humanity comes down to empathy. In *Blade Runner* and its sequel, *Blade Runner 2049*, the police apply the fictional Voight Kampff test to measure empathy and determine whether someone is a human or an android 'replicant'. It is ironic, then, that empathy is often a quality deemed lacking from the traditional definition of the lawyer's role. Especially in a world defined by technology, "Who or what counts as human?" could be reworded as "Who or what counts as lawyer?"[1]

The innovation revolution which is redefining the industry itself involves a redefinition of what it is to be a lawyer. As technology accelerates and machine learning becomes more sophisticated, the human qualities that lawyers bring – and that technology cannot replicate – will be crucial.

2. Do we even need lawyers?

In some of the earliest attempts to make the practice of law more creative – such as the DuPont Legal Model and Jeff Carr's focus on the value equation at Univar – a key focus was to establish what lawyers were actually necessary for. This is not about making lawyers redundant, but rather about asking where they can add most value: essentially, what is the real purpose of being a lawyer?

It is interesting that – particularly for in-house lawyers – the more senior they become, the more empathy trumps legal skills such as technical drafting and knowledge of case law. Understanding, communication and judgement are all vital tools in the general counsel's toolbox.

Alex Dimitrief, formerly general counsel at GE, observes: "There's a huge benefit to thinking like a lawyer. We're taught to evaluate the strengths and weaknesses of a position, but also to respect and hear out the other side." But does the overspecialisation that characterises the legal profession preclude a recognition of what other disciplines can bring to the table, in terms of complementary skill sets and ideas? Do we need to look more closely at what a lawyer is not to understand what the lawyer of the future could be?

Notes

1   This idea was adapted from Lorraine Boisseneault, "Are Blade Runner's Replicants 'Human'? Descartes and Locke Have Some Thoughts", *The Smithsonian Magazine*, 13 October 2017, www.smithsonianmag.com/arts-culture/are-blade-runners-replicants-human-descartes-and-locke-have-some-thoughts-180965097/.

"Large financial services institutions are often hampered by their size and the bureaucracy that inevitably results from this. The legal teams that serve them are often similarly challenged when trying to adapt or change."

28. Case study: playing with your head up – the Royal Bank of Scotland's outsourcing, technology and IP legal team

Developing different ways of thinking is crucial to bring greater creativity to how legal departments approach their role. Kenny Robertson, general counsel for the Royal Bank of Scotland's (RBS) outsourcing, technology and IP (OTIP) legal team, agrees that creative thinking is vital for modern legal teams and often uses the football analogy of "playing with your head up" to describe this.

Headquartered in Edinburgh, RBS is a major bank served by a large legal team, subdivided into smaller teams which service different areas, but also report into a central legal department executive committee.

Large financial services institutions are often hampered by their size and the bureaucracy that inevitably results from this. The legal teams that serve them are often similarly challenged when trying to adapt or change. The silos that tend to exist within major companies can seem ineluctable – given the sheer size and scale of these institutions, working seamlessly is difficult, if not impossible. As a result, many larger organisations are seeking to learn from the ways of working pioneered by smaller, more agile and often more entrepreneurial companies. Eric Ries, who wrote *The Lean Startup* in 2011,[1] followed up in 2017 with *The Startup Way*,[2] looking at how larger companies could use some of the ideas and methodologies of smaller, more entrepreneurial businesses. Ries highlights that in this mindset, innovation and transformation are seen as constant, iterative processes, not one-off events focused on a single innovation or change.

However, individual teams within a larger institution can seek to apply creative and innovative ideas in more manageable ways, approaching day-to-day tasks from a fresh perspective. And this is exactly what has happened in the OTIP legal team. The team handles legal matters relating to technology, outsourcing and intellectual property, primarily from RBS's headquarters in Edinburgh – although members are also based in London, India and Poland. One approach which the team has successfully adopted to reframe its perspective is design thinking.

But why did a legal team in a large traditional bank decide to take a more creative process approach to how it worked? "Peer pressure is probably the honest answer!" laughs Robertson:

> *I had been at various conferences and events. Mo Ajaz of National Grid had done a session on design thinking and I had been at various other events where it was mentioned. There comes a point where you need to make it work for you and give it a try. I'd also had a meeting with Cat [Moon from Vanderbilt University School of Law] and attended a session she did in Toronto. That was good, because it took a real-world problem that we worked through in groups; so I could start to see how it might work in practice. When enough people are doing something that I respect, it piques my interest, so I thought: "Well, we'd better look into this more."*

While Robertson had not yet come across the application of design thinking in real-world legal situations, the RBS innovation team was applying this technique on a regular basis. This was another impetus – particularly given that his team's remit includes supporting the innovation functions in the bank: "One of the benefits of using a methodology like this is that – for any in-house lawyers, but particularly those who are working in a business where there is a premium on innovation – if you are able in any way to talk the language of your stakeholders, it's a real advantage. They don't expect lawyers to know what design thinking is."

The legal team's adoption of design thinking established common ground when working with the innovation team on issues where regulatory certainty is still some way off, says Robertson:

> *Our use of design thinking provides an extension to some of the work we have been doing on the technical side, with blockchain; APIs, open banking and AI – it's been important to be able to demonstrate to the innovation teams that we are aligned with their technology roadmaps and initiatives, and to invite them into our own design thinking sessions. Showing that we are using the same principles to examine these areas does our credibility no harm. We have an alignment with them that otherwise would be quite hard to get; so it has really worked. It's been really good for us, in a completely unexpected way.*

As one example of this process, the team explored what a document assembly tool might look like. The session threw up new ideas, such as having a tool automate the compilation of regulatory checklists. "I would never have thought of that," Robertson admits. "And when we spoke to some vendors about that, they didn't know anything about it and you could see a lightbulb moment of, 'I get it – it's quite easy to build in that functionality.' So as clients or potential clients, we're enhancing the product suite by coming up with these ideas."

So how has design thinking been most useful to Robertson and his team, and how does it actually work in practice?

1. Design thinking in practice

In August 2019 I sat in as the RBS OTIP legal team conducted a design thinking exercise. The process of design thinking involves five stages:

- empathy;
- definition;
- ideation;
- prototyping; and
- testing.

To conduct design thinking exercises, the team usually breaks out of its normal working environment. This might be as simple as booking a meeting room at RBS headquarters or might involve travelling to an offsite venue. This physical separation from their everyday workplace signals a shift in what they will be doing and how they will be thinking about it.

The exercise I observed took place in a meeting room away from the team's normal working area. The atmosphere was more relaxed than a traditional meeting: Robertson put on some music from his iPhone, which was plugged into a speaker. Four flipcharts and a variety of pens and Post-it Notes were placed in the corners of the room, and team members divided themselves into groups of four or five and congregated around the flipcharts. The music played throughout the brainstorming component.

The objective was to figure out what might work in terms of devising a fortnightly anonymous 'pulse survey' to understand employee engagement, separate from the bank's own biannual engagement survey. The aim was to create a simple survey that was easy to use on mobile devices, asking half a dozen questions that would track engagement over an extended period in order to identify trends, pain points, areas where greater support could be provided and so on.

One thing I was struck by during the brainstorming session was how focused the team were and how many ideas they churned out. After 10 minutes of concentrated idea generation, the teams began to categorise the ideas into themes on their Post-it Notes.

The teams then presented their key ideas on the focus of the survey to the wider group.

Next, they moved onto the ideation section, in which they started to look at functionality and how the survey could be delivered. This considered not only how the survey would be presented and would operate, but also when it should be delivered to secure optimum engagement.

Following the session, the next stage was to produce a prototype of the survey using an existing channel that the team was already familiar with (eg, WhatsApp), and test it out before its official launch.

2. A closer look: working through the stages

Watching a session in action, it was fascinating to see how working through the different stages produced a very disciplined and democratic engagement with, and sharing of, ideas. The first stage of the design thinking process, centred on empathy, involved working out the problem statement which is closely linked to the second stage, centred on definition: defining it and unpicking its components and contributing factors. While the empathy staged focused more on understanding the need for the survey, the definition stage was much more about outlining the parameters of what needed to be included in it.

It can be easy to conflate empathy and definition, or just to skip straight to defining the issue, but Robertson suggests that empathy is fundamental to any task in the legal industry:

> *Having a curious mindset and wanting to understand the client's focus, to understand its problems, is an excellent means to develop empathy. This goes to a number of areas that we try to put a premium on. To me, it's essentially about client-centricity. Whether they are internal clients or, if you're a firm, external clients, the premium is on curiosity – on trying to understand what the client's drivers are, what the pain points are, putting yourself in their shoes... I don't think you'll ever go too far wrong as a lawyer if you try to understand that.*

This also helps in developing emotional intelligence: "This curious mindset and wanting to understand the client's focus; sometimes sitting down and interviewing stakeholders to try to get under the skin of a problem – that discipline is only good for lawyers to have. They must continually work on their emotional intelligence and their empathy skills; so having that straight off the bat in the design thinking process was attractive." It's also a skill that is integral to the redefined notion of leadership in today's more connected, fast-paced business world: understanding your team and your colleagues as people.

The next key stage involves ideation: generating ideas and brainstorming as many potential solutions as possible. Robertson suggests that in this phase, leaders can empower their teams to practise self-leadership:

> *Having an ideation session takes a lot of the pressure off my role as team head. Instead of being expected to be the guy who comes up with all the ideas and just produces something, which the rest of the team is then told to go away and execute, it allows the democratisation of the team. Everyone in the team now has a stake; the brains of everyone in the team are being pooled. Now we can tap into ideas and solutions and creativity that previously just weren't there; and that gives team members a stake in the process.*

The next stage is prototyping: developing and refining concrete solutions, which may be anywhere from the early stages to almost complete. Or as Robertson summarises it: "Having something that is okay to deliver – it might be a bit rough and ready, but that's okay, because it's a prototype and it's there to generate feedback."

The prototyping stage is not focused on perfection, but rather on producing something that is simply good enough and that can open up a dialogue with stakeholders and end users. This is particularly valuable in the legal industry, suggests Robertson:

> *There's a wellbeing aspect to this as well – it pierces the expectation that everything that's produced by lawyers needs to be absolutely perfect and gold-plated. You can produce something and you can share it as, "This is a bit rough and ready; it's not necessarily*

intended to be the final product." That then creates a cycle of feedback – it gets something out there quickly that you can get feedback on and refine and iterate, rather than the model that I think all lawyers are more comfortable with, which is, "I'll wait until I produce something that looks beautiful and hope that it's there or thereabouts."

3. General counsel as client

Robertson suggests that applying design thinking techniques can also lead to more productive relations with external counsel:

More creative and collaborative ways of working result in a mindset which is not, "I pay you money and therefore I expect something that's incredible," but rather, "I'm paying you money and expect something quickly that I can then give you feedback on and you can iterate, and we'll have a two-way dialogue that is beneficial for both of us." Outside lawyers will better understand where we are going because there is an investment in empathy earlier on; and that investment then pays a dividend at the prototype stage – much of the inefficiencies can be removed because the external counsel better understand what the exact question is.

The benefits of design thinking are thus abundant: it facilitates a fresh perspective; democratises the team and boosts team engagement; results in iterative models of working rather than a focus on a detailed, 'perfect' finished product; and can transform processes and practices both within the team itself and with external partners.

4. Design thinking versus legal excellence – settling for 'less than perfect'

In practice, the crux of design thinking is co-creation and the ability to understand that the prototype should not be perfect; instead, the prototype stage should leave considerable room for co-creation. Robertson suggests that this can run counter to the lawyer mentality, which makes it far too easy to stifle creativity in the service of perfection:

At the risk of sounding like an amateur psychologist, when the principal means of assessment is quite often your written product – your written advice, your drafting, your pleading – there really isn't scope to get that wrong. And a lot of lawyers also come from a background where they are used to being praised for perfection. That's their currency. They are used to being praised for being academically strong, and in the main in academia, you don't usually get A+ for coming up with prototype A, and "This feels good enough." No – you're delivering pristine content, and that is the tailwind that has guided you to a point in your career. So trying to introduce a concept that allows for space for work which is prototyping is potentially uncomfortable.

But by applying design thinking to a variety of problems, the team has gradually become accustomed to this new approach. While there was initially a natural tendency to work the questions to within an inch of their lives, the approach has changed now the team has gone through the process more regularly and become comfortable with it. "It's now, 'Let's just get some questions out there. Yes, apply some brain power to it; but let's not over-sweat it. We'll try it; we'll see what data we get back. Inevitably, we'll need to refine it; but we're best to do that and learn from experience rather than guessing what's going to work. Let's get on with it,'" says Robertson.

5. Empathy and creativity

In many ways, the really ground-breaking aspect of design thinking is its focus on empathy as fundamental to how work is approached. Indeed, empathy is a crucial building block for almost all the business issues which are discussed in this book.

Robertson acknowledges both the value and the challenges that working as an empathetic ally with other stakeholders has presented at RBS:

I think the stakeholders are grateful that you want to help, and that you want to get under the skin and understand their problems. But in developing our approach to human-centred design, we found this easier when dealing with a team-facing issue. Effectively, we're the stakeholder and we know the pain points, so the empathy piece is more easily addressed. But when we're trying to move into engaging the stakeholders, empathy becomes the real priority. Trying to understand where their pain points are – whether it's the contracting process or how advice is given – is a much better starter for 10 than preparing a five-page advice note on clearance searches for a branding proposal, for example. That's probably not such a great experience for the stakeholders, who would rather have something more digestible and pictorial.

Here Robertson is citing the team's recent use of design thinking to reassess how advice on trademark clearance searches was delivered. They realised that this would likely resonate more in graphic form than in a dense five-page report. In this situation, empathy informed a move from a traditional legal response based on lengthy, risk-weighted opinions to a solution which better suited stakeholder needs.

Thus far, the team's application of design thinking has primarily related to business of law issues or internal operational problems around how service is delivered. But could design thinking ever be used as a means to solve actual legal problems? Robertson suggests the answer is a cautious – but qualified – yes:

In a contract, for example, the initial versions of a charging schedule or a service description, or a transition schedule in a big outsourcing contract, are effectively prototypes. But in some areas of legal advice, it would be difficult, because there are instances where you do need it to be perfect – you do need it to give you the right answer. When you go out for external legal support, sometimes you're looking for the absolutely correct, polished, dense answer, rather than an answer that will lend itself to creating something. So there are obviously instances where 'there or thereabouts' isn't good enough; but there are other occasions where you would rather work up something iteratively that, operationally, is an improvement.

6. Co-creation and democratising the culture

Another advantage of design thinking, reports Robertson, is that it empowers the team and can feel much more democratic:

People like to be engaged in improving things, rather than this being imposed on them. And most of the sessions we do have been fun. Quite often, we go off-site. We'll make it different: we'll get some music on; we'll have flip-charts; we'll have groups of three or four; we'll have break-out sessions; we'll try to keep it energised and keep it fun. It never feels like hard work.

We also try to make sure that it's not the seniors in the team who constantly run these sessions. If there's something that would benefit from the application of these principles, then anybody can do so and we encourage them to do so. We use something called a T bar, which is essentially a metric to track delivery of what's important to the team. The frequency of design thinking sessions is part of what we track. Everyone is incentivised to get involved, and the team understands the value in the sessions and can see the benefit being derived from them.

The real proof of the pudding is that now others in the team are trying to come up with their own design thinking sessions.

Securing such enthusiastic buy-in for this new type of creative thinking from an initially hesitant team bears testament to the culture that Robertson has developed at RBS. Members feel psychologically safe, and that they are free to try and to fail. His model for creating this culture is not unlike that of design thinking itself: an iterative process in which all ideas are considered and failures are allowed:

We try to share a lot with each other: that's a big part of the cultural piece. But there's no point having a culture if it's just words. So in our team meetings and touch points, we're quite open with each other in sharing what's gone well and what's not gone well. Not all of this is focused on creativity – there's a big risk element to it as well, in disclosing what could have gone better: "Oh, I did this; it went quite well", or "I did this – I tweaked the way I operate and this was the result."

Robertson feels strongly that this openness to sharing, to exploring and to approaching things differently has been a game changer for the team:

Excuse the football analogy, but it is like playing with your head up. It also means getting out there and keeping an eye on the external market and what's going on – whether that's attending a conference and listening to people talk, reading articles or listening to podcasts. We do this thing called 'managing our performance' on a weekly basis. A topic is chosen each week, and we each identify relatively short, easily delivered, straightforward actions that we will take that week to raise our performance incrementally in the relevant area. A number of those sessions have focused on creativity – we had one on creative confidence, for example, and we have one coming up on personal brand. These have helped us drive that focus on what's going on out there – particularly when there's a premium on thought leadership; and the disruptions in the market right now have created fairly fertile ground for people to try new things and do things differently. It's not that we just see something shiny and charge towards it; but it's useful for people to go out there and bring ideas back to the team.

The team also runs a book club, which for the most part is completely unrelated to law. Robertson feels that learning from beyond the law pushes the team to be more creative:

A lot of that comes back to culture. When you have a culture that puts an emphasis on playing with your head up and understanding what else is happening out there, it tends to become self-fulfilling – an energy is built up where team members will engage with each other asking, "Did you see that? Did you read that?" We've got a WhatsApp group that is focused on this sort of content; so rather than the normal nonsense about what people are doing at the weekend, we have a separate one that is focused on things like future law, creativity and leadership, wellbeing, whatever – thought leadership, in a nutshell. And not everyone completely digests that; I totally get that. But you have enough people for it to pique curiosity, and that helps.

7. Bringing creativity to the business of law

One key reason why creative thinking and related innovation often fail is because too much time is spent on the solution (the innovation) and too little on understanding the problems that the innovation is solving. You can't start to create or innovate until you understand the whole piece. As Steve Jobs has said: "To design something really well, you have to get it. You have to really grasp what it's all about. It takes a passionate commitment to really thoroughly understand something, chew it up, not just quickly swallow it. Most people don't take the time to do that."[3]

7.1 Contrast

Think about everything you do, and particularly those areas that need to change. Interrogate and question every aspect of what you do. If the automatic response that springs to mind is, "We can't do that differently" or "We've always done this that way", force yourself to ask why and break out of that way of thinking. Try a brainstorming exercise – perhaps with colleagues from outside of your area or with clients. Take a process and try to brainstorm how it could look, beginning with a blank slate.

7.2 Connections

Start training your brain to think differently. For example, take a different route to work, as Balder Onarheim suggests (see Chapter 25); try to think of as many random word associations as possible while performing a mundane, everyday task, such as brushing your teeth; or use the Wikipedia "Random" button to see if you can connect what Wikipedia throws up to your original problem. It may be impossible; but even trying to do so is effectively training your brain to be more creative.

You could also apply the technique used by Roger Beaty (see Chapter 25), by taking an idea or process used in a department that is very different from legal and considering how this could be applied to what lawyers do.

7.3 Contexts

As the experiences of the OTIP legal team at RBS bear out, regular exposure to ideas from outside legal can be energising and can lead to the adoption of new ways of doing things which have worked in other industries. This is where collaboration and networking with internal colleagues can be incredibly helpful. Learning about the ideas and innovations that other departments are pioneering – whether through formal company communications or informal catch-ups over coffee – can prove a useful source of inspiration, as well as helping to build your internal network and thus your influence.

Meanwhile, away-days for your team focused on new activities – such as design thinking exercises or LEGO Serious Play – can also provide a different context for inspiration.

7.4 Constraints

Most in-house teams will already be working with these, to some degree. However, setting tight deadlines and challenging teams to think differently with limited resources can produce startling results. It can also help to kick-start collaboration – for example, discussing potential technical and process-driven hacks with internal IT teams before considering external solutions can be transformative.

Personnel constraints and work demands mean that creative solutions must be found among the day to day. They also help this sort of thinking to become intrinsic to what you do – not a 'nice to have' that is indulged in only on special occasions.

Notes

1   Eric Ries, *The Lean Startup* (Portfolio Penguin 2011).
2   Eric Ries, *The Startup Way* (Currency 2017).
3   Steve Jobs, quoted in Gary Wolf, "Steve Jobs: The Next Insanely Great Thing", *Wired*, 1 February 1996, www.wired.com/1996/02/jobs-2/.

Part VI: Collaboration

Only connect.

EM Forster

29. Working together

Most of the business ideas that we have discussed in this book are dependent on people, but not just on people working in isolation – these ideas really take off when they are applied by people working together.

Collaboration is one of the most pressing issues for all organisations and has become increasingly important in the legal profession, as the ways in which clients work and their demands of suppliers evolve. The main blocks to collaboration are silos.

1. Silos

A 'silo' is a mentality and a way of working that prevents certain teams from sharing information and operating symbiotically with others. Instead of working towards the common goal or purpose of the organisation, the specific business unit is viewed as unique and potentially as in competition with others. Silos are a fundamental threat to business, as they stifle the creativity and diversity of perspectives needed for true innovation. Many business thinkers recognise the dangers of siloed thinking and working, particularly as the world becomes more connected, information moves more quickly and the workforce becomes increasingly global and mobile.

In terms of legal and risk factors, silos also increase the likelihood of risk events of all sorts and make it much more challenging to deal with the fallout of crisis situations.

The larger an organisation, the greater the number of employees and departments, the higher the level of specialisation and the more diverse the incentives used to motivate employees, the more likely it is that silos will arise. Deep specialisation and diverse incentive mechanisms are both features of law firms. In previous chapters, we have also discussed how the specialisation required of lawyers at the beginning of their careers – usually in law firms – is often at odds with the requirements of an in-house career.

Harvard Law School's Heidi Gardner has conducted research into collaboration in the legal industry and has found that many large law firms are undercutting their efficiencies, effectiveness and profitability through a lack of collaboration and overspecialisation.[1]

As in-house legal departments and the lawyers who work in them are usually more generalist – hence the designation 'general counsel' – their structures may lend themselves more readily to collaboration. In practice, however, in-house lawyers can often feel isolated –whether due to historical practices and views of the legal team in the business, their own learned behaviour from training and private practice or a mix of the two. In many companies, the stereotype of legal as cloistered away in an ivory tower, separate from the concerns of the wider business, still persists – even where the reality contradicts this. This also leads to the pervasive notion of legal as the 'department of no'. And when legal is characterised (rightly or wrongly) as a blocker in this way, it becomes a self-fulfilling prophecy: if the legal team is not included in strategic planning, it cannot offset regulatory, compliance or legal issues before they become catastrophic.

When considering legal departments and collaboration, there are three factors to consider:

- internal collaboration within the legal department – generally only a factor within larger legal teams;
- internal organisational collaboration with business departments by the legal team; and
- external collaboration with legal suppliers.

Another emerging collaborative trend, which is becoming more significant for the modern general counsel, is the sharing of information among peers. Increasingly, general counsel from different organisations seek opportunities to compare best practices and share their experiences of how to run a legal department.

Collaboration is integral to all of the business ideas discussed in this book: in driving culture change; in creating a shared vision of purpose; in facilitating effective leadership; and in promoting creativity and innovation. A failure to collaborate results in silos, where people work in separate units and do not necessarily think about the bigger picture for the wider organisation. *Financial Times* journalist Gillian Tett has written about the dangers of silos and examined how different organisations have implemented methods that help to break down silos and create more efficient organisational cultures.[2] Her ideas will resonate with many legal departments, in terms of both internal and external collaboration.

2. Barriers to collaboration: why do silos arise?

The silo mentality arises when certain departments or units are reluctant to share information with others in the same organisation. This reduces the efficiency of the overall operation, reduces trust and morale, and may contribute to the demise of a productive company culture.

However, the creation of silos is a natural human instinct. Our brains continually seek to sort and organise information in order to make sense of it. Numerous psychologists have shown that this is an essential facet of brain activity; otherwise, our brains would be overwhelmed by the vast array and complexity of information that is thrown at them. In *The Silo Effect*, Tett references a 1950s psychological study by Harvard professor George Miller examining the short-term memories of telegraph system and telephone system operators. Miller found that there is a natural limit to how much information the human brain can naturally retain when it is shown a list of numbers or letters, ranging from between five and nine data points. But when the information is organised into chunks or groupings, the brain's capacity for retention increases. More generally, organising information into chunks makes it easier to process that information in many ways. As Tett defines it, "This is the neurological equivalent of creating files of ideas inside an old fashioned filing cabinet with colorful, easy-to-see (and remember) labels on the topic."[3]

And this applies not only to information, but also to external and social interactions. It is interesting that the first thing that many new managers – including general counsel – look at is the structure of their team. This is where silos intersect with cultures. Organisations and groupings have their own cultural norms and behavioural codes. In the chapters on culture, we explored how these can produce cohesion and psychological safety, and can stimulate individuals to work cohesively, leading to enhanced performance. But what also unites many great cultures is the ability to collaborate effectively, both internally and externally.

If these cultural norms and behavioural codes become too entrenched, or if the building blocks for psychological safety and shared vulnerabilities are not in place, silos can develop. Silos and overspecialisation are often hallmarks of both large law firms and large legal departments. While some degree of specialisation is obviously useful, a lack of cohesion or collaboration around a greater shared purpose can lead to challenges and operational failures.

The emergence of legal operations as a discipline is in large part an effort to combat the effects of overspecialisation and the creation of silos. Many legal operations professionals and consultants begin with a diagnostic overview of how the legal team or law firm currently works. Identifying silos and areas where a lack of collaboration is resulting in the replication of work is a significant part of this early diagnostic work.

Part of the process of identifying new routes to collaboration involves asking why. In the chapters on creativity, we observed that one facet of creative thinking which is linked to innovation involves questioning how things are currently done. Silos often build up through processes which may seem logical at the time of implementation, but which over time can mitigate against collaboration, as the mentality of 'that's just how things are done' becomes entrenched. A key factor of creative thinking is challenging the status quo; and this is also vital in establishing a collaborative mindset and culture.

Tim Murphy, general counsel at Mastercard, moved into this position after spending five years as chief product officer and then two as president, US market. This broad business experience meant that when he assumed leadership of the legal team, he could apply operational thinking and efficiencies to how the team worked. In large part, this involved breaking down silos and introducing more opportunities for collaboration both within the team and externally. Murphy agrees that lawyers tend towards siloed thinking and are not natural collaborators because of their training and early experiences in law firms:

> *Many lawyers live their work lives in this very project-oriented way: the work comes in, you do the work, then you're done and the next work comes in. If that's all you're thinking about, you know how to do that work well, but you're never going get to operational efficiency. As a result, the [Mastercard] legal department was built like a medieval craft guild! Here's my IP lawyer working on IP; here's my M&A lawyer working on M&A... That sort of thinking is just not operationally efficient and it's not how businesses think.*

This mirrors the way in which most law firms are structured: departments of specialists working on those aspects of law that relate to their particular specialism. For most lawyers – as for other professionals – what Gardner terms the 'expertise gap'[4] is at the heart of the client relationship, ensuring that clients come back for more. What can cause friction in this relationship is not paying for the best specialist expertise, but rather paying for higher-volume, less specialised work. One general counsel once told me that he didn't mind paying £800 per hour for a particular lawyer, because that lawyer knew so much it would likely only take him a couple of hours to come up with a result that might take others 20 hours to arrive at. The friction over cost and collaboration is generally due to the charges levied for junior legal talent and non-expert tasks. To avoid this – especially given the budgetary constraints they face – general counsel and their teams should thus investigate whether there are more creative and innovative ways to process certain tasks than through lawyer hours.

The billable-hour model also creates a siloed approach, particularly in larger firms. In her recent book *Legal Upheaval*, Michele DeStefano points out that collegiality is often erroneously conflated with collaboration in many law firms. But collaboration is about much more than just getting on together; it's about working together towards the greater purpose of meeting clients' needs. However, many law firms still reward the individual endeavours of star players over collaboration across teams and departments.[5]

3. The cost of silos: risk blindness

Something that always makes me cringe is when I hear an in-house lawyer say, "The legal team at [insert name of company] is like an internal law firm serving the needs of its clients in the business." While this might be true in some respects, in others it seems far off the mark – especially given the vocal complaints of many in-house teams about their relationships with outside counsel! The designation of internal colleagues as clients also sets up an 'us and them' mentality. Many of the next generation of general counsel now regard this way of thinking and classification as counterproductive to their evolving role and that of the legal team. Traditionally, this separation was to some degree informed by a desire to maintain the lawyers' objectivity and ensure they could give impartial advice and preserve their professional integrity, thus fulfilling their fundamental purpose as officers of the court rather than employees of the company. But this also sets up a dichotomy which runs counter to the way in which the general counsel role has developed.

Murphy likewise objects to much of this rhetoric around the need for objectivity: "It's also based on the premise that the business is somehow predisposed to do wrong or be corrupt, which is rubbish – most failures are down to lack of knowledge. And if the legal team are trying to separate themselves in an ivory tower, then that will just make things worse."

A lack of collaboration not only hinders creativity, innovation and a positive culture, but can also lead to systemic failures in identifying and responding to risk events. And if general counsel and their teams are not included in key discussions and decisions, this can lead to missteps which might ultimately prove fatal for an organisation.

In Tett's analysis in *The Silo Effect* of the failures at UBS during the subprime mortgage crisis, the key theme that emerges is a lack of communication. Many senior managers and board members had no idea of the existence of an office in New York to trade collaterised debt obligations. The UBS risk function, which was meant to oversee such activities, was heavily siloed and decentralised. When the subprime crisis hit, UBS's loss on mortgage-backed securities was revealed to be more than $30 billion.

The crisis at Royal Bank of Scotland during the same period was likewise attributed to both lack of collaboration and a 'tick-box' approach to compliance. A 2010 report by the Chartered Institute of Management Accountants found: "The risk process ticked all the compliance boxes, but was rarely reviewed in terms of judgments, rather than just mathematical models." Moreover, warnings fell on deaf ears: "Professional risk managers appear not to have had either the authority or the influencing skills to change the approach to risk."[6]

Following the global financial crisis, the risk functions at both banks were centralised, so that they could oversee risk in a much more holistic way.

This trend is likewise being followed by many legal departments and – crucially – by their leaders, the general counsel. The general counsel role is becoming much more holistic and more closely aligned with the risk function. To work successfully in this way, the focus must be less reactive – as has historically been the case for lawyers, both internally and externally – and much more proactive, with legal and business risks identified and acted upon before they even become an issue.

Many general counsel around the world now identify ethics and compliance as an essential part of their role. This is distinguished from traditional compliance, as it is focused much more on culture creation and maintenance than simply on adherence to rules and regulations.

Univar's Jeff Carr is a firm believer that today's general counsel and their teams should primarily focus on proactively spotting risks and avoiding legal problems, rather than spending time and money on costly litigation down the line:

> *That's where this prevention concept comes in – we believe we can prevent all disputes. That's where we aim to get to – not just efficiently managing disputes, that's not the same thing. Litigation and the risk of litigation end many deals and are value destructive. But too often, our response is not to understand why the process of litigation has come about, but only to negate the process. The ability to understand why it's happening and potentially stop it happening is rooted in an understanding of your company's culture and business models. It can be hard, but it provides extreme value to your company.*[7]

This involves analysing trends and data to identify the factors that cause legal issues to arise in the first place. To work successfully in this way and produce the sophisticated risk analysis that modern businesses need demands access to information from, and collaboration with, other departments. In our case study on DXC Technology, where the legal team is implementing a diverse range of innovations in trying to create a model of the digital legal department of the future, a key tool is the use of data and trends to drive a more proactive response to both legal and business risk.

Collaboration is crucial to arrive at a holistic view of legal and business risk and a full understanding of the business, and to promote a perception of the general counsel as a colleague, not just 'the lawyer.' While it may seem counterintuitive to shake off the trappings of lawyerly expertise, given the years of study and expense spent in attaining them, collaboration ultimately produces a business professional who has legal training, but who can see the bigger picture.

Rupa Patel – currently general counsel at Awaze and previously in the same role at Exterion Media – agrees:

> *I believe it's important to participate fully – to step up and step out of being the lawyer in the box... That's been a key learning for me: participate fully, not just as a lawyer. That means understanding and getting to know the business, which is as much your responsibility as the CEO's, to make sure that you are heading in the right direction and to add value beyond your immediate remit. That is what makes a general counsel: it's understanding the big picture for the business. You can make better decisions because you know the strategic sectoral impact, the financial impact and so on.*[8]

This is a delicate balance to strike, as recent corporate scandals bear out. In the News International phone hacking scandal, for instance, it was alleged that a lack of oversight resulted from too much complicity between the executives and the lawyers over bad behaviour. Conversely, the VW emissions scandal is thought to have resulted from the legal team being kept in the dark – perhaps not deliberately, but because nobody thought to consult it.

Writing about such scandals in the *ABA Journal*, Paul Lippe, CEO of Legal OnRamp,[9] observes that greater knowledge, and by extension greater collaboration, could even be regarded as a professional tenet of duty:

> *The real question is "were the lawyers engaged enough in the business to know what was going on?" If they were, it seems certain that they could have prevented this manipulation from occurring.*

So how can lawyers truly be effective in managing risk?

Maybe spend less time broadly claiming to reduce risk, and more time really understanding the business and the sources of risk. Skilled lawyers can combine the roles of a trusted problem solver with independent judgment and integrated understanding, working with the people making risk-based decisions. Since these kind of corporate shortcuts almost always result in disaster in a transparent world, it's just common sense and enlightened self-interest that any manager can apply to avoid them... In Volkswagen, not knowing was just as bad as knowing and acquiescing. Maybe we should start talking about a duty to know what's going on.[10]

Notes

1   Heidi K Gardner, *Smart Collaboration* (Harvard Business Review Press 2017).
2   Gillian Tett, *The Silo Effect* (Abacus 2016).
3   *Ibid*, p34.
4   Heidi K Gardner (n 1), p5.
5   Michele DeStefano, *Legal Upheaval: A Guide to Creativity, Collaboration, and Innovation in Law* (American Bar Association 2018) location 1057.
6   Chartered Institute of Management Accountants, "Reporting and Managing Risk: A look at current practice at Tesco, RBS , local and central government", *CIMA Research Executive Survey* Volume 6, Issue 8, July 2010, www.cimaglobal.com/Documents/Thought_leadership_docs/R267%20Manage%20risks.pdf, p6.
7   Interview with the author, August 2019.
8   Interview with the author, June 2019.
9   Legal OnRamp is a Silicon Valley-based initiative founded in cooperation with Cisco Systems to improve legal quality and efficiency through collaboration, automation and process re-engineering.
10 Paul Lippe, "Volkswagen: Where Were the Lawyers?", *ABA Journal*, 13 October 2015, www.abajournal.com/legalrebels/article/volkswagen_where_were_the_lawyers.

30. Internal collaboration

For many general counsel and their teams, the ability to collaborate with other departments is essential in order to know what is going on in the business and provide more sophisticated risk analysis. The ability to ensure that outside suppliers collaborate effectively is another key factor for internal success, due to the greater efficiencies and cost reductions this may yield. One long-held prejudice against procurement professionals, when it comes to the sourcing of legal services, is that the sophistication of these services sets them apart from others. "It's not the same as buying toilet paper!" I have heard lawyers – both internal and external – insist. This reflects a perception of law as somehow special and different which, when taken to extremes, can end up with legal teams being siloed – whether through the lawyers' attitudes, the perceptions of business colleagues or a combination of the two.

And while buying toilet paper is indeed very different from procuring legal services, there are still principles that may be effectively applied to both, as work such as Heidi Gardner and Silvia Hodges Silverstein's ground-breaking case study on GlaxoSmithKline shows.[1] Here, collaboration between the legal team and the procurement function produced innovative changes in how legal services were viewed and purchased.

It may perhaps seem like semantics, but – as discussed in the previous chapter – the characterisation of business stakeholders as clients and the legal team that works with them as an internal law firm sets up an automatic division between the two. It also suggests that the aims and objectives of business stakeholders are distinct from those of the legal department – a scenario in which the latter seems to assume the guise of an autonomous entity.

During my career, I have interviewed thousands of general counsel and I often ask them what advice they would give a lawyer who is about to move in-house. The most consistent response is to get to know the business. Equally, one of the most common complaints about external lawyers is that they don't understand the client's business. Generally, this means that they don't understand the client's specific issues and pain points; although I have heard some horror stories of law firm pitches that were so generic and focused on the firm itself that the client wondered whether the lawyers even knew what company they were pitching to! What is needed here is connection and empathy – the ability to see the situation from someone else's viewpoint.

1. Only connect: empathy, influence and collaboration

One of my favourite quotes is the epigraph from EM Forster's *Howard's End:* "Only connect." It has served me well as a mantra both in life and in business: building connections and trying to understand people are essential tools for a consultant, writer and editor. But for all professionals, including lawyers, building your network – both internal and external – will improve your ability to influence and to collaborate effectively. There is no point in coming up with a great idea or suggesting a collaborative project if the main gist is lost in an undercurrent of whispers from colleagues asking, "Who's that?"

Developing personal connections with your colleagues also makes it more likely that they will listen to you and may ultimately adopt your ideas, suggests Dorie Clark, the author of *Entrepreneurial You*.[2] This needn't be a popularity contest, advises Clark: "You just need to have good rapport with your colleagues. This won't translate directly into influence, of course, but it does make it more likely that others will at least hear you out."[3]

However, in today's fast-paced digital economy, we have to fight for people's time and attention – which makes personal influence, connection and collaboration more important than ever.

Personal connection can initially be forged through projects that cut across departments, particularly where these involve something that you are passionate about. Your passion will also help with building trust and ultimately influence. Sharing ideas with colleagues or an interesting article on a relevant topic is another good way to make conversations and connections. This can even be done by email in the first instance and then followed up with a meeting or something more personal, such as a coffee. For colleagues who are active on LinkedIn or other content networks, looking at the contents of their feeds and trends on what they follow can be helpful in identifying mutual points of connection.

In making a connection through a shared passion, however, take care to ensure that you don't get carried away by your enthusiasm and end up just speaking about yourself and your thoughts on the issue. Listening is vital in establishing trust, influence and collaboration. Listening is also inextricably linked to empathy, which underpins many of the other issues we are looking at, such as leadership, culture and innovation. For example, empathy is the starting point for collaborative creative thinking exercises, such as design thinking. And it is also crucial in breaking down silos and promoting collaboration more widely.

Writing in the *Harvard Business Review* in 2009,[4] Katherine Bell argues that empathy is certainly not a soft skill, and that characterising it as such diminishes its power: "I've learned that empathy isn't about being nice or tolerant. It's not about feeling sorry for people or giving them the benefit of the doubt. It's an act of imagination in which you try to look at the world from the perspective of another person, a human being whose history and point of view are as complex as your own." This skill is critical to successfully bring together different groups with different skill sets and different world views.

The creative arts can teach business a lot when it comes to empathy. My background before legal journalism, editing and consulting was in drama and performance. As an actor, you have to put yourself in the shoes of the character you are playing. You may not always like that character or have sympathy for him or her, but the key to a successful performance is unlocking a way into the character. This is often achieved through workshops and rehearsals, which might involve theatre games or improvisation in character. In trying to respond in the moment as your character, you must extrapolate beyond the words on the page to imagine how your character might behave in a certain situation. One popular theatre game involves the actors standing in a circle in character and then interacting with each other non-verbally, endeavouring to embody and inhabit their characters without the words on the page.

Thinking in the moment in these ways can encourage our brains to be more creative. One famous example of this which has gained currency in the business world is the "Yes and..." exercise developed by Chicago-based improvisation group Second City. The purpose of the exercise is to stimulate both creative thinking and collaboration. As Second City executive Kelly Leonard shares in *Fast Company*, this exercise not only generates new ideas, but also encourages people to share these ideas and work together: "What you learn about improvisation when you apply 'Yes and...' is that there's a bounty of ideas, way more than will ever get used. Everyone in the ensemble produces hundreds of ideas, so even though most of (the ideas) will die and never be seen again, people don't hold on out of fear that they'll have nothing to offer at the end."[5]

In *Legal Upheaval*, Michele DeStefano recounts her experience of using this exercise: "The reason 'Yes, and...' works in real life (in addition to improv) is that saying, 'Yes, and...' forces you to listen to what the other person is saying before you respond as opposed to simply interjecting what you want. Apparently, we spend most of our time forming our response when we are supposed to be listening, which is why we don't remember a great deal of what we hear."[6]

Listening creates genuine connections between both parties: the speaker feels heard and the listener feels engaged and may begin to see things from the other party's perspective – even if he or she does not agree with everything being said. Considering those legal teams that successfully work with procurement, this is an example of "Yes and..." thinking in practice, in its recognition that not all aspects of external legal work are different, complex and special. Some are, and can thus be treated differently; but for others, the priority is to seek out the best prices and efficiencies of scale by exploring and learning lessons from the ideas tried and tested by other business units.

2. From client to colleague

Just as actors step into their characters' shoes, literally walking in colleagues' shoes can be a great way to enhance collaboration between legal and other business units. Experiencing exactly what the business does can be transformative for some legal teams.

For many years, the legal team at Network Rail – which oversees the maintenance and running of the UK rail network infrastructure – suffered from siloed thinking: the perception was that they were 'just the lawyers' and did not understand the realities of the business. To combat this, they introduced a number of measure which literally placed them on the front lines. The genesis for this was a survey of the wider business on the relationship with the legal team. They found that the most positive responses came from business areas where lawyers were working directly with the team. So the decision was taken to replicate this way of working – even in the central business team. In this way, the lawyers demonstrated their interest in, and understanding of, the different business units; while their presence on the ground ensured that colleagues involved them more, both formally and informally.

Dan Kayne, Network Rail's general counsel (routes), explains: "We have often said: 'Let's go and see what people in the business do.' Not just go to the office and sit there, but: 'Let's go and see what a level crossing manager actually does,' for example. If someone is advising on something to do with, say, performance and they don't really understand how that works, I say: 'Go and spend a day with the performance team.'"

Being present allows for collaboration to happen organically. "It's one of those things that builds on itself," says Natalie Jobling, formerly general counsel for corporate. "You may not have arranged any meetings; but once you're there, people want to talk to you. They'll just bounce something off you because they've caught you in the corridor or by the coffee machine. It's getting them into the habit of thinking, 'Actually, there might be a legal issue – I'll just check.'"[7]

Similarly, when Julio Avalos became the first lawyer and general counsel at coding platform GitHub in 2013, he realised that the key to success was to think and work in the same way as the rest of the company. Given that GitHub itself is a collaboration platform for sharing code, the company also works around this principle, using a common operational platform called Inner Source. Avalos started working in real time across this shared platform, like all his other colleagues; the only exceptions were confidential issues such as employment disputes. This also saved him time and replication of work: he was able to ask questions on the platform and get swift responses on how things had been done previously or whether draft policies might already exist. Working in this collaborative way also gained him the trust of his colleagues and meant that the arrival of the first lawyer in what was still a start-up environment was not so challenging for them.

GitHub was sold to Microsoft in 2018 in a $7.5 billion deal. Its collaborative platform for writing code is now one of the tools of choice for coders round the world. And equally, collaboration is still a defining aspect of the legal team, which uses Inner Source to work in a much more open way than even many of the most joined-up teams, both internally and externally. The openness and transparency this afforded the rest of the company, in terms of understanding what the lawyers were doing, has helped to promote integration and avoid duplication of work.

Getting out and about in the business to understand priorities is one thing; but for legal teams which are seeking to encourage the wider business to work with them in a more transparent way, establishing collaborative work processes such as this is likewise crucial.

3. Collaboration and influence

Another vital factor for effective collaboration is influence: that is, the ability not only to understand and empathise with colleagues, but also to put this understanding into action – often by enlisting people's help or changing how they do or think about something. General counsel and senior in-house lawyers are increasingly considering how best to acquire and use influence. In moving away from the stereotype of the 'department of no', this involves couching refusals in a way that shows a holistic understanding of the business and finding workable outcomes through collaboration. When this succeeds, lawyers are seen as welcome additions to strategic discussions and as key colleagues to collaborate with.

General counsel will usually find themselves influencing in all directions: upwards, downwards and sideways. While upwards influencing is obviously crucial, downwards and sideways influencing can be just as important in promoting successful collaboration. A significant motivation for cross-departmental collaboration is to get a full view of the big picture and bring different perspectives to an issue. By understanding who they are working with and building relationships upwards, downwards and sideways – both within their functions and cross-functionally – general counsel can lay the groundwork for successful collaboration.

For all leaders, the ability to get their message across to a variety of different stakeholders is fundamental. This relies heavily on emotional intelligence (EQ), rather than IQ; but most lawyers are much more comfortable with IQ than with EQ. This ability to connect with colleagues and understand their perspectives from a human viewpoint, rather than from a strictly legal viewpoint, is what sets many successful general counsel and their teams apart. And these qualities are also fundamental in facilitating effective, long-lasting collaboration. However, while 'soft skills' such as empathy and influence can pave the way for collaboration, practices and processes that underscore this are also needed.

4. Agility: breaking down silos

Tett cites Facebook as an example of one company that has actively built into its structures mechanisms that break down silos and promote more effective cross-team collaboration. One theory that proved incredibly influential in how it approached this is Dunbar's number. Robin Dunbar – a British evolutionary psychologists and anthropologist – studied how humans interact and build socially functioning groups, and concluded that the optimum size of an effective socially functioning group is 150; any larger and teams must rely on additional methods for cohesive functioning, such as rules and bureaucracies. One organisational culture that relies heavily on collaboration is the military and Dunbar's theory seems reflected in the protocols here: "Company size in the British army is 120 troops, and it's 180 in the American army. These sit nicely on either side of 150, the number of friends per person my research identified. There's just something special about these numbers, something to do with the structure of relationships that makes them very stable."[8]

As Facebook grew, this gradually became unfeasible; but the company has still maintained this practice through its boot camp training programme, which aims to facilitate inter-departmental collaboration by training cross-team cohorts together so that they build up their own social networks. It also introduced the concept of 'Hackamonth', when those who have spent 12 to 18 months working on one project are encouraged to spend a month or two doing something completely different. The idea is that this rotation mitigates against the creation of silos while also promoting collaboration and the flow of new ideas.

McKinsey works with its consultants in a similar way, encouraging them to move on to a different industry focus once they have spent a certain period of time studying one subject; the thinking is that overspecialisation can lead to burnout and can stunt creativity. However, this idea has yet to gain currency in many large law firms, which are reliant on specialisation and increasingly entrench this in lawyers' professional lives. Indeed, a significant reason why many lawyers move in-house is in a bid to escape this overspecialisation.

Alternative ways of working are also being utilised in in-house teams, both to mitigate against increasingly heavy workloads and to promote greater collaborate with the wider business. In our DXC Technology case study, the company's business units had to get used to working with a global team of both lawyers and non-lawyers – some employed by an external company – who collaborate using technology to get more done and work more efficiently. Initial scepticism from some corners was gradually replaced by a soaring Net Promoter Score for the legal department.

These new working practices are often inspired by agile and lean ways of working that were initially pioneered by technology teams. I will consider these in more detail in the chapters on innovation and customer-centric innovation. However, a key objective of agile working is to manage workflow in a way that is both more productive and more transparent and collaborative.

Agile software development and the 12 agile principles were developed 20 years ago in response to industry-wide frustrations over the lag between commencement of a software development project started and delivery of results. This often prompted frustrated clients to cancel projects midway through. A group of 17 thought leaders – including Jon Kern, Kent Beck, Ward Cunningham, Arie van Bennekum and Alistair Cockburn – met first at a resort in Oregon in 2000 and then the following year at a ski resort in Utah. It was at this second meeting that the Agile Manifesto and the 12 principles were formally written. The Manifesto reads:

> *We are uncovering better ways of developing*
> *software by doing it and helping others do it.*
> *Through this work we have come to value:*
>
> **Individuals and interactions** *over processes and tools*
> **Working software** *over comprehensive documentation*
> **Customer collaboration** *over contract negotiation*
> **Responding to change** *over following a plan*
>
> *That is, while there is value in the items on*
> *the right, we value the items on the left more.*[9]

The ideas of collaboration and co-creation are central to the manifesto. It describes a customer who engages and collaborates throughout the development process. Agile methods have only recently been adopted by legal teams, but these are likewise designed to ensure that the process of how lawyers engage with work is more clearly defined and visible to internal clients. An article posted on the website of transformation consultant Luna Tractor details how its professionals worked with the legal team at Lonely Planet to design more agile ways of approaching legal work that would better meet customer expectations and result in a more collaborative process:

> *Other teams requiring legal work now bring their cards/stories to the Legal Affairs board – leaving a placeholder card back on their originating agile board. These are fed into the board by the team from a 'daily news' section at the left side – mostly weekly (but sometimes daily) by re-prioritising other tasks.*
>
> *Prioritisation by business value is largely delegated to the Legal Affairs team, who act as the trusted broker for the many business stakeholders. The transparency of their priorities on the board helps this considerably.*

The team have grown their internal Net Promoter Score consistently, and most importantly of all, regularly head home early in the evening after highly productive working days. The focus on end-to-end process and the adoption of the final customer as their own customer (rather than a traditional shared service mentality with internal customer focus) resulted in about a 25% improvement in productivity overall for the team. This was reflected in the ability to absorb a reduced headcount in 2011, in a period where demand for the team's services was continuing to grow.[10]

Here, transparency and trust are central, making the legal department more effective through collaboration: the legal team would not have succeeded in this initiative if its internal clients had not understood the purpose behind what it was doing. In addition, a methodology such as agile is a recognised and respected way of working that other departments can relate to, even if they do not use it themselves.

5. Walk the talk

One practical way to ensure that collaboration is truly valued is to reward it. Lou Gerstner was the CEO who successfully turned around IBM's business. A defining aspect of this turnaround was his decision not to disaggregate IBM's businesses, which seemed to be the logical trajectory that the company was following. Rather, Gerstner felt that success lay in encouraging the different divisions to work together and to unite around a strategy for the whole company. A significant tool in achieving this concerned how business unit executives were compensated. While traditionally, executives' bonuses reflected how well their own units had done, this was now linked to overall profitability. The key for Gerstner was to measure and reward the future – where everyone was trying to get to – not the past: "When a CEO tells me that he or she is considering a major reintegration of his or her company, I try to say politely, 'If you are not prepared to manage your compensation this way you should probably not proceed.'"[11]

However, in most law firms the remuneration structure is the inverse of this, with the success of star individuals determining the success of the whole. Writers such as DeStefano and Heidi Gardner have shown that this can prove counterproductive to collaboration, whether internal or external. It can also potentially make it harder for law firms to understand the bigger picture when it comes to clients' needs. One general counsel friend of mine reports that although he sets strategies and goals for his legal team each year and then shares them with its external advisers, he has yet to see any of his main law firms refer to this strategic plan or make an effort to discuss it. For him, this lack of interest means that any claims of collaboration made by those firms ring hollow.

Notes
1   Heidi K Gardner and Silvia Hodges Silverstein, *GlaxoSmithKline: Sourcing Complex Professional Services* (Harvard Business School, 2013).
2   Dorie Clark, *Entrepreneurial You: Monetize Your Expertise, Create Multiple Income Streams, and Thrive* (Harvard Business Review Press 2017).
3   Rebecca Knight, "How to Increase Your Influence at Work", *Harvard Business Review*, 16 February 2018, https://hbr.org/2018/02/how-to-increase-your-influence-at-work.
4   Katherine Bell, "Empathy: Not Such a Soft Skill", *Harvard Business Review*, 28 May 2009, https://hbr.org/2009/05/empathy-not-such-a-soft-skill.
5   Hugh Hart, "Yes and ... 5 More Lessons in Improving Collaboration and Creativity From Second City", *Fast Company*, 26 February 2015, www.fastcompany.com/3042080/yes-and-5-more-lessons-in-improving-collaboration-and-creativity-from-second-city.
6   Michele DeStefano, *Legal Upheaval* (American Bar Association ebook 2018), location 1984.
7   *GC*, "From Client to Colleague: The John Lewis Partnership", Winter 2014, www.legal500.com/gc-magazine/feature/from-client-to-colleague-network-rail/.
8   Aylin Woodward, "With a Little Help from My Friends", *Scientific American*, 1 May 2017, www.scientificamerican.com/article/with-a-little-help-from-my-friends/.
9   www.agilealliance.org/agile101/the-agile-manifesto/.
10 Luna Tractor, "Lean Lawyers", http://lunatractor.com/not-just-an-it-thing-our-book/lonely-planet-legal-affairs-smart-people-lean-work-practices-innovation/.
11 Lou Gerstner, *Who Says Elephants Can't Dance* (Harper Collins 2003), pp250–252.

31. External collaboration

Improving working practices and promoting collaboration with external suppliers – particularly law firms – are significant challenges for many general counsel and legal departments. To address this, some of the new law companies are now incorporating different ways of working into their DNA, based on collaboration and even co-creation. This is resulting in unique new approaches, driven by a rethink of how lawyers work and a focus on both working collaboratively and working digitally. This is exemplified by the cutting-edge model discussed in our case study on DXC Technology, whose success hinges on seamless collaboration.

While many traditional law firms claim that they understand their clients and work in partnership with them, the vast majority of general counsel maintain this is illusory and express dissatisfaction with the law firm-client relationship. The prevailing sentiment is that the relationship is purely transactional and focused exclusively on the lawyer's own specific area of expertise. There is little, if any, understanding of the bigger picture for clients and the contexts within which they operate – and in many cases, little, if any desire to change this situation. As a good general counsel friend of mine once quipped over drinks: "Dealing with law firms is like being on a bad date: 'But enough about me; what do you think about me?'"

To some degree, the specialisation and siloed thinking in evidence in large legal teams, and even more so in large law firms, are a response to today's increasingly complex world, with increasingly complex problems. As the work of Heidi Gardner[1] shows, firms increasingly have more narrowly defined practice groups and practitioners have greater specialisation. Meanwhile, globalisation means that teams are dispersed around the world, presenting considerable geographical challenges. Put all of these factors together and you have a veritable bastion of silos to break down. In law firms, this is compounded by the billable-hour and 'eat what you kill' models. If partners are predominantly compensated only for the business that they bring in and execute themselves, there is little, if any personal incentive to become more collaborative. Gardner's research shows that when lawyers do collaborate, the rewards are manifold; but this seems counterintuitive to the prevailing structure and how lawyers are encouraged to operate within it.

The focus on annual profit per equity partner (PEP) as a metric of success can make it less attractive to focus on longer-term collaborative projects which might ultimately yield greater benefits:

> When they do [collaborate], my research shows, their firms earn higher margins, inspire greater client loyalty, and gain a competitive edge. But for the professionals involved, the financial benefits of collaboration accrue slowly, and other advantages are hard to quantify. That makes it difficult to decide whether the investment in learning to collaborate will pay off. Even if they value the camaraderie of collaborative work, many partners are hard-pressed to spend time and energy on cross-specialty ventures when they could be building their own practices instead.[2]

It is often down to clients – that is, in-house legal departments – to make it clear to external firms that collaboration is both needed and expected. For example, collaboration is a key component of the DuPont Legal Model – one of the earliest examples of how a large legal department reconfigured its working relationship with law firms. Tom Sager, former general counsel and one of the architects of the model, recalls that this did not come naturally to all outside counsel: "Initially, we had too many lone rangers; everyone thought they were better and more successful, and didn't need to collaborate. Collaborate or die – we had a big push on this. What we learned from the DuPont model was that collaboration is key. If you don't have true collaboration between internal and external lawyers, then the change cannot be sustainable."[3]

Collaboration between legal departments and external providers can encompass:
- the client's ability to collaborate with external providers;
- the ability of external providers to collaborate both with the client as a legal team and internally across departments and practices; and
- the ability of external providers to collaborate with other external providers beyond their own organisation.

As previously discussed, there often seems to be a significant disconnect between clients and law firms when it comes to collaboration. Many law firms make much-vaunted claims in their marketing materials that they are true partners to clients and fully understand their issues. But on the client side of the equation, many feel that law firms approach engagements from a purely transactional perspective: "What's in it for me? How can I get more work?" Some suggest that many law firms are missing a trick in not thinking more laterally about how they offer services and what they have which is of value.

This is particularly true with regard to their view of what 'good' looks like in other in-house teams. Many legal departments are wondering how best to structure themselves and how they can work differently and more efficiently. Some are teaming up with law firm professionals who have expertise in these areas, but are not themselves practising lawyers. For some clients, the secondment of a process and technology expert might be more valuable than the secondment of a junior associate.

Our case study for this part of the book and the next focuses on DXC Technology. It is presented as the final case study because it draws together many of the themes identified in this book, while also suggesting what the legal department and the outside counsel relationship of the future might look like, so referencing both collaboration and innovation. Importantly, it also calls into question a host of accepted ways of doing things.

DXC's innovative solution of moving a large part of its in-house team to a managed services set-up under law company UnitedLex – badged as United Lex for managed services and Marshall Denning for law firm matters – brings collaboration between internal and external resources to a whole new level.

One reason why this outcome was achievable may be cultural: unlike law firms, law companies do not have a PEP structure, and many have embraced a truly collaborative and empathetic mindset. They see the pain points for clients; they see that clients are being overcharged for high-volume, commoditised work which, even kept internally, would be a huge drain on resource and potentially force many lawyers to work below their pay grade.

John Croft, president and co-founder of Elevate, agrees that most law companies have brought a fresh new take to the legal profession:

> *In a way, what law companies like ours have done differently is to start by asking why. We started thinking about what law needed to be and who needed to deliver it, and realised there were different ways to approach this. These different ways of thinking about legal solutions were rooted in looking at the problems that general counsel, their teams and the wider company face in a much more holistic fashion. What many of us do which is different is to consider law as part of a broader ecosystem where cost, delivery and digitisation are parts of the solution, not just legal advice.[4]*

One key feature of how many law companies work is through the integrated use of digital tools and process-driven ways of working. To this end, many of the larger platforms – such as UnitedLex and Elevate – offer consulting services to assist legal teams in their own efforts to increase engagement in this area. Their offerings are often predicated on a collaborative approach: to deliver their services most effectively, they must often do so in conjunction with other service providers, including traditional law firms.

A deconstruction of the legal services industry makes clear the need for collaboration to deliver future-ready services.

1. External to external

Perhaps one of the most interesting developments of the last 10 years is the recognition in business and social enterprise that the best results often come by joining forces – not just internally, but also externally. As Nelson Mandela once famously declared in relation to the fight to end apartheid in South Africa, "Together we are stronger."

Writing in the *Harvard Business Review* in 2013, Ben Hecht – CEO of Living Cities, an organisation that harnesses the collective knowledge of its 22 member foundations and financial institutions to benefit low-income people and the cities in which they live – sets out the case for cross-organisational collaboration:

> *Leaders and organizations are acknowledging that even their best individual efforts can't stack up against today's complex and interconnected problems... While collaboration is certainly not a foreign concept, what we're seeing around the country is the coming together of non-traditional partners, and a willingness to embrace new ways of working together. And, this movement is yielding promising results.*[5]

Successful collaboration with organisations that might historically have been viewed as competitors demands an ability to be creative and innovative, and to work across skill sets to come up with more integrated solutions for clients.

Writing in *Fast Company*, Bob Mudge – then president of consumer and mass business at Verizon – acknowledges that cooperating with other companies in your own industry may seem counterintuitive to competitiveness, but it actually needs to become the new normal:

> *At Verizon, we are committed to the concept of 'co-opetition.' For example, Verizon is collaborating with content providers and software developers to provide live TV and video-on-demand content both inside and away from home to FiOS TV customers. Through these partnerships, we have developed the FiOS Mobile app which delivers a simple, seamless way for our customers to watch their favorite programming and content wherever they are, whenever they want. We have also started engaging with developers and start-ups through 'meet-ups' in select cities, aimed at creating an environment that showcases the newest innovations to solve the challenges facing today's connected home.*[6]

Many of these innovations and new delivery options would not have happened, or would not have happened so quickly, if Verizon had not been willing to look beyond its own boundaries and actively seek to work with others.

So is the legal industry ready for co-opetition? Maybe; but maybe not.

For many general counsel, open and honest dialogue with peers – even from competing organisations in the same sector – is fast becoming a necessity. Some of the reasons for this are operational; but a key driver is the desire to share pain points and potential solutions. An increasing number of offerings have sprung up to meet this need – some organic and peer led; others created by third parties. For senior in-house lawyers and general counsel in particular, these have become increasingly important. Indeed, for many general counsel who are sole lawyers or in small legal teams, such collaboration can be vital to success (and sanity!) in their roles.

A few years ago, I carried out an audit of a law firm's in-house training and education offering. One key concern was the dwindling number of senior in-house lawyers attending its events – although they were still happy to appear as speakers and panellists. The overwhelming feedback from a number of interviews with general counsel around the world was that they didn't want to listen passively, but rather wanted to share with peers – ideally in a small, psychologically safe setting where they could speak freely. Collaboration with peers was seen as crucial – primarily because their peers understood the whole range of issues and challenges they faced, and not just the legal issues.

2. Supplier collaboration

Cross-organisational collaboration and sharing of insights and data are now facts of life for businesses and are being embraced by law firm clients. However, traditional law firms have been slower on the uptake. Much of this is down to the inherent competitiveness built into their structures. Frankly, given that it can be challenging within some permutations of this model to get partners and teams from the same firm to collaborate, what chance is there of achieving this with organisations perceived as competitors?

This is all linked to law firms' inertia with regard to innovation. While in recent years, law firms may have recognised the importance of innovation, their efforts in this regard tend to be predominantly focused on technological solutions. Technology is often seen as a magic bullet, offering solutions that can simply be layered on top of existing structures. Scant attention is paid to those structures themselves, or to how they could be redefined to put the client experience and client needs front and centre. When this does happen, it is generally driven by those in-house legal departments with sufficient scale and purchasing power to push this through.

But in many different disciplines, the best outcomes are achieved when experts who traditionally might have worked separately join forces. In her book *Smart Collaboration*,[7] Gardner shares a case study on the Dana Farber Cancer Institute. Over the years the research labs at Dana Farber had become autonomous entities, focused on attracting the most talented scientists, almost without any thought to how this could further the goals of the institute as a whole. Primary funding for cancer research was abundant in the 1990s; but in the early years of the 21st century, questions began to be asked about the lack of translational therapies resulting from this funding. Dr Edward Benz, the president of Dana Farber, realised that change was needed, in the form of greater collaboration managed against a set of institutional goals. This resulted in the establishment of new integrative research centres, which had substantive autonomy and were open for faculty from outside the centre to use – but only as long as they were willing to collaborate on projects with centre members. Each centre had a five-year plan and a budget which was subject to metrics outlined in its approved business plan. Success depended on collaboration and the ability to mobilise talent.

Admittedly, such initiatives may be harder to implement in the professional services environment, given its traditional reliance on a star culture. But while this could mitigate against successful collaboration, the two need not be mutually exclusive. Just as general counsel such as Bill Deckelman and Jeff Carr are redefining the role of the in-house lawyer to be more general and strategic, clients increasingly see law firms as part of a broader ecosystem of legal solutions, rather than a one-stop shop.

Having had to critically examine their own structures, operational efficiencies and use of talent, legal departments now expect their outside suppliers to do the same, and to look beyond the confines of their own organisations where necessary. A good example of this new mode of thinking was seen in the earlier case study on the Crown Estate: under its new purpose-driven model, the legal team is actively forging partnerships with outside suppliers which involve working both with the team itself and with other suppliers to maximise the different perspectives on issues. As general counsel Rob Booth is often fond of saying, five less intelligent people will always produce a better solution than one brilliant person.

This can also be seen in the "Bionic Lawyer" project established by Booth, Stephen Allen – head of innovation and digital at Hogan Lovells – and Stéphanie Hamon, head of legal operations and consulting at

Norton Rose Fulbright. The project brings together people from across the legal ecosystem – including in-house lawyers, academics, private practitioners and those who work for law companies, as well as legal journalists and commentators – to reimagine what the lawyer of the future looks like. Interestingly, many of the participants are not lawyers and in some cases never have been lawyers. This is one of a number of groups that have come together over the last couple of years in order to gather a range of viewpoints and perspectives on what the future of law might look like.[8]

3. Imagining more

At the end of her book on collaboration, Gillian Tett draws an analogy between how we must think to break down silos and how an anthropologist views the world. Tett identifies six aspects of thinking like an anthropologist, including looking from the bottom up; listening and looking with an open mind; examining what people don't want to talk about; comparing what people say to what people do; and comparing different societies and cultures. The sixth aspect – and for Tett, the most important – is that the anthropologist's discipline "celebrates the idea that there is more than one valid way for humans to live".[9]

The ability to imagine different ways of doing things is enhanced by working with others and considering diverse points of view. This also requires vision and purpose – and ultimately, a vision and purpose which can be shared. Innovation and collaboration are inextricably linked and come together in our final case study, which points to one vision of what the legal department of the future and the digital lawyer might look like.

Notes
1   Heidi K Gardner, *Smart Collaboration* (Harvard Business Review 2017).
2   Heidi K Gardner, "When Senior Managers Won't Collaborate", *Harvard Business Review*, March 2015
     https://hbr.org/2015/03/when-senior-managers-wont-collaborate.
3   Interview with the author, October 2019.
4   Interview with the author, December 2019.
5   Ben Hecht, "Collaboration is the New Competition", *Harvard Business Review,* 10 January 2013
     https://hbr.org/2013/01/collaboration-is-the-new-compe.
6   Bob Mudge, "Why Collaboration is Crucial to Success" *Fast Company,* 2 January 2014
     www.fastcompany.com/3024246/why-collaboration-is-crucial-to-success.
7   Gardner (n 1).
8   Others include Michele DeStefano's *Law Without Walls* and Dan Kayne's *The O Shaped Lawyer.*
9   Gillian Tett, *The Silo Effect* (Abacus 2016) p312.

Part VII: Innovation

If you want something new, you have to stop doing something old.

Peter Drucker

32. Innovation: starting with the right question

I am writing this chapter in January 2020, just after the death of Clayton Christensen. Christensen's name became synonymous with the understanding and application of theories of innovation in the late 20th and early 21st centuries across many industries.

His ideas are equally relevant to innovation in legal departments and in law firms. What is significant in his thinking – and that of many others who write on innovation – is a focus not so much on the *what*, but on the *why* and *how*: on asking the right questions and understanding the situation. Karen Dillon, former editor of the *Harvard Business Review* and a frequent collaborator with Christensen, recalls:

> *To Clay, a great question was worth more than a great answer. Because without the great question, we would never get to the right answer.*

> *In an era of "add-water-and-stir" solutions to problems, Clay provided something much more enduring. He wanted to help people understand the causal mechanism of those problems, because until*

you understand what caused your problem, its solution is, at best, hit or miss in its success.[1]

To be truly effective, therefore, innovation must be rooted in an understanding of what needs to change and where the opportunities are.

Innovation has become the lifeblood of modern business; 'innovate or die' seems to be the modern mantra. The legal industry is not immune from this drive to innovate – although it has come later to the party than many others and is thus scrambling to catch up. But innovation can't be rushed. To do so risks getting much of the fundamentals of innovation wrong: focusing too quickly on the solution before fully understanding the problem. Innovation for innovation's sake, without a solid grounding in the purpose of the innovation, seldom yields positive results.

The other ideas we consider in this book – purpose, culture, leadership, talent, creativity and collaboration – must be present in varying degrees before innovation can be approached successfully. But what is fundamental is a clear understanding of what exactly is needed and how innovation can help to satisfy this need.

Famously, Harvard marketing professor Theodore Levitt used to tell his students, "People don't want to buy a quarter-inch drill. They want a quarter-inch hole!" This is why the notion of understanding your customers and their needs is so fundamental, both in law and in all other fields.

1. Why do we need to innovate?

Simply put, innovation is needed to grow your market share and distinguish yourself from the competition. While companies may be doing what they have always done very well, the pace of change and acceleration of R&D cycles mean that markets are no longer as stable as they might previously have been. Companies that fail to innovate may find that when an S curve appears that fundamentally changes the conditions of the market, they are completely unprepared.

Innovation also yields better returns. One US study found that the overall rate of return for some 17 successful innovations made in the 1970s averaged 56% – compare that with the 16% average return on investment for all American business over the past 30 years.[2]

Innovation is additionally an important way to differentiate yourself from competitors in an increasingly crowded marketplace, where consumers have more choice than ever before.

Innovation aims to give consumers what they need – in the most successful cases, even before those consumers have realised they need it!

Innovation is also increasingly correlated with talent. Companies with a reputation for innovation tend to attract top talent more easily: creative people want to work in an organisation that will nurture, challenge and encourage them. This is arguably even more important today, when a steady job for life is no longer the norm – or even the goal – for the new generations entering the workforce.

Finally, it's important to remember that innovation need not always involve doing something new. It often simply involves doing something better, more efficiently or more cost effectively; or even stopping doing something that isn't working. Many of the innovations in the legal industry are not completely new – they are rather more effective and efficient ways of solving the same old problems.

Barclays Eagle Labs – a space for innovation

Barclays Eagle Labs were set up in empty retail bank branches as a network of incubators and co-working spaces across the United Kingdom. In the chapters on creativity, we discussed how both temporal and physical space can facilitate creativity. The Eagle Labs aim to provide physical and temporal space for young enterprises and innovative endeavours in more established companies. They are also linked to Barclays' commitment to small business, as Chris Grant, LawTech director at Barclays Ventures, explains:

Eagle Labs started in Cambridge. Ultimately, it's about giving back to the community. It started where we had empty space that we wanted to re-purpose. Staff were often on the road; they can work remotely and don't need desks etc. So we had all this space. Given the relationships we have with many start-ups and small businesses, we brought those two things together to give young businesses a space and a network of support.[3]

This initial incarnation has since grown into a network of 25 labs which is one of the biggest incubators of small businesses in the United Kingdom. This has led to a realisation that ideas and support can be grouped around industry verticals, explains Grant:

As we started to do more in that space, we identified that there are industry verticals that we can start to look after: pulling together healthcare technology; pulling together agricultural technology; pulling together law tech; and bringing in corporate partners, industry bodies and universities to effect real change in those industries. We know that it can strengthen many of these young organisations to work together with others in the space.

The Eagle Lab in Notting Hill Gate is dedicated to legal technology and innovation. It is currently close to full capacity. As well as start-ups, the legal-focused Eagle Lab hosts the innovation arms of several established law firms. "The lab is a focal point where people can come and benefit from having conversations, having law firms in, having our change and transformation people through the door, to really help us to drive change in the industry," says Grant.

2. What's in a word?

'Innovation' has become a buzzword in every line of business. Until the 1980s, it was more likely to be confined to the R&D departments of companies with a strong scientific or engineering focus. But today, it has permeated every industry, including legal.

Canadian historian Benoît Godin has studied the history of innovation and how its use and meaning as a word have shifted over the centuries. Prior to the Industrial Revolution in the 19th century, 'innovation' was a dirty word. Godin shows how in its earliest uses, from the 13th century onwards, it referred to something new, often with an imitative aspect; but also something that was revolutionary and produced catastrophic change. The word became highly politicised during the religious upheaval of the Reformation and Counter-Reformation in the 16th and early 17th centuries. As Godin defines it: "Innovators were those who transgressed the disciplinary order and intend to change it for evil purposes."[4] The charge was levied at both Protestants and Catholics. In the 17th and 18th centuries, the word was further politicised in its use against advocates of republicanism. It was generally used as a pejorative by those who opposed change.

This gradually began to change in the 19th century, with the advent of the Industrial Revolution; but the modern understanding of the word, and its connotations of positive change and creativity, only began to emerge in the 1940s. 'Innovation' now refers to planned and intentional change, linked to creativity and progress. An innovator is seen as someone who thinks differently – but this is now considered a positive in business:

> *The novelty (the 'innovation') of the twentieth century is to enrich the idea of innovation with thought, dreams and imagination. Innovation takes on a positive meaning that had been missing until then, and becomes an obsession.* "Il arrive que la nouveauté comme telle, à certaines heures de l'évolution sociale, devienne à son tour une valeur en soi" *[At certain stages in social evolution, innovation becomes, in turn, its own value] (Bouglé, 1922 : 113).*[5]

Notes

1 Karen Dillon, "What Clayton Christensen Taught Me", *Harvard Business Review*, 27 January 2020, https://hbr.org/2020/01/what-clayton-christensen-taught-me.
2 Nicholas Valéry, "Special Report: Industry Gets Religion", *The Economist*, 18 February 1999, www.economist.com/special-report/1999/02/18/industry-gets-religion.
3 Interview with the author, October 2019.
4 Benoît Godin, "Innovation: A Conceptual History of an Anonymous Concept" 2015, www.csiic.ca/PDF/WorkingPaper21.pdf.
5 *Ibid*, p28.

"Innovation is powered by a thorough understanding, through direct observation, of what people want and need in their lives and what they like or dislike about the way particular products are made, packaged, marketed, sold, and supported."

33. Theories of innovation

One common theme that runs through most major theories of innovation is that it is less about *what* you innovate than about *why* and *how* you innovate. While there is an obvious link to creativity, as explored earlier in this book, there is much more to creativity than simply waiting for inspiration to strike. Mindset, preparation and process are also crucial; and this is even more true of innovation.

1. Peter Drucker: the discipline of innovation

Peter Drucker is generally considered the father of modern management theories. In Drucker's analysis, "Innovation requires knowledge, ingenuity, and, above all else, focus."[1]

For Drucker, innovation involves a methodical analysis of seven key areas of opportunity which are evident not only in business, but also in social and demographic trends. It also involves thinking creatively and differently to come up with what Drucker describes as 'functional inspiration'.

The seven key areas that Drucker identifies are as follows.

1.1 The unexpected

This can variously encompass both unexpected failures and unexpected successes, whether of your own or of others. Unexpected events are very powerful, according to Drucker, as they allow leaders and innovators to take a different perspective and think differently about a situation. This mindset facilitate innovation.

1.2 Incongruities

Many companies develop new products or innovations without researching what customers might need or want. This is also the central tenet of the 'jobs to be done' theory. While this incongruity between what is developed and what is actually wanted may lead to failures, it can also be a great source of innovation. Analysing what customers or clients did not like or felt did not work can lay the groundwork for future success.

1.3 Process need

This source of innovation is more task focused than situation focused. It involves looking at what is being done and figuring out whether there is a way to do it better. Many of the innovations in law have been significant wins relating to how work is carried out.

1.4 Industry and market structure change

For Drucker, to ensure they are not derailed by disruptive innovations, organisations must constantly keep a weather eye on the bigger picture, both in their own industries and beyond. An up-to-date awareness of developments and trends will ensure that, as changes happen both outside your industry and within it, you can figure out how your organisation can keep pace.

1.5 Demographics

Demographics can affect both client base and talent pool. Companies that monitor demographics can potentially explore new directions and identify new opportunities. For example, over the next 10 years, more millennials will start to move into management positions in legal departments and law firms. These leaders will have a much more seamless relationship with digitisation than previous generations. Rather than digitisation being seen as a threat to the role of the lawyer, it will be seen as a natural corollary.

1.6 Changes in perception

Changes in perception can relate to how the world works (eg, globalisation) or, on a smaller scale, to how specific industries and companies operate. A significant example here is climate change: significant innovations are now being driven by environmental concerns which some years ago would not have been perceived as pressing.

Changes in perception open up opportunities for businesses to develop new products and services that align with their customers' new perspectives. For example, given consumers' heightened focus on ethical concerns, today's general counsel must look at risk much more broadly and ask not just "Is it legal?'", but also "Is it right?"

1.7 New knowledge

New knowledge is often conflated with innovation, but the two are not the same – although they can have a symbiotic relationship. In legal innovation, it is the use of algorithms and artificial intelligence (AI) to process and apply knowledge much faster than any human that has proved most seductive. For many in the legal profession, despite much discussion and hype, the full promise of technological developments such as AI has not been realised in practice. In Drucker's theory of innovation, keeping apprised of how new knowledge is developing is key to avoid being left behind – albeit that such developments may not in fact be the innovation you need.

2. Disruptive innovation

The term 'disruptive innovation' has gained increasing currency over the last 10 years. It refers to innovations which do not sustain an industry, but rather change it forever. The term was first coined in 1995 by Clayton Christensen. A disruptive innovation is one pioneered by a smaller company with less resources that succeeds in changing the prevailing market conditions. As incumbents focus on improving their products and services for their most demanding or profitable customers, they often overlook key segments of the market – particularly lower-value, lower-cost segments. Disruptive innovations provide new solutions which target those overlooked segments, often at a more competitive price. The incumbents often do not respond at first, because they are too focused on their most profitable segments. The new entrants then move upwards, delivering the performance that the market's key customers require, while preserving the advantages that drove their early success. When mainstream customers start adopting their offerings in volume, this constitutes disruption innovation.

In a 2015 article for the *Harvard Business Review*,[2] Christensen discussed how the term 'disruptive innovation' has become overused to describe any new innovation in a marketplace. To be truly disruptive, an innovation must seize on either a low-end foothold or a new market foothold; it cannot just be new or different. As Christensen describes it:

> *Low-end footholds exist because incumbents typically try to provide their most profitable and demanding customers with ever-improving products and services, and they pay less attention to less-demanding customers. In fact, incumbents' offerings often overshoot the performance requirements of the latter. This opens the door to a disrupter focused (at first) on providing those low-end customers with a 'good enough' product.*

This trend is clearly playing out in the overlooked segments of the legal market: high-volume, low-cost legal work was the obvious target for market disruption. Clients learned that they were paying more for or spending more time than was necessary on work which could be handled more efficiently by non-legal experts or even by technology. Having gained a foothold in the neglected lower end of the legal market, many of the new law companies and agile staffing solutions – such as UnitedLex, Elevate and Axiom – have now expanded their offerings.

3. The 'jobs to be done' theory

Christensen developed the 'jobs to be done' theory from his work on *The Innovator's Dilemma*[3] and *The Innovator's Solution*.[4] The theory was first outlined in a 2005 article in the *Harvard Business Review* co-authored with Scott Cook, CEO of Intuit, and Taddy Hall.[5] Christensen and Hall went on to collaborate with Karen Dillon and David S Duncan on the 2016 book *Competing Against Luck*,[6] which aimed to unpick why some innovations work and others don't. This book also provides a more thorough examination of the use and application of the 'jobs to be done' theory.

It might appear that whether an innovation catches on is in large part down to luck. But Christensen *et al* suggest that the crucial factor for success is whether companies really understand what their customers need and want. In other words, what job is the innovation intended to do? The 'jobs...' theory aims to take the notion of disruption to the next stage by adding in the *why* and *how*, not just the *what*.

Going back to Levitt's drill analogy discussed in Chapter 32, in the legal profession's approach to innovation, there is often too much focus on the drill, rather than on the desire for a hole. This is particularly evident when we look at the discourse around legal technology. As Dillon told me: "There is the wrong sense that innovation means investing in tech. Those things might be helpful, but they are not the same as fundamentally figuring out what your customer needs."[7]

This detailed understanding of customers and their context, rather than simply on the means of delivery, is key to innovation success – and is at the heart of the 'jobs to be done' theory. As with disruptive innovation, incumbents can have too narrow a focus on what they perceive as the higher end of the market and lose sight of the lower end, with low-hanging fruit ripe for disruption. In the jobs to be done theory, the key fallacy is assuming that you know what clients want. Sometimes clients can't even articulate this themselves; but their struggles and their actions can be revealing. You have to start by observing what they are struggling with, when and why. For Karen Dillon this is at the heart of innovations that don't work:

I really think the biggest part is this lack of understanding customers, which is at the heart of innovations that are not working. We talked to a consultancy client, a large company, that wanted to introduce a new line. The idea came from what the company assumed its clients would want; but in reality, there was no insight into clients. My feedback to the client was, 'You decided it; it was not figured out from watching behaviour.' Unless you actually truly understand customers and their choices, you cannot understand what jobs they might need to be done.[8]

This is also a key tenet of Drucker's pillars of innovation. Given the ubiquity of technology, making it second nature to use is a fundamental component of success – but this depends on a function that makes sense and facilitates ease of adoption. In the technology space, the gap between the specialist knowledge of software engineers and the experience of the end user has long been a focus. No matter how wonderful a technological innovation is, if it is too difficult to use, it won't stick with consumers.

One field in which there has been significant B2C technology innovation in recent years is financial services – especially by consumer challenger banks, whose primary or only interface with customers is digital. This surge in fintech has left many of the larger consumer banks struggling to catch up.

In 2015 Barclays hired Noel Lyons of Kent Lyons as its digital design director, to ensure that its new banking apps were doing the right job. Lyons told *Designweek* that for him, the opportunity to translate the emotional charge of money into useable solutions was a big draw of the role: "Money is very emotional. It can feel good, bad, calming, all sorts of things. How can we use digital products to help people with those feelings – maybe they just want to check their balance, or increase their financial stability. I want to look at what people's ambitions are and help them achieve their goals through service and interaction design."[9]

Lyons addressed a Barclays Bridge Ventures event (see box opposite), which aimed to bring together innovators and start-up founders with those working in the innovation space in law. For Lyons, the 'jobs to be done' theory is fundamental to the innovations around mobile banking he is working on. 'Jobs to be done' has been central to this, as it involves thinking about people and emotional connection. Much of the strategic investment in the bank has been based on the delivery of ideas through the 'jobs to be done' theory. What has been central to this, according to Lyons, is design, researching and testing. Interviewees test ideas live, watched by designers and developers, who can get real-time feedback on what works and what doesn't.[10]

This kind of first-hand insight is especially valuable for larger organisations, which lack the agility of start-ups. In larger organisations, innovations can often get booted down by committees; and the time, emotional and financial investment is such that creators may have become blind to their failings by the time their innovations are launched to market.

As a result, certain innovations that seem logical to their creators may fall flat in reality. Lyons cites a tool introduced in the Barclays app to help customers keep track of spending and suggest more economical alternatives. For example, if someone spent £3 on a coffee, it might show options for cheaper coffees nearby. However, as Lyons shared, while this seemed like a good idea in theory, in practice test users reacted very negatively to it, finding it somewhat patronising.

The key lesson from the 'jobs to be done' theory is to think about the functionality of the innovation, but also about how and why users will interact with it, as well as the emotional effect on users.

Barclays LawTech Bridge: cross-fertilising ideas for innovation

LawTech Bridge had its inception in Barclays Eagle Labs and is designed to stimulate the cross-fertilisation of ideas from technology, innovation and law.

LawTech Bridge serves as a meeting point for people from across the legal ecosystem who are frustrated with the pace of change in the industry. It encourages representatives from large legal organisations and from the start-ups that might become the legal service providers of the future to come together to share their experiences and perspectives. Crucially, it also gives them insight into the perspectives of non-legal tech start-ups and venture capital investors, so that they can learn from the experiences of entrepreneurs and innovators from outside their own industry.

LawTech Bridge is open to people who work in law firms, law departments and legal start-ups, and is the first in a series of industry-specific ventures. Luke Christoforidis – vice president at Barclays Ventures, who runs LawTech Bridge – explains that one reason why they started this initiative by focusing on legal is because law is such a horizontal profession:

The main idea of LawTech Bridge is to bring together these law tech start-ups on the one hand, and those affected by disruption – legal teams and law firms – on the other. The event is hosted by a technology company. It's disrupting the usual paradigm by bringing in someone from the tech industry who has experience in either building software or making partnerships; bringing the best of what you have and getting a distribution brand halo with someone else who has the right tech or the right people, or who has investment experience.[11]

As an example of this, one LawTech Bridge session was hosted by Andy Robertson, who runs an agency that makes software products for companies that need delivery and payment systems. His agency, Cultivate, was acquired by Deliveroo in 2019, having previously designed the food delivery company's payment systems. The LawTech Bridge session provided first-hand insight into how start-ups and incumbents in the technology delivery and logistics industries can work together and learn from each other, says Christoforidis: "Andy has experience in running a start-up. Currently, most law-tech start-ups in the UK have some way to go in terms of the maturity of their business models and their ability to partner with the incumbent law firms. Andy's thinking and experience could be very valuable – for example, what are the playbooks that Andy used to put himself in a position to be acquired by Deliveroo?"

By initiating these conversations and connections across different sectors of the legal ecosystem, LawTech Bridge aims to "create a similar kinetic energy in the legal industry", says Christoforidis. "Can we help all the component parts to think about things in better ways? Can we help start-ups and law firms to come together to make changes in their cultures which could benefit each other?"

Christoforidis believes that this dialogue could significantly boost the synergies between law and tech, which are currently embryonic. Looking at this through the prism of the 'jobs to be done' theory, it is clear that many of the jobs in this space have not even been conceptualised yet: "As software eats the world, that will highlight more and more jobs that law can do for software." Christoforidis gives the example of the role that technology can play in fraud protection: one tech company has begun working with a leading global fashion house, scouring social media for posts that show fake goods. This task is normally outsourced to humans and is very labour intensive and slow; but now tech can handle this 'job to be done' more expediently.

Christoforidis believes that such synergies could revolutionise the delivery of legal services: "What we are hoping to do with LawTech Bridge is to change partnerships between law firms and start-ups, so it isn't just about law firms' processes, but is rather disruptive in bringing technology or new ways of thinking and law together to create wider market innovation."

4. A start-up mentality

Barclays' recruitment of Lyons illustrates how many incumbent institutions are seeking to harness the energy and creativity that characterise start-ups. Eric Ries – the author of *The Lean Startup*[12] and *The Startup Way*[13] – developed the Lean Start-Up methodology both to help start-ups scale up and to help larger companies tap into their innovation dynamics. The methodology relies on much shorter research and development cycles to determine whether a product is viable through iterative product releases and validated learnings – in other words, testing out an initial idea and then measuring the response of potential customers to validate its effect. This methodology relies on agility and the ability to fail fast and change direction as necessary.

In *The Startup Way*, Ries recognises that the challenges facing large companies and start-up scaling are essentially no different:

> *I have come to realize that today's organizations – both established and emerging – are missing capabilities that are needed for every organization to thrive in the century ahead: the ability to experiment rapidly with new products and new business models, the ability to empower their most creative people and the ability to engage again and again in an innovation process and manage it with rigor and accountability, so that they can unlock new sources of growth and productivity.*[14]

In his Lean Start-Up methodology, which also draws on the work of Silicon Valley entrepreneur Steve Blank,[15] Ries suggests that innovations should be developed on the basis of the expressed desires of the market – echoing the principles of Drucker's thinking and Christensen's disruptive innovation and 'jobs to be done' theories. What is new in this methodology is its primacy of validated learning – a process by which companies assess consumer interest and then apply this to the next iteration of their innovation. The methodology is also characterised by an agile approach, in which experimentation is favoured over adherence to a fixed plan.

5. First mover or category creator?

In *Start With Why*,[16] Simon Sinek explores what has made Apple the world's market leader in terms of innovation. He suggests that this is not necessarily down to discovering the *what*, but rather to linking the *what* with the *why* – which is often an emotional sell. For example, Apple did not invent the first MP3 player; in fact, the first portable multi-gigabyte hard drive that could play music was produced by Singapore company Creative Technologies Ltd, which specialised in digital sound products. Apple followed suit with its iPod 22 months later, building its marketing strategy on the powerful tagline: "1,000 songs in your pocket." By contrast, observes Sinek, Creative Technologies advertised its product as: "A '5GB mp3player'. It is exactly the same message as Apple's '1,000 songs in your pocket.' The difference is Creative told us WHAT their product was and Apple told us WHY we needed it."[17]

So rather than a first mover, Apple was in fact a category creator. Writing in the *Harvard Business Review*, Eddie Yoon, Christopher Lochhead and Nicolas Cole reveal the crucial distinction between the two:

> *Creating a new category is about educating the market about not only new solutions, but often new problems that are not top of mind. This kind of education can't be done merely with a great product or service or traditional marketing. This often needs to be experienced, which requires a breakthrough in the business model as well. The emphasis should be on creating the first high functioning flywheel, which is the combination of 1) a radical product/service innovation, combined with 2) a breakthrough business model innovation, and finally greased by 3) a breakthrough big data about future category demand.*[18]

So success does not necessarily hinge on being first to innovate, but rather on understanding the ecosystem within which your innovation will operate and defining your business model to suit the delivery of your innovation. Uber is another exemplar of this: it is not just the concept that is innovative, but also the delivery – the ability to order and pay for rides with your phone. Uber's business model has transformed the market: as a result, even standard taxis accept credit cards today.

Similar transformations are needed in the legal industry, where the conversation is still too focused on innovation that merely sustains the status quo. Although a number of new players are beginning to chip away at the traditional models of legal service delivery, these are not being fundamentally challenged. However, in-house legal teams are ramping up the pressure on law firms to innovate and are increasingly challenging the status quo.

Notes

1   https://hbr.org/2002/08/the-discipline-of-innovation.
2   Clayton M Christensen, Michael E Raynor and Rory McDonald, "What is Disruptive Innovation?" *Harvard Business Review*, December 2015, https://hbr.org/2015/12/what-is-disruptive-innovation.
3   Clayton M Christensen, *The Innovator's Dilemma* (Harvard Business Review Press 1997).
4   Clayton M Christensen, *The Innovator's Solution, Revised and Expanded: Creating and Sustaining Successful Growth* (Harvard Business Review Press 2013).
5   Clayton M Christensen, Scott Cook and Taddy Hall, "Marketing Malpractice: The Cause and the Cure", *Harvard Business Review*, December 2005, https://hbr.org/2005/12/marketing-malpractice-the-cause-and-the-cure.
6   Clayton M Christensen, Karen Dillon, Taddy Hall and David S Duncan, *Competing Against Luck: The Story of Innovation and Customer Choice* (Harper Collins 2016).
7   Interview with the author, November 2019.
8   Interview with the author, November 2019.
9   Tom Banks, "Kent Lyons rebrands to Why as co-founder Noel Lyons joins Barclays", *Design Week*, 12 June 2015, www.designweek.co.uk/issues/8-14-june-2015/kent-lyons-rebrands-to-y-as-co-founder-noel-lyons-joins-barclays/.
10 Noel Lyons' speech at LawTech Bridge Event, 30 November 2019.
11 Interview with the author, November 2019.
12 Eric Ries, *The Lean Startup* (Portfolio Penguin 2011).
13 Eric Ries, *The Startup Way* (Currency Books 2017).
14 *Ibid*, p3.
15 Steve Blank, "Why the Lean Startup Changes Everything", *Harvard Business Review*, May 2013.
16 Simon Sinek, *Start With Why* (Portfolio Penguin 2011).
17 *Ibid*, p44.
18 Eddie Yoon, Christopher Lochhead and Nicolas Cole, "The Difference Between a First Mover and a Category Creator", *Harvard Business Review*, 21 November 2018, https://hbr.org/2019/11/the-difference-between-a-first-mover-and-a-category-creator?referral=03759&cm_vc=rr_item_page.bottom.

34. Why legal teams need to innovate – and how they can do so

Innovation in the legal profession is a more recent phenomenon than in wider business. The movement started about 25 to 30 years ago, when legal departments and law firms began to explore new ways to work differently, more efficiently and more cost effectively. These efforts were inspired by the initiatives of colleagues in other departments, as well as by a desire to try to control the waves of litigation – and the associated costs – that many were facing. As Tom Sager, former general counsel at DuPont recalls, these were the key drivers behind the development of the Dupont Legal Model:

DuPont went through a convergence process in engineering and it made sense for them, so we thought it should make sense for us. Their focus in engineering was on creating accountability, driving collaboration and being able to do what they did better. So, if legal started to look at these metrics, we would be judged via similar metrics to other departments. Lean Six Sigma was a key part in the corporate initiative and our GC at time selected me to be a Six Sigma champion; he saw I could learn from the work of other leaders and apply it in right way. I was sent to Arizona with two other business leaders so we could learn Six Sigma and find ways to translate this to lawyers.[1]

Lean Six Sigma is a process efficiency tool, but it can assist when it comes to innovation by helping to identify problem causes and potential solutions. At DuPont, it led to the identification of areas of accepted practice that were ripe for innovation – even disruption.

The team also applied business management expert Harold Leavitt's model for organisational change, which looks at people, process and technology (PPT). The PPT framework is underpinned by the premise that to drive transformation, you first must ask three questions:

- What is the work that people are doing?
- Through what processes do they perform this work?
- How can those processes be improved by the intelligent application of technology?

The lawyers at DuPont needed to understand their own *why*; as did the law firms and external suppliers that they worked with. On the internal side, in-house lawyers were given much more responsibility for strategic budgeting and greater scope to think about process and project management. In terms of their partnership with law firms, this involved increased use of alternative fee structures, where the financial incentives for suppliers were linked to the legal team's own goals. This produced a sense of true collaboration and partnership. As a result of this realignment, the number of law firms that DuPont was using dropped dramatically from 350 to just 38, and the number of other suppliers from 150 to nine.

The final piece considered in the DuPont Legal Model was smarter use of technology and data, such as for early case assessment. Given that, even today, the application of data in legal departments is still uncommon, its use in the early 1990s was nothing short of revolutionary. In our case study on DXC Technology, one key innovation is the use of technology to generate data on trends in terms of legal risk, which allows the legal team to be much more proactive as risk managers, not just as lawyers.

The integration of data into strategic decision making is still in its infancy in law. Mark Cohen, writing in *Forbes* in 2019, shares the findings of a survey by leading business analytics provider RELX Group, which "polled 1,000 U.S. senior executives across the health care, insurance, legal, science, banking industries as well as government. Law finished last among industries – just ahead of government – in utilizing big data in some form. Of the law firm leaders surveyed, only 44 percent said they offer employee training on big data, artificial intelligence, and machine learning".[2]

Big data is nothing new: it has been around as a business trend for more than 15 years. It is thus unsurprising that the legal teams of businesses which have been applying process, data, digitisation and other innovations for some time now were first to see the value of importing these to law. Considerations such as outsourcing, digitisation, rationalisation of services and costs and innovation affect all businesses and, by extension, their legal teams.

Since the 1980s the business world – and therefore its lawyers (and their lawyers) – have faced increasing complexity. As experts such as Rita Gunther McGrath have observed, this means that traditional competitive advantage is no longer enough. The ecosystems within which business takes place have become increasingly complex and interdependent. McGrath identifies the following key aspects of this complexity:
- the digitisation of information;
- smart systems that increasingly work and communicate interdependently;
- the decreasing cost of computing power;
- the increasing ease of communicating content around the globe;
- increased wealth, which means that more individuals are part of the formal economy; and
- ultimately, the complete rewriting of industry norms and business models.

All of these changes mean that organisations can't have a 'business as usual' ethos: "Not surprisingly, that unpredictability creates a need for organisations to be far more aware of, and responsive to, changes in their own environment and in the world around them."[3]

1. Doing more with less

A fundamental driver of innovation for in-house departments – both their own and that increasingly demanded of external suppliers – is the need to do more with less. In many, if not most cases, innovative solutions are born as much of necessity as of desire.

The chapters on talent[4] highlighted the stark message from Schlumberger's CEO to its general counsel after the oil price crisis of 2016: adapt or have someone else do it for you. This has been the driving force behind many innovations in the in-house legal sphere: if legal teams don't find different ways of doing things, then someone else will. Likewise, the chapters on culture[5] explained that the starting point for Pearson's legal team was a consideration of what was unique to what they did and how they did it, and why this function should rest with them rather than being outsourced to an external provider.

But why this need to adapt or be replaced? Historically, in-house legal teams have been seen as a cost centre. In the earliest days of the role, the in-house lawyer was seen as a mere post-box function, simply sending work out to external law firms. As the sophistication of the role increased, so too did the cost. When Ben Heineman overhauled the legal function at GE, he hired the best talent from major US law firms and offered comparable salaries.

In our case study on DXC Technology, falling stock prices and a series of mergers led to drastic reductions in workforce and a rethink of how to do things differently. Nothing was sacrosanct; a big, bold vision was needed to produce a future-ready legal department. Many of the innovations embraced by DXC were a response to the fact that too much time, money and personnel were being taken up by commoditised tasks. While this case study focuses on a large legal department, the catalysts for many of the innovations that general counsel Bill Deckelman introduced are universal: the need to work with budgetary constraints and become more efficient. The starting point is also something that any legal department can apply: thinking differently and learning quickly.

But understanding what to focus on requires a strategy, underpinned by an appreciation of *why* and *how* you can best innovate, rather than simply taking what you can innovate with as your starting point.

Notes
1   Interview with the author, October 2019.
2   Mark A Cohen, "Why Is Law So Slow to Use Data?" *Forbes*, 24 June 2019,
     www.forbes.com/sites/markcohen1/2019/06/24/why-is-law-so-slow-to-use-data/.
3   Rita Gunther McGrath, "The World is More Complex Than it Used to Be", *Harvard Business Review*,
     31 August 2011, https://hbr.org/2011/08/the-world-really-is-more-compl.
4   Chapters 16–21.
5   Chapters 7–10.

"Understanding what to focus on requires a strategy, underpinned by an appreciation of why and how you can best innovate, rather than simply taking what you can innovate with as your starting point."

35. Innovation strategy

The various innovation theories outlined in the preceding chapters all share the same starting point: innovation cannot be simply about a new or different way of doing something, but must rather be driven by strategy. Arguably, legal departments have generally had a much clearer vision in this regard than many law firms. In recent years, legal teams have been laser focused on cutting legal spend; taking a creative approach to who does the work; outsourcing high-volume, less complex work; and introducing more self-service capacity for routine work such as contracts, where internal clients might not even need a lawyer's assistance if the process is relatively straightforward.

The first steps for many legal departments in considering how to add more value was to examine what they were doing and identify areas that were ripe for change and improvement. Many of these improvements focused on issues of cost and efficiency, often through the introduction of process methodology – hence the development of legal operations. These innovations curtailed the organic individualistic growth of many legal teams, which in some cases led to replication of work, excessive spend and a general lack of awareness of the broader landscape – in other words, insufficient strategy. As Tim Murphy at Mastercard characterises it, the traditional legal department looked more like a medieval craft guild than an operational business unit.

Taken to their logical conclusion, these advances have resulted in solutions such as Mastercard's shared services unit; DXC Technology's partnership with UnitedLex; and Univar's partnership with Elevate – innovative models that are underpinned by the mantra of 'people, process, technology' (PPT).

The PPT model is often described as the 'golden triangle'. The 'people' element reflects the importance of securing emotional buy-in for change from internal stakeholders, from the C-suite down to the most junior employees. It can also refer to the external stakeholders that impact on your business, such as customers and suppliers. 'Process' refers to the ways in which these stakeholders work. 'Technology' is the hardware that can yield efficiencies in terms of who does the work and how it is done; but this cannot be considered separately from the first two elements in the equation. As legal departments are primarily based on human knowledge and expertise, managing both the most effective way to deploy this talent and the transformation and change process is fundamental. Another reason why the model begins with people is because this is the most expensive element of the equation.

Neither of the earlier models of in-house teams – the 'post-box' that merely sent work out to external counsel and the internal law firm staffed with highly qualified (and expensive) lawyers, supplemented by equally highly qualified (and probably even more expensive) external lawyers – was cost effective. As a result, legal was traditionally viewed as a cost centre. This is why so much innovation in the legal space has begun by interrogating the use of human resources and figuring out how they can be used more effectively or replaced through process and technology.

1. Mapping the landscape

As the Karen Dillon quote at the beginning of Chapter 32 highlights, innovation must begin by asking the right questions and fully understanding the problem before potential solutions can be considered. Many general counsel start by considering the legal risks to which a company is exposed and how best to respond to them. Increasingly, however, legal risk now intersects with business risks; so conversations and collaboration with colleagues in other departments are also vital here.

The next step is to identify the different stakeholders in the business who use the services of the legal team and examine how they interact with it. In many companies, the sales and commercial departments interact with legal on contracts; this is an obvious candidate for more innovative approaches. Legal process outsourcing to jurisdictions where qualified lawyers can work much more cost effectively has become increasingly popular, both among legal departments and among law firms themselves (in the latter case, often at the demand of their clients).

Many legal teams are also introducing self-service portals for standardised contracts, which host templates drawn up with appropriate clauses based on standard practice and accepted exposure to risk.[1] This approach may well become the norm, not least thanks to its success outside the legal sphere. For example, if we consider Amazon's customer services: it is incredibly difficult to find a contact telephone number for Amazon's customer services, as almost every stage of the sales process – from reporting issues to printing off prepaid labels for returns – is driven by customers themselves; yet Amazon consistently gets top scores in customer service satisfaction surveys.[2]

2. Innovation strategy versus legal technology

When considering innovation strategically in the legal profession, it is crucial not to succumb to the thrill of the new – in other words, the technology. As Chris Grant at Barclays Eagle Labs explains: "Everybody forgets that there are three things underneath, and that it's not just the technology piece – it's also the people and the process. The three are positioned in that order for a reason."[3]

There is a plethora of new legal technologies out there, each touting itself as a magic bullet solution. However, from speaking to general counsel – even those at very large companies – it is clear that many are not fully exploring these options or are confused as to how best they might be utilised in practice. For the unwary general counsel, this can be a minefield – ironically, a very expensive one, given that the initial promise is generally to cut costs and save money. Again, it is vital to ask the right questions and fully understand the problem before jumping in.

Writing in 2018, Max Huber – himself a former general counsel – succinctly summarised the dilemma for general counsel with regard to innovation and legal technology. You need to begin with a roadmap of your legal risk and an understanding of the expectations of your clients and stakeholders. However:

> Many GCs jump past this step entirely and assume that new technology is what they need. They read something on LinkedIn; they saw something at a conference, they spotted something at their external counsel's office and they want it. But following the legal technology explosion to a software solution that promises efficiency and effectiveness without taking a hard look at where your legal services map should take you, is amongst the worst mistakes a GC can make. Software alone won't help you – not without a strategy and road map to guide you.[4]

General counsel should also understand that innovation is a journey and a continuous endeavour, not a one-off event. As Dillon explains, this realisation is also crucial in striking the right the balance between people and technology:

> Clay [Christensen] always pointed out that innovation is not an event; it's a constant. Innovation and change take time – if you always understand that, you will be able to take the time to track the jobs to be done.

This is especially relevant in law, where the human and social components are central. The jobs to be done are often very human centred and often nothing to do with technology. It is so much easier to understand how to improve if you start by looking at your clients' needs and the different jobs to be done: the law firms' jobs to be done; the clients' jobs to be done; those of their end clients and so forth.[5]

Another aspect that is crucial to innovation strategy, and to viewing innovation as a journey, is the ability to deal with mistakes: to see what hasn't worked and to learn from and refine it. Small failures and corrections along the way can prevent full-scale failure further down the line, as Dillon explains:

Failure is what happens when the focus is on finding the perfection at the end of the rainbow. It becomes a much more expensive and impactful failure, rather than process failure – which still matters, of course; but then you can correct and check your assumptions. Toyota has a control process where, if any worker sees something that is not going right, he or she can stop the whole production line. I think that's a really good model for lawyers and for all service industries: empower people to spot mistakes and fix them before they become too big.[6]

3. A note on stack fallacy

The notion of stack fallacy is rooted in technology, but is equally relevant to law and innovation. We often think of innovation as being synonymous with technology or as something 'new and shiny'; but as the 'jobs to be done' theory bears out, this can be a fallacy. A 'stack fallacy' is where engineers overweight the technology at the expense of the process that it enables or the needs of the end user. The phrase was coined by Anshu Sharma, a serial entrepreneur and a former venture partner at Storm Ventures.

So what does this mean for legal services? The rise in automation and the emergence of alternative law firms are classic examples of the 'jobs to be done' theory in action. The focus is not on the technology itself, but rather on the jobs that legal teams need done – which are essentially those of the company or the CEO. Illustrations of this in this book include the reorganisation and cuts made at DXC Technology as a result of a merger; Rob Booth's promise to his CEO regarding the purpose of the Crown Estate legal team; and the Pearson legal team's redefinition of why it was needed.

4. Changing client expectations

The main driver of innovation in legal is client expectations. For in-house legal teams, these are the expectations of their own stakeholders.

The client ecosystem is like a line of dominos and what happens at one end of the chain will ultimately affect those who exist to service this ecosystem. The focus in-house on doing things differently and realising greater efficiencies and cost savings has naturally begun to change the wider ecosystem. For one thing, the landscape has become considerably more diverse, including not only traditional law firms, but also legal process outsourcing companies and service providers – whether as standalone companies, parts of wider law companies or divisions of law firms.

However, some would argue that this evolution is still not as radical as it should be. For those seeking to drive change, it seems as though there is still too much tinkering around the edges, rather than completely rethinking the proposition. Those in-house maintain that this is particularly true on the law firm side of the equation, as Barclays' Chris Grant observes: "No one is thinking outside the box. Plus, the partnership model doesn't lend itself towards that need to shake things up. Lots of innovation is purely a knee-jerk reaction to client demands; firms are not doing the most that they could be able to help everybody on that journey." But Grant is under no illusion that transformative change is inevitable for law, just as it was for financial services: "We'll go through cycles of making hay while the sun shines; and then suddenly the sun won't be shining anymore and we'll have to work out how to do things differently."

Increasingly, clients such as Barclays, Schlumberger and the Crown

Estate – which have all had to think differently and deconstruct the fundamentals of how things are done in their teams – expect that same agility from their suppliers. The response can vary significantly, suggests Grant:

We see a huge difference in law firms between those that are labelling things as innovation, and those that are truly changing the way that they are built and operate so that they can become more innovative. And it's not even those in the top band; it's in the next band that we see this. It's the DWFs of the world that have done this: they're not called a law firm anymore; they don't have a managing partner anymore. I think that's the interesting part – you have to set yourself up to be innovative.[7]

For Grant, collaboration is crucial to this movement, to ensure that the wheel of innovation is not constantly reinvented: "We bring these people who are innovative together, who all have common issues and common challenges; who are starting to think about the big picture; who are saying, 'Actually, if we do something collectively, then we're saving money' – rather than each law firm going out and doing its own thing."

But it's a fact that for many law firms, 'innovation' is still just a buzzword. The challenge for many clients is to identify those innovations that are based on the actual jobs to be done, rather than on legal suppliers' perceptions of what those jobs should be. Much of this comes down to whether law firms are brave enough to question the fundamentals of their own business models and ways of operating. This has implications not only for process and technology, but also for people. As Vanderbilt University's Cat Moon states:

I think our talent drain – why we lose so many women and diverse lawyers – is because of this inability to innovate. There are people who look like they are innovative from the outside, such as focusing on process improvement. But then if you start asking why and digging into the strategy, a different story emerges. I had a conversation with a partner in an AMLaw 200 firm that looked very innovative; but when I asked why it was doing this, it was to perpetuate the old leverage model and to capitalise as much as possible off the backs of others, such as associates.

Currently, many firms still find that the old models are working fine and thus have little real incentive to rethink them. But Grant warns that the writing is on the wall:

I do think the time is coming for the traditional law firms in the world. They have a five to six-year window where, if they have not fundamentally changed the way that they operate, other firms will step into their shoes which can do things more effectively, more efficiently and more profitably, because of how they set themselves up. It's not about the billable hour. The new entrants will be fundamentally structured in a way that allows them to provide those services in a way that those that haven't bothered to change will never be able to. If they're not able to engage with that change process, they'll be left behind.

5. Doing a job and creating value – applying innovation theory in practice

To be more than a theoretical concept, innovation must create value for customers and for the organisation itself. But how does this play out in legal departments? How can you understand the right questions to ask and figure out the jobs to be done in order to inform your innovation strategy?

Christensen *et al* categorises the ways in which innovations can fulfil needs into a series of jobs, as follows.

5.1 How do people live?
This involves observing day-to-day activities and operations. In the legal setting, it might involve asking: what do your lawyers do? What do your customers do? Is there something that's not working so well? It can even start with an examination of your own day-to-day activities: "Understanding the unresolved jobs in your own life can provide fertile territory for innovation."[8]

5.2 What jobs aren't people doing?

This is trickier to consider, as it requires you to think about what your organisation does or could do in a completely different way, and look beyond the parameters of traditional competition. Christensen at al consider the example of Airbnb, which might initially have been regarded as competition to hotels. However, research subsequently revealed that 40% of Airbnb bookers would not have made their trips in the first place or would have stayed with family instead; while almost 100% of hosts would not previously have considered renting out some or all of their property.

Looking at the DXC/UnitedLex tie-up discussed in the case study in Chapter 36, if general counsel Bill Deckelman had not considered the innovative solution of captive outsourcing to UnitedLex, there might have been even more swingeing job cuts at DXC. Some of the lawyers previously employed in the legal team might have ended up in suppliers that advised DXC; but much of this would have been left to chance. DXC's unique model of having legacy lawyers work under a brand-new external structure is now being explored by other legal teams.

5.3 What compensating behaviours or workarounds are clients adopting to solve problems?

According to Christensen *et al*, this can be a major red flag for the need for some sort of innovation. In legal teams, this could involve people creating Word document templates for contracts as a first stage to automation prior to the introduction of a contract management systems. People may innately realise that something is missing and try to create that themselves. Again, by understanding the whole context of how your lawyers and your legal team are working, significant opportunities and ideas can be identified.

5.4 What are the jobs that people don't want to do?

These should not be confused with the jobs that people aren't doing discussed in section 5.2 – in most cases, people are unaware of the existence of the jobs in that category. Rather, these are jobs that people are aware of, but don't want to do. Here Christensen at al cite the example of the Minute Clinics located in CVS drug stores in the United States. These walk-in clinics provide prescriptions for minor ailments to consumers who do not want to take the time out to see a doctor.

In law, a good example is the DoNotPay robot lawyer created by former Stanford student Joshua Browder. Browder worked with lawyers to create a bot to help consumers challenge parking tickets on legal technicalities. Many would not previously have challenged the tickets because it would have involved too much work – hiring a real lawyer would be too expensive, but the DoNotPay program is free. DoNotPay has since expanded into other areas of law, although it currently takes on claims of up to £25,000 only. Browder's mission is to use technology to make legal advice available to all. The platform currently uses IBM's Watson, a computer system that can answer questions posed in natural language.

5.5 In what jobs are people using an existing product in a new way?
The example cited by Christensen *et al* is Arm and Hammer baking soda, which consumers use for many purposes other than baking, such as teeth cleaning, fridge deodorising and carpet cleaning. In-house, one example is the use of secondees – newly qualified lawyers from law firms – not just to advise on legal, but also to input data and test legal technology and process tools. This has led to the development of consultancies focused on helping legal departments to onboard process efficiency and technology tools.

6. Understanding context

Ultimately, Christensen *et al* caution that the difference with the 'jobs to be done' theory is the need to understand the context in which your customer is using or will use an innovation.

Sometimes, by observing what their legal teams do and how they are working, general counsel can gain insights into what is needed and what isn't. For example, Nick Boymal – who runs the UnitedLex side of DXC Technology's legal capabilities in Australia and Asia-Pacific – tries to sit in with his teams on all training in new technology, to get a sense of its complexity and the possibilities afforded by its practical adoption. Is it doing the job that needs to be done? Is it doing that job in the right way? By looking at the real context of user experience and engagement, Boymal can identify the shortcomings of certain innovations and suggest to leadership that some may cause more problems than they solve.

Successful innovation strategy thus hinges on an appreciation of the purpose of what you are doing and why an innovation might be needed.

Notes

1 Interview with the author, October 2019.
2 Josie Clarke, "Amazon Tops Customer Satisfaction Ratings For Five Years in a Row", *The Independent*, 23 January 2018, www.independent.co.uk/news/business/news/amazon-customer-satisfaction-ratings-spotify-prezzo-british-gas-a8172501.html.
3 Interview with the author, October 2019.
4 Max Huber, "Service delivery and alternative support models: How satisfied is your internal client?", *Legal Operations* (Juro Online Limited) 2018, p23.
5 Interview with the author, November 2019.
6 Interview with the author, November 2019.
7 Interview with the author, October 2019.
8 Clayton Christensen, Taddy Hall, Karen Dillon and David S Duncan, *Competing Against Luck* (Harper Business 2016), p75.

"[An] aspect that is crucial to innovation strategy, and to viewing innovation as a journey, is the ability to deal with mistakes: to see what hasn't worked and to learn from and refine it."

36. Case study: DXC Technology – a new blueprint for legal teams

Our final case study considers innovation and collaboration. It reimagines the structure of the legal department and outlines how legal teams can collaborate with outside suppliers in a uniquely different way. I suspect that the ideas examined in this case study will become increasingly influential in the industry. The case study also weaves together the other ideas discussed this book: the need for purpose; for a culture which supports that purpose; for leadership which can drive and sustain the vision; for talent to support this; and for collaboration with others – both internally and externally – to make the vision a reality.

DXC Technology's legal team has undergone a radical transformation as a result of the biggest managed shared services deal the legal industry has ever seen. Its change journey has evolved significantly since it began in 2017; and the purpose of that journey has also evolved from a straightforward value creation exercise to become a blueprint for the truly digital legal department of the future.

DXC was born of the April 2017 merger between Computer Sciences Corporation (CSC) and the enterprise services arm of Hewlett Packard Enterprises (HPE). The merger created the world's biggest B2B technology services company, worth a total of $25 billion. But the merger also brought with it an urgent need for consolidation, to reduce the number of offices and headcount across the new company. General counsel Bill Deckelman had worked for the legacy CSC for more than 12 years. As the new general counsel of DXC, he was presented with the challenge of meeting an aggressive 35% cost reduction target while also merging the two legacy legal teams and supporting the needs of the new and evolving business.

The first item on the agenda was to map the landscape and identify both the synergies between the two legal teams and those areas where there was replication of skills and efforts. While this yielded some cost savings, they were nowhere near the amount that was needed. It became increasingly clear to Deckelman that nothing short of a complete rethink of how legal work was traditionally handled and how the legal teams were traditionally organised was required: "PWC came in and they were recommending, at the time, that the contract management function needed to grow from 286, when we were in the first stages of the transformation, to 325. The challenge was saying, 'No, we're not going to grow in headcount, but we need to do more through technology and process.' It's just a really stark example of old thinking versus new thinking."[1]

Much of this focused on increased use of digitisation. However, Deckelman recognised that – given the speed of change needed, the cost of purchasing digital technologies and the time, money and effort required to onboard them – this was no magic bullet and in fact would prevent him from meeting his cost reduction target:

> *The traditional approach is to look internally and we worked on that for three months; but really, it got us nowhere and was not even coming close to where we needed to be. My people were saying, "We can develop the technology; we just need $5 million!" To be honest, we didn't have it and never would have it – legal is always near the*

bottom of the list of priorities for technology investment. I have been doing outsourcing since the beginning of my career, so I thought, "I can spread the cost and make a significant process and technology investment for us."

1. Legal 2.0

Instead, Deckelman partnered with UnitedLex, a leading enterprise services business focused on the legal industry. In recent years law companies such as UnitedLex have begun redefining the legal services landscape, driving disruption by focusing on the low-hanging fruit of high-volume, low-cost work.

The legacy CSC had previously worked with UnitedLex, so this was a logical move. It also coincided with UnitedLex receiving a huge injection of capital from private equity investment firm CVC Partners, giving it all the resources needed to realise the kind of bold innovative partnership that Deckelman had in mind.

Deckelman began by discussing with UnitedLex CEO Daniel Reed what a new operating model for DXC's legal department might look like in terms of people, process and technology (PPT) – what Deckelman called Legal 2.0. Nothing was sacrosanct; in destroying the old models, they sought to build a future-ready legal function for a 21st century digital company. With sparkling credentials, Reed was just the man for the job. He started his career as a corporate lawyer and for a time was also an accountant, before serving as general counsel in a technology start-up during the dot.com boom of the late 1990s. He then became managing director of Capgemini in the areas of supply chain and finance, arriving just after its acquisition of Nasdaq-listed company Kanbay and subsidiary Adjoined Consulting. Thanks to this diverse background, Reed has a deep understanding of how PPT can be used to transform how organisations work. He founded UnitedLex in 2006 with the objective of applying these concepts to the legal industry.

The planning phase began before the merger was finalised, giving UnitedLex the opportunity to conduct a comprehensive review of the legacy law departments and the needs of the organisational stakeholders they would serve. UnitedLex began engaging with DXC as consultants, partnering with McKinsey & Company. As the emphasis was on value capture rather than pure cost containment, there was also a focus on optimising both performance and risk management. UnitedLex reviewed every resource, process and technology used by the legacy law departments to design the new enterprise legal services model. In other words, as Clayton Christensen would advocate, it asked the right questions and took the time to fully understand the problem before looking at potential solutions.

The result was a unique model that blended internal and external expertise and focused not on *who* was doing the 'jobs to be done', but rather on *why* those jobs were being done and *how* they could be done best. Undergoing such a radical rethink in the middle of a merger was a herculean undertaking, as Deckelman explains: "The challenge for us was the merger. I didn't know anything about the other side's legal team. We had an 11-month due diligence period, during which we had to both learn about the heritage organisations and also do the predictive analysis of both what day one of the new model would look like and what day 366 of the new model would look like."

2. The vision

The vision statement for the new legal department is: "To be the preeminent global innovator in digital transformation and world-class delivery of legal, commercial, and compliance solutions to advance the mission of DXC Technology Company." Thus far, this has been achieved by divesting a large portion of the legal function to a captive shared services operation owned and managed by UnitedLex, but run as though it is part of the DXC legal team. Many of the regional and departmental leaders of the legacy CSC and HPE legal teams are now as likely to be badged UnitedLex as DXC. The purpose of this was to remove headcount cost from DXC, while maintaining access to the service levels and legacy knowledge that many of those staff members possessed. It also allowed for the function to be truly agile and for staff numbers to be scaled up and down as needed.

Inevitably, some people left as a result of these dramatic changes; but many of those who subsequently joined were energised by this rethink of legal service delivery and reimagining of the role of the in-house lawyer. The mix of legacy knowledge from remaining staff who embraced the change and new blood who were attracted by this unique challenge proved an ideal blend.

The tie-up also gave DXC unfettered access to UnitedLex's vast bank of technology and its ability to implement this through process efficiency. A major growth area for law companies such as UnitedLex and Elevate is consulting for legal teams on the identification and implementation of process and technology improvements; at DXC, the deal effectively allows this to happen continuously. For example, professionals such as director and practice lead of digital solutions Timothy Igoe has advised DXC since he arrived at UnitedLex and is a member of the leadership team, but he also works for other clients – experience which informs his approach to mapping the transformation journey for DXC.

3. Leadership

Visionary leadership – the ability not only to set a vision, but also to communicate it and confirm it daily, through behaviours big and small – is vital to the success of such a transformative project. For Deckelman, this meant that he had to be fully invested and supportive at all times, even through setbacks and challenges. Paul Lanzone – senior vice president enterprise legal services at UnitedLex and a core member of the DXC legal leadership team – suggests that Deckelman's honesty and engagement were integral to securing wider buy-in for the initiative. What has made the difference, thinks Lanzone, is the leadership team's mix of honesty and engagement, generating a positive sense of urgency, which has come from the top with Deckelman's own attitude. What is key, according to Lanzone, is "investing in the department's culture, encouraging energy and passion to get the most out of people, so they in turn can get the most out of DXC… and I think that's different to other leadership. A lot of leadership is about taglines – there's no real follow through, whereas with Bill there's a lot of follow through, patience and forgiveness for mistakes, to a point."[2]

Lanzone identifies the leadership's willingness to listen and to show vulnerability during this period of change as another key differentiator. A pulse survey conducted by the team at the end of 2019 exemplifies this:

> *The good news for us is that unlike some departments we are not too nervous to conduct a pulse survey. Or if they did do a pulse survey, they might curate the questions, so that you could never get a bad answer. If they got bad answers, they might not release the results; and then they probably wouldn't even care about the results enough to make fundamental changes. We haven't done any of that; when we do the surveys, we communicate the results and then we try to hit changes hard, to listen and act accordingly.*

For the new model to succeed, it also had to be truly seamless, from the top down. In traditional shared services, it can seem as though the service centres are subordinate to the core legal department. By contrast, at DXC the legal department leadership team includes members from both DXC and UnitedLex, as well as from captive law firm Marshall Denning.[3] This presents a united front not only across the business, but also to the outside world, as Mike Woodfine, vice president legal at DXC in the United Kingdom, explains: "The message is we are as one and there is no chink of light between UnitedLex and DXC."[4]

4. People

Perhaps the biggest change introduced by the new model concerns how DXC deploys and uses its people – the first and most important element of the PPT equation. UnitedLex now provides legal support in more than 26 jurisdictions worldwide. In the first wave of transformation in 2017–2018, 209 DXC legal personnel became UnitedLex employees – a move that allowed DXC to save money while retaining institutional knowledge and a 'one department' mindset. Today, some 464 UnitedLex senior attorneys, contract and commercial professionals and subject-matter experts support DXC globally on sales transactions, legal operations, litigation, immigration and other corporate legal activities. They include both legacy CSC/HPE legal staff who have been rebadged as UnitedLex and new hires. Overall headcount across both DXC and UnitedLex has dropped from 695 to 537 – a reduction of 23%. Their five-year agreement is the largest managed legal services transaction ever inked.

The new model is far more sophisticated than traditional outsourcing and shared services structures, as even complex deals and negotiations are handled by lawyers from all areas of the combined legal function – not just those at DXC. Today, just 70 staff are still badged DXC legal. This approach is truly radical, especially given that for many business departments, headcount is sacrosanct: many executives equate the headcount they command to how influential they are and are seldom willing to countenance a drop in numbers.

But are talent and headcount the same thing? Increasingly, effective use and deployment of talent in the digital age runs counter to increasing headcount (even if the latter were possible). Rethinking talent strategies for the digital age is a significant challenge for all businesses, as a report from Wharton Business School outlines: "First leaders need to consider the skills and capabilities required to execute their strategy in the digital world. Comparing these requirements to their current employee skill base will enable them to develop a workforce plan and robust talent strategy, defining when to buy, build or borrow skills and how to create an enabling culture. What do employees need to do differently to adapt to a digital culture?"[5]

The main obstacle to legal departments and law firms in replicating the DXC model may be their perceived 'special' status, as discussed in the chapters on talent. True innovation in the legal industry demands a realisation that the delivery of legal services need not be the responsibility of traditionally trained lawyers – or even humans. The DXC model jettisons outmoded dichotomies and divisions between lawyers and non-lawyers, and between internal staff and external providers. The guiding purpose is that, conceptually, there is no difference between whether the service is delivered by a UnitedLex badged lawyer or a DXC lawyer; or even by a contract manager rather than a lawyer. Instead, the focus is on getting the job done.

Continuous learning is also integral to the success of the DXC model. Research has shown that, particularly as businesses become more digital, knowledge and learning must be a continuous strand throughout the working lives of all employees. Writing in the *Harvard Business Review*,[6] Jacques Bughin, Susan Lund and Eric Hazan of McKinsey suggest that companies will need to think differently about how they acquire talent and what skills that talent will need. Crucially, they must also appreciate that these skills will inevitably need to change over time and help employees to upskill and reskill accordingly through continuous learning: "The starting point for all of this will be a mindset change, with companies seeking to measure future success by their ability to provide continuous learning options to employees."

At DXC, the team has developed a digital learning platform through BriefBox, providing access to all learning and professional development content. BriefBox is a proprietary tool developed by DXC that can store a vast cache of learning materials, from webinars to videos and guided exercises. Employees can access both selected and assigned learning materials directly from a personal learning diary. Additional training sessions which are not available through the digital learning platform, such as conferences, can be added manually to the diary. The platform also provides access to DXC-specific 'pathways' designed to develop expertise in particular focus areas (core competencies). Using these digital tools, employees can map their learning journeys and suggest where additional help is needed.

This is supported by a one-to-one mentoring programme, launched through a pilot in March 2019, which aims for an average of two monthly meetings per pair.

The third pillar of DXC's continuous learning programme is focused on cross-training and allows employees to sign up for new opportunities or stretch assignments to facilitate lateral professional development. There are similarities here with the programme at Pearson discussed in the part of this book on culture.[7] Rather than enlisting external help, both legal teams first seek more creative ways to deploy and develop their existing talent. Recent examples of cross-training include a 'BriefBoxer' role, to support the rollout of BriefBox within DXC.

The continuous learning programme aims to cultivate the skills and attributes of a digital lawyer, as envisioned by Michele DeStefano: "The world is changing, and clients are asking their lawyers for help. Clients are asking their lawyers to utilize tech, to be more efficient, and to add value at every step, to cross-collaborate and partner with them and other legal service providers, to solve problems, and to innovate with them. In other words, clients need lawyers with new and different skills."[8]

Or as Deckelman would characterise it: "It's about being agile, aware and curious. We need to explore, experiment and test. It's about embracing change and implementing that, in training and in practice." Digital lawyers are aware that they don't have all the answers and actively embrace the ability to explore a range of solutions.

5. Process

The second element in the PPT equation is process. For many general counsel who are now thinking more operationally about how their teams function, a crucial step in this was gaining a full understanding of what everyone did and how long it took them to do it. And it is often through the third element, technology, that this can be measured in a meaningful way.

The relationship between process and technology adoption at DXC is very symbiotic; in practice, the two can be inextricably interlinked, as Deckelman explains:

> *For example, thinking about our contract management group, we're looking at how they typically work. So we ask, "What kind of data have we been missing that we would like to have?" And now, with the technology, they're able to upload data in real time; we're able to see it on a dashboard in real time. As part of the process, we will say, "You will upload the separate data points and this is how you do it. Here's the tool you use and here's how that's going to report data back to us."*

So there's the process that supports the technology; but by using that digital tool, you're fulfilling the process piece. But at the same time, you're thinking, "Okay, what does this technology allow us now do in terms of data and how do we use our people and our process to make sure we're optimising that technology?"

Deckelman emphasises not only that this approach has made the legal department's work much more structured and focused, but also that the resulting efficiencies in contracting solutions have given DXC a competitive advantage in wooing new customers. In a sales environment in which customers almost always demand requests for proposals and usually at least four companies are submitting them, success often hinges on how quickly and fairly you can contract. This is why a laser focus on effective process can produce wins not just for the legal team, but for the wider business.

6. Technology

As discussed throughout the chapters on innovation, understanding the legal tech landscape proves a challenge for many legal teams. Too often, they begin analysing tech solutions before mapping their own status and processes to identify exactly where technology might best be utilised. This means that the money, time and effort spent in acquiring and embedding new technologies are often spent in vain. And in some cases – not least that of DXC, as discussed earlier in this chapter – these resources may simply be unavailable. Instead, the blended model that Deckelman developed allows the DXC legal team to effortlessly plug into UnitedLex's technology stack.

One piece of tech which proved immensely valuable from the start is UnitedLex's ContractRoom contract management platform, which integrates with leading customer relationship management solution Salesforce. ContractRoom supports more than $26 billion worth of DXC contracts and provides automated end-to-end contract support, as well as real-time information on workflow and deal status. When a contract is generated via Salesforce, this also links to BriefBox, DXC's proprietary tool for information sharing and workflow management.

The digital workflow in Briefbox allows the legal team to triage workflow to see where assistance is most urgently needed. It also produces effective metrics and facilitates reporting on workflow.

BriefBox was developed by DXC with UnitedLex to serve as a legal and business portal for the whole technology stack. It is effectively a digital 'one-stop shop' for all legal professionals, functioning as a platform for communication between the legal team, the business and its customers. It is both a central repository and a facilitator of legal work. As well as ContractRoom, the software is integrated with Legal Tracker, which coordinates e-billing and financial management processes with external legal vendors. Ultimately, it will integrate with all of the technology tools that the legal team uses.

7. Data

The use of data has been crucial in knitting together the PPT efficiencies generated by the new legal model, with impressive results, says Deckelman: "It's been amazing to watch because, at the end of the day, we have fewer resources, but the quality of the work has increased, because we have visibility on data."

Smarter use of data means that everything being done by the legal team is now being measured and has become more tangible as a consequence. This approach also mirrors how the wider business operates: based on actual, real-time information and measurable standards. This synchronicity has transformed the day-to-day working relationship between legal and the wider business, and how legal professionals are perceived by the business. The insights and efficiencies that it yields have also helped to assuage concerns about the change among business clients who might previously have been accustomed to having a lawyer working closely with them on the ground.

Greater visibility on the data also allows the legal team to focus more closely on risk management by spotting recurring issues and managing these proactively through training solutions; and has helped to reinforce the change management which is fundamental to the whole project.

8. Change and facing the future

"No battle plan ever survives first contact with the enemy," observed Helmuth von Moltke, chief of staff of the Prussian army in the nineteenth century. Taking a similarly realistic view to change and innovation, legal leaders must accept the need to pivot as necessary and modify their blueprint accordingly.

Naturally, careful change management was crucial to ensure a successful transition at DXC. Early in the process, Deckelman sought to garner support from the CEO and the executive team, which proved a fairly easy sell: "I was presenting the idea to our CEO and within seven seconds he was nodding enthusiastically. As someone who had spent his whole life around technology and outsourcing, he got it."

What was more challenging was managing this change among business units that previously might have had a lawyer sitting with them. Here, Deckelman secured buy-in by pointing both to the inevitability of digital change and to the quick wins in terms of efficiency and process it would bring for the business.

For those members of the legal team who were transferring to UnitedLex, Deckelman emphasised that they were being offered a unique new career trajectory at a company with both a deep understanding of digital and a diverse client base; and that the move could open up a plethora of new career opportunities in a world which will only need more digital lawyers. Inevitably, however, divesting such a large amount of people triggered a whole range of emotions among the team and managing this was not always easy, as Deckelman admits:

> From the beginning it was very hard to make the decisions about letting people go. It was hard managing through that for the people who remained, and there were a lot of emotions. As we came through, we started to develop qualities such as the culture of the new blended

department. That does not happen overnight, though – it takes a lot of repetitive messaging about what digital is and what has changed and why it needed to. It's repeating ad nauseum.

The pace of transformation was another challenge, given the extent of the change to be achieved in such a short timeframe and the introduction of a whole new suite of digital tools – some of which turned out not to be fit for purpose. And all while the team was still doing its day job of providing legal services.

But ultimately, it has all been worth it. Today, many members of the DXC/UnitedLex team are astounded at how far they have progressed in their change journey compared to their peers across the profession. Seamless integration between the different stakeholders makes the tie-up much more innovative than the traditional shared services models; and Deckelman suggests that such smart collaborations will inevitably come to characterise the market: "I think by the middle of this decade – when technology has leaped ahead, with the promise of AI catching up with reality – I cannot imagine lawyers being able to run a legal department and figure out the implications of all this use of technology, process and data on their own. If you want a holistic viewpoint, it's got to be with help from other experts."

Notes
1   Interview with the author, February 2020.
2   Interview with the author, December 2019.
3   Marshall Denning is the law firm arm of UnitedLex. The firm was created and structured so that it could operate in countries where law firms not owned by lawyers and unregulated legal businesses are not allowed. It takes its name from leading figures in US and UK jurisprudence – John Marshall, the longest-serving chief justice of the US Supreme Court; its first black justice, Thurgood Marshall; and Lord Denning in the United Kingdom.
4   Interview with the author, December 2019.
5   "Rethinking Talent in the Digital Age", *Wharton Business Consulting Insights*, 14 June 2018, https://whartonbc.co.uk/insights/rethinking-talent-in-the-digital-age/.
6   https://hbr.org/2018/05/automation-will-make-lifelong-learning-a-necessary-part-of-work.
7   Chapters 7–10.
8   Michele DeStefano, *Legal Upheaval* (ABA Publishing 2018 Kindle e-book), location 740–741.

Conclusion

··

Change is the only constant in life.

Heraclitus

Conclusion

The discussions in this book confirm that this is a crucial time of change for the legal profession. Much of the drive for change has come from in-house legal teams, which are seeking to follow the examples set by their business colleagues in achieving enhanced efficiencies, greater cost savings, increased use of digital solutions and more astute deployment of talent. The broader business concepts discussed in this book are vital to realise this change.

A number of groups and initiatives in the legal industry have been established to explore this further. Many of these groups bring together a diverse range of perspectives in their efforts to shape a vision of the future of law. Whatever this may be, one thing is certain: it will not be shaped exclusively by the views of lawyers.

Our final case study on DXC Technology finished with a thought from transformational general counsel Bill Deckelman, who suggests that while legal departments need to change, they cannot do so alone – they will need the help of other experts to succeed.

It is interesting for me, as a non-lawyer, to have made a career out of researching, studying, debating and perhaps even in some small way driving the debate on the future of the profession. But, as many of these ideas we discuss in the book highlight, it will be ideas from outside the law – and increasingly, a recognition of the skills of professionals from outside the law – that will shape the transformation of the legal industry. It is clear that the term 'non-lawyer' is not fit for purpose, based as it is on a binary definition which privileges one term over the other. This cannot work either conceptually or in practice. The traditional sense of lawyers being different from everyone else and operating in a specialised sphere has changed. In many of the examples discussed in this book, the catalyst for applying some of these business ideas was a pivotal moment when the legal team re-examined its very reason for existence, reconsidered what it had traditionally done and how this was traditionally done, and questioned whether this could be done in other ways or by other people.

Given the pace of change both in business and in the wider world, the *why* and *how* of *what* you do will increasingly be the focus of scrutiny. Many of the in-house teams profiled in this book are using these broader business concepts both to stimulate and to cope with perennial change.

1. How business ideas are changing the legal profession

The rethink of how law is delivered has been driven by the users of legal services – first by business stakeholders and then by their legal teams, which have cascaded this different way of thinking down to legal services providers. Many of the broader business concepts discussed in this book are dramatically reshaping the legal services landscape. What kick-started much of this change was a rethink of the *why, how* and *what* of the work of legal teams. As what takes place internally has a symbiotic relationship with the services offered by external providers, it is no surprise that the evolving world view of general counsel and their teams is rippling outwards. This is radically changing the landscape of who offers services and how they do this.

Some years ago, a general counsel friend and I asked a law firm leader about what his firm's purpose was. He had obviously never really thought about it. Today, more and more firms are stating their purpose and using this as a springboard for a range of activities, including designing and implementing innovation strategies and offering services beyond traditional legal work to clients.

The traditional law firm partnership based on the billable-hour model is still very much alive and well; but for how long? Many of the challenger models have arisen to meet the specific and evolving needs of in-house counsel; and increasingly, these new ways of doing things are being adopted by the incumbent law firms.

2. The impact of new ways of working

It is also evident that the new ways of working being implemented by many innovative in-house teams are forcing their outside counsel to work in very different ways. This can sometimes be an uphill struggle, as traditional law firms are still hugely profitable. But the feedback of many of the general counsel interviewed for this book confirms that the gap between the skills needed in-house and those needed to work in private practice is widening. This has significant implications for talent strategies, and for identifying those lawyers with the right mindsets and skill sets to succeed in the new in-house reality. However, the ramifications extend far beyond this: if your external providers are offering services which are increasingly divorced from your own lived reality, then where is the service in that model?

Just as in-house legal departments have had to adapt to the new business realities that their wider organisations face, so too must the wider legal profession face up to the future – and perhaps to a day of reckoning for obsolete models and outmoded ways of thinking.

About the author

Catherine McGregor
Chief executive officer, Catherine McGregor Research
catherine@catherinemcgregor.co.uk

Catherine McGregor runs her own company focused on thought leadership, strategic consultancy, content creation, events and training for businesses and professional services companies. She specialises in the intersection between law and business, particularly in the role of the general counsel, the future of the legal profession and diversity and inclusion.

Dr McGregor frequently curates content focused on and about inside counsel. She is an experienced keynote speaker and moderator covering topics such as the future of the legal department; the changing role of in-house counsel; innovation and disruption in legal services; inclusion and diversity in the law; and social mobility.

Dr McGregor was previously the founding editor of *GC Magazine* and director of in-house counsel initiatives at Legalease, a London-based legal publishing company. Before she moved into legal publishing, she completed a PhD in English and drama and taught drama and performance at UK and US universities.

Index

About Globe Law
and Business

Globe Law and Business was established in 2005, and from the very beginning we set out to create law books which are sufficiently high level to be of real use to the experienced professional, yet still accessible and easy to navigate. Most of our authors are drawn from Magic Circle and other top commercial firms, both in the UK and internationally. Our titles are carefully produced, with the utmost attention paid to editorial, design and production processes. We hope this results in high-quality books which are easy to read, and a pleasure to own. All our new books are also available as ebooks, which are compatible with most desktop, laptop and tablet devices.

We have recently expanded our portfolio to include a new range of journals and Special Reports, available both digitally and in hard copy format, and produced to the same high standards as our books. We'd very much like to hear from you with your thoughts and ideas for improving what we offer. Please do feel free to email me at sian@globelawandbusiness.com with your views.

Sian O'Neill
Managing director
Globe Law and Business